SET YOUR LIFE ON A SUCCESSFUL COURSE!

Sydney Omarr, America's most accurate astrologer, will help you turn all your dreams into wonderful realities. Beginning in July, 1991, his on-target horoscopes and sound advice will counsel you in all aspects of your future—from romance to health and career.

A year of heavenly possibilities awaits you. Look up your planets . . . find out what makes a lover of each sign stay around, stray or get jealous. . . . Know when to play it cool—and when to go for it! Discover the secrets to a great 1992 and make it your most fulfilling year ever!

SYDNEY OMARR'S DAY-BY-DAY ASTROLOGICAL GUIDES FOR YOU IN 1992

- ☐ **ARIES** ....(169980—$3.99)
- ☐ **TAURUS** ....(169999—$3.99)
- ☐ **GEMINI** ....(170008—$3.99)
- ☐ **CANCER** ....(170016—$3.99)
- ☐ **LEO** ....(170024—$3.99)
- ☐ **VIRGO** ....(170032—$3.99)
- ☐ **LIBRA** ....(170040—$3.99)
- ☐ **SCORPIO** ....(170059—$3.99)
- ☐ **SAGITTARIUS** ....(170067—$3.99)
- ☐ **CAPRICORN** ....(170075—$3.99)
- ☐ **AQUARIUS** ....(170083—$3.99)
- ☐ **PISCES** ....(170091—$3.99)

Price slightly higher in Canada.

SYDNEY OMARR'S

DAY-BY-DAY ASTROLOGICAL GUIDE FOR

GEMINI

MAY 21-JUNE 20

·1·9·9·2·

A SIGNET BOOK

SIGNET
Published by the Penguin Group
Penguin Books USA Inc.,
375 Hudson Street, New York, New York 10014, U.S.A.
Penguin Books Ltd, 27 Wrights Lane,
London W8 5TZ, England
Penguin Books Australia Ltd, Ringwood,
Victoria, Australia
Penguin Books Canada Ltd,
2801 John Street, Markham, Ontario, Canada L3R 1B4
Penguin Books (N.Z.) Ltd, 182-190 Wairau Road,
Auckland 10, New Zealand

Penguin Books Ltd, Registered Offices:
Harmondsworth, Middlesex, England

First published by Signet,
an imprint of New American Library,
a division of Penguin Books USA Inc.

First Printing, July, 1991
10 9 8 7 6 5 4 3 2 1

 REGISTERED TRADEMARK—MARCA REGISTRADA

Printed in the United States of America

Contents

Introduction

The scene is a New York courtroom in the year 1914. The woman on trial for fortune-telling is an astrologer, the proper Bostonian descendant of two American presidents, who learned her technique from a noted Boston physician who used astrology in his diagnoses. Into the courtroom she comes, laden with piles of reference books, tracing the history of astrology back to the ancient Babylonians. As the trial progresses, she challenges the skeptical judge to let her cast a chart to demonstrate the accuracy of astrology. The judge agrees and gives her the birth date, time, and place of an unnamed subject. Evangeline Adams consults her books of tables and draws up a chart, then confidently gives the first public reading of a horoscope in the United States.

The judge's verdict: not guilty. He needed no experts to verify the accuracy of the stunning insights into the character of the subject—the birth date he had given Miss Adams was that of his own son. That trial, which was reported in newspapers across the country, was the beginning of astrology consciousness in America.

Astrology has come a long way since that time. Now it has entered the high-tech era with computer programs, nationwide networks of astrologers, conventions, seminars, and lectures attended by thousands of astrology fans.

Who's following the stars in the 1990s? An estimated 32 million people, according to a recent Gallup Poll, believe that the movements of the planets affect their daily lives. And as national barriers break down, astrologers around the world are discovering a kinship. By the time this guide is published there will have been the first international conference of astrologers in Russia, where

7

an astrological community has survived through all the years of tumultuous political changes.

New areas of astrology are opening up as other professionals are incorporating astrological insights into their work. Psychotherapists are using astrological charts for accurate information about the personalities of their patients—and astrologers, in a fair turnabout, are becoming more aware of the techniques and responsibilities of being counselors. Businesses are analyzing the horoscopes of their employees for successful job matchups and financiers are retaining astrologers for advice on timing and markets.

This book is for you if you want to learn more about astrology and how to use it every day in your personal and professional life. There are tips on how to take control of your life and steer it on a successful course by moving in harmony with planetary cycles. You'll learn which are the most powerful planets in your chart and the special qualities that enhance your chances for success in your career. You'll not only learn about your sun sign, but about the nine other planets in your horoscope. You can find out what celebrities share your birthday, too.

Astrology can help you put the increasingly complicated lifestyle of the 1990s into perspective, help you achieve a more fulfilling love relationship, and guide you in timing and decision making. Let this be your guide to following the stars in 1992—and may you have a year of growth, happiness, and prosperity!

1

Clearing Up the Mystery of Astrology

Over the years, I've gathered the most frequent questions asked about how astrology works. Once you get beyond sun signs, the symbols and terminology of this subject can often be confusing to the beginner. I'm also often asked about how to find an astrologer or if you can do astrology on your personal computer at home. The answers should help to solve some of astrology's mysteries for you. And you'll find that it's easy to get hooked on astrology: the more you know, the more deeply you'll want to investigate this fascinating subject.

What is the difference between sign and a constellation?
This is one of the most frequently asked questions. Everyone knows that the constellations of the zodiac are specific configurations of stars. But not everyone knows that the sign the constellation represents may be in a different place!

A sign is actually a 30-degree division of a circular belt of sky called the zodiac, which means "circle of animals" in Greek. Originally, each division was marked by a constellation, some of which were named after animals—a lion, a bull, a goat, a ram—or sea creatures—fish, a crab. But as the earth's axis changed over thousands of years, so did the signposts. Even though the "animals" have moved, however, the division of the circle—which is what astrologers call a "sign"— remains the same.

Then what is a sun sign?
That is the sign (or division of the zodiac) the sun was passing through at the time of your birth. This is really the foundation of your horoscope, the base of your astrological character. It takes on color and nuances with nine

other planets (the moon is most often referred to as a planet) and the signs in which they fall.

What does it mean that Pisces is a water sign, Aquarius is an air sign?

The definitions of the signs evolved systematically from four components, which interrelate. These four different criteria are: a sign's ELEMENT, its QUALITY, its POLARITY or sex, and its ORDER on the zodiac "belt." These all work together to tell us what the sign is like and how it behaves.

The system is magically mathematical: The number 12—as in the 12 signs of the zodiac—is divisible by 4, by 3, and by 2. Perhaps it is no coincidence that there are four elements, three qualities, and two polarities. The signs follow each other in sequence around the zodiac, starting with Aries.

The four elements (earth, air, fire, and water) are the "building blocks" of astrology. The use of an element to describe a sign probably dates from man's first attempts to categorize what and who he saw in the world. Ancient sages believed that all things were composed of combinations of earth, air, fire, and water. This included the human character, which was fiery/choleric, earthy/melancholy, airy/sanguine, or watery/phlegmatic. The elements also correspond to our emotional (water), physical (earth), mental (air), and spiritual (fire) natures. The energies of each of the elements were then observed to relate to the time of year when the sun was passing through a certain segment of the zodiac.

The fire signs—Aries, Leo, and Sagittarius—embody the characteristics of that element. Optimism, warmth, hot tempers, enthusiasm, and "spirit" are typical of these signs. Taurus, Virgo, and Capricorn are "earthy"—more grounded, physical, materialistic, organized, and deliberate than fire people. Air signs—Gemini, Libra, and Aquarius—are mentally oriented communicators. Water signs—Cancer, Scorpio, and Pisces—are emotional and creative.

Think of what each element does to the others: water puts out fire or evaporates heat. Air fans the flames or blows them out. Earth smothers fire, drifts and erodes

10

with too much wind, becomes mud or fertile soil with water. Those are often perfect analogies for the relationships between signs of these elements! This astro-chemistry was one of the first ways man described his relationships. Fortunately, no one is entirely "air" or "fire." We all have a bit, or a lot, of each element in our horoscopes; it is this unique mix that defines each astrological personality.

Within each element there are three qualities that describe how the sign behaves, how it works. Cardinal signs are the activists, the go-getters. These signs—Aries, Cancer, Libra, and Capricorn—begin each season. Fixed signs are the builders that happen in the middle of the season. You'll find that Taurus, Leo, Scorpio, and Aquarius are gifted with concentration, stubbornness, and stamina. Mutable signs—Gemini, Virgo, Sagittarius, and Pisces—are catalysts for change at the end of each season; these are flexible, adaptable, mobile signs.

The polarity of a sign is its positive or negative "charge." It can be masculine, active, positive, and yang like the air and fire signs. Or feminine, reactive, negative, and yin like the water and earth signs.

Finally, we consider the sign's place in the order of the zodiac. This is vital to the balance of all the forces and the transmission of energy moving through the signs. You may have noticed that your sign is quite different from your neighboring sign on either side. Yet each seems to grow out of its predecessor like links in a chain and transmits a synthesis of energy gathered along the "chain" to the following sign, beginning with the fire-powered active positive charge of Aries.

What if a person has no planets in an element?
Usually that person will be especially challenged in the areas of that low-function element. For instance, someone who has no planets in earth signs may have to work very hard to manifest the material side of life. Or the person may overcompensate in that area and want to be around earthy things—near a beautiful garden, for instance.

It's appropriate here to remember that, in astrology, there are no pat answers. How a chart works out depends on the individual—a missing element could be an area of great self-expression and self-development, as well as a

11

difficult area. One example is a famous television commentator, renowned for his intellectual approach, who has no planets in air signs. The missing element could also be emphasized in the placement of the houses. Someone with no water might have a water sign in a powerful angular position.

Does my sign have a special planet?
Each sign has a "ruling planet" that is most compatible with its energies. Mars rules the fiery, assertive Aries. The sensual beauty and comfort-loving side of Venus rules Taurus, whereas the more idealistic side rules Libra. The quick-moving Mercury rules both Gemini and Virgo—showing its mental agility in Gemini, its critical analytical side in Virgo. Emotional Cancer is ruled by the moon, while outgoing Leo is ruled by the sun. Scorpio was originally given Mars, but when Pluto was discovered in this century, its powerful magnetic energies were deemed more suitable to Scorpio (though many astrologers still consider Mars the co-ruler of Scorpio). Disciplined Capricorn is ruled by Saturn, and expansive Sagittarius by Jupiter. Unpredictable Aquarius is ruled by Uranus and creative, impressionable Pisces by Neptune.

What does an astrologer need to know to cast a horoscope?
First, an astrologer needs to know the date and time of birth, as accurate as possible, and the subject's place of birth. A horoscope can be cast about anything that has a specific time and place.

An astrologer may use a book of tables called an ephemeris to determine the exact placement of the moon and planets at that moment. Today, however, many astrologers prefer to use one of several computer programs available that calculates the exact information very quickly, saving much time and effort.

Once the chart is set up, there is the matter of interpretation. Most astrologers have looked at hundreds of charts and have a ready frame of reference. Each will have a unique point of view, based on experience and interests. Some astrologers may be more literal, some more intuitive, whereas others are also trained psychotherapists. But, although some may seem to have an almost psychic ability, extrasensory perception or any other parapsychological talent is not necessary to be a good astrologer. You can draw a very accurate picture from factual data.

An astrologer may draw up several charts for each client or date—one for the time of birth, one for the current date, and a "progressed" chart showing the changes from that person's birth time to the present. According to your individual needs, there are many other possibilities, such as a chart for a different location, if you are contemplating a change of place.

An astrologer may also be called upon to interpret relationships. Then they will do a special "synastry" chart, which compares the chart of one date with the chart of another date. The relationship can be between any two people or things or events.

An astrologer will be particularly interested in transits—planets passing over the planets or sensitive points in your chart during the upcoming year. These will signal important times for you.

If someone has the same birthday as mine, why aren't our lives similar? What about twins?
Even a few moments difference in time can change a horoscope chart. However, the difference in development of the charts involves how the individual uses the energies. Over and over again, we point out that, though astrology may indicate certain strengths and weaknesses, every person can choose positive or negative ways to express them. We often see strikingly similar charts, belonging to people who bear little resemblance to each other, who have used their energies in radically different ways. Twins may often choose to express different facets of very similar charts, simply from the desire not to be alike.

Besides my "sun sign," how many other signs do I have?
In compiling your astrological data base, we consider eight planets, besides the moon and sun. The phrase "as above, so below" is often used to describe a chart as a microcosm of the universe. The three closest planets to the earth—Mercury, Mars, Venus—and the moon affect

13

your personal character. The next farthest out, Jupiter and Saturn, affect influences from others, turning points, and significant cycles in your life. As we get farther out, the slower-moving planets Uranus, Neptune, and Pluto deal with mass trends that affect your whole generation.

In the western systems of astrology, we confine our charts to the planets and stars within the zodiac. We would not consider the influence of the Big Dipper or Orion or black holes and supernovas.

What about the asteroids and Chiron?

Between Saturn and Uranus lies a ring of thousands of oddly shaped bodies, called asteroids. There is much conjecture about their origin. Some astronomers think they are pieces of a planet or several planets that exploded in the past. Others feel that these are random, floating pieces of matter that never came together to form a planet. Most asteroids are quite small; the larger ones are only about 200 miles in diameter. The asteroids have recently been noticed by astrologers who have begun to chart the effects of the larger asteroids in the horoscopes of clients and have found a correlation with the reemergence of feminine consciousness.

Many astrologers now use the four major asteroids—Pallas, Vesta, Ceres, and Juno—to supply an extra feminine dimension to the chart. Ceres, "the great mother," symbolizes the principle of nurturing, both of ourselves—in terms of self-love—and others. Pallas is the significator of creative intelligence, the healing arts, and the role of woman in a man's world. Vesta deals with the way we use our personal sexual energy and how we integrate it with our focus on work. Juno rules over intimate relationships and our lessons to learn from one-on-one commitments. Astrologer Demetra George has provided an in-depth study of the asteroids in her book *Asteroid Goddesses*, which also contains tables where you can look up the placements of sixteen asteroids.

Chiron is a small body orbiting the sun between Saturn and Uranus. Discovered in 1977, it is thought to be a comet. It travels slowly, taking between 49 and 51 years to make a full transit of the zodiac. In Greek mythology, Chiron was the chief centaur, half man and half horse, who was a teacher to both the Gods and man. In your natal chart, Chiron is thought to relate to your life quest. Its symbol, the key, reflects its power to unlock higher consciousness. As such a small body, Chiron has not been definitely assigned to any astrological sign. However, its teaching and healing energies are thought to be most related to Virgo. A definitive in-depth book on Chiron has been written by astrologer Barbara Hand Clow and is available at your nearest astrological bookstore.

With ten planets to juggle, what more do astrologers need? The answer could come from our quest for depth, richness, and a relationship to the issues of today, which emerges in the archetypes and symbolism of the most recent discoveries. Women's consciousness, deep psychological issues, healing, and ecology, as well as our approach to the afterlife, all have a place in astrological readings and can be clarified by the components discovered in our own time. Whatever is out there or whatever we put out there has a place in the energies that affect us all.

Will astrology conflict with my religious beliefs?
Many religious people disapprove of astrologers, first because they confuse modern-day astrologers with charlatans or fortune-tellers of the past or because they feel someone interested in astrology will turn away from religion. However, the study of astrology actually brings one closer to a religious understanding of the dynamic interchange between the universal plan, the material world, and man's place in it.

There is no religious dogma attached to astrology—although it has deep roots in all religions and can be found in the spiritual history of all races. It is an objective study with no definite rules for behavior, moral codes, or concept of a particular god. Most astrologers stress strongly that you are in charge of your horoscope. It is a diagnostic tool for enlightenment, a helpful method of analysis, but by no means an arbitrary dictator and should not conflict with other forms of spiritual self-development.

I own a personal computer and would like to use it to learn more about astrology by doing some charts for

friends. What kind of program would you recommend for a nonprofessional student of astrology?

If you have a PC, the world of astrology can really open up for you. No longer do you have to spend hours on tedious calculations or rely on guesswork when you set up a chart.

There is software available for every make of computer, at all levels of astrological expertise. Some will calculate a chart in a few seconds and provide pages of interpretations. Others simply run off a chart with technical information. Still others give you mind-boggling menus of different zodiacs, house systems, and types of charts to choose from.

If, like most of our readers, you will be using the program only occasionally for fun, then you don't need an expensive and complicated program. Many options are available that don't require a complicated computer setup to run. The easiest start at less than $100 and can be ordered from one of the several companies specializing in astrology programs. It's a good idea to contact one of these companies and tell them what your needs are and the type of hardware you use.

Some of the names to know are:

MATRIX SOFTWARE
315 Madison Avenue
Big Rapids, MI 49307
1-800-PLANETS, extension 22

ASTRO COMPUTING SERVICES
Dept. AA689, P.O. Box 34487
San Diego, CA 92103-0802

ASTROLABE
Department A.
P.O. Box 28
Orleans, MA 02653
1-800-843-6682

I would like to study astrology—how can I find a good teacher?

There are several ways to find a good teacher. You might

contact one of the regional astrology groups across the country, which have regular meetings; ask at your local metaphysical or "New Age" bookstore.

Astrological organizations such as the National Council for Geocosmic Research may also hold classes in your area. Several times a year, these organizations sponsor regional astrology conferences where you can meet some of the best teachers. Write to the N.C.G.R. for more information:

N.C.G.R. Headquarters
105 Snyder Avenue
Ramsey, NJ 07446

You can also investigate the study-by-mail courses offered by astrological computing services and astrology magazines.

2

How the Planets Operate

To decide who "you" are, an astrologer must weigh and balance nine other planets besides the sun (the moon is considered a "planet," too). Each planet represents a basic force in your life and the sign where it is placed represents how this force will manifest itself. It may be easier to imagine the planet as a person with a choice of twelve different roles to play. In some roles, the person will be more flamboyant or aggressive, in others the more thoughtful or spiritual side of his nature will be expressed.

Interpreting a planet's personality changes according to the different signs is one of the most basic skills in astrology. It's one you can begin to practice yourself with the help of the charts in the "Look Up Your Planets" chapter in this book and the following descriptions. Let's consider first the basic personality of the planet and its function in your life, then the possible roles it can play in each sign.

THE SUN

Because the sun shows your basic will and ego, it's always the strongest planetary personality in your chart. That is why sun sign astrology is so accurate for so many born under the same sign. In chart interpretation, the sun can also play the paternal role. It rules the sign of Leo, gaining strength though the pride, dignity, and confidence of the fixed fire personality. It is also strong in "me-first" Aries. In Aquarius, the sun-ego is strengthened through group participation and social consciousness rather than self-centeredness. In Libra, the sun needs the strength of a partner, an "other," for balance and self-expression.

THE MOON

The most emotional function in your chart is the moon, which represents your subconscious "hidden" side. The moon's function is to dig beneath the surface to reflect your needs, longings, the kind of mothering and childhood conditioning you had. The moon is strongest in Cancer and Taurus—both comforting, home-loving signs where the natural emotional energies of the moon are easily and productively expressed. But, when the moon is in the opposite signs, Capricorn and Scorpio, it leaves the comfortable nest and deals with emotional issues of power and achievement in the outside world. Those of you with the moon in these signs will find your emotional role more challenging in life.

(Because accurate moon tables are too extensive to include in this book, I suggest you consult an astrologer or have a computer chart made to determine your correct moon position.)

MERCURY

Mercury reveals your logical mind, how you think and speak. It stays close to the sun and often shares the same sign as the sun, reinforcing the sun's communicative talents. Mercury operates most easily in the sign it rules—Gemini and Virgo—naturally analytical signs. Yet Mercury in Sagittarius and Pisces, signs where logic often takes second place to visionary ideas, can, when this planet is properly harnessed, provide great visionary thinking and poetic expression.

Since Mercury never moves far from the sun, check the signs preceding and following your sun sign, to see which Mercury position is most applicable to you.

VENUS

Venus is the planet of romantic love, pleasure, and artistry. It shows what you react to, your tastes, what (or who) turns you on. It is strongest in Libra, the sign of partnerships, or Taurus, the sign of physical pleasures. In

19

Pisces, where Venus is exalted, this planet can go over-board, loving to the point of self-sacrifice.

You can find your Venus placement on the chart in this book. Look for the year of your birth in the left-hand column, then follow the line across the page until you read the time of your birthday. The sign heading that column will be your Venus. If you were born on a day when Venus was changing signs, check the signs preceding or following that day.

MARS

This planet is your driving force, your active sexuality. Mars is what makes you run. In Aries, Mars is at his most powerful. Yet this drive can be self-serving and impetuous. In Libra, Mars demands cooperation in a relationship. In Capricorn, Mars becomes an ambitious achiever, headed for the top—but in Cancer, Mars' aggression becomes tempered by feelings, which are always considered. The end can never justify the means, for Mars in Cancer. To find your Mars, refer to the Mars chart in this book and the description later in this chapter.

JUPITER

Jupiter is often viewed as the Santa Claus of the horoscope, a jolly happy planet that brings good luck, gifts, success, and opportunities. Jupiter also embodies the functions of the higher mind, where you do complex, expansive thinking, and deal with the big overall picture rather than the specifics (the province of Mercury). Jupiter functions naturally in Sagittarius, the sign of the philosopher. In Gemini, Jupiter can be a scattered jack-of-all-trades or a lighthearted, effective communicator. In Cancer, Jupiter becomes the protective "big brother." In Capricorn, Jupiter is brought down to earth, its vision harnessed to practical goals.

Be sure to look up your Jupiter "lucky spot" in the tables in this book. But bear in mind that Jupiter gives growth without discrimination or discipline. It's also the place where you could have too much of a good thing, resulting in extravagance, excess pounds, laziness, or carelessness.

SATURN

Saturn has suffered from a bad reputation, always cast as the "heavy" in the chart. The flip side of Saturn is the teacher, however, the one whose class is the toughest in school, but, when you graduate, has taught you lessons you'll never forget. And the tests of Saturn, which come at regular seven-year "exam periods," are the ones you need to pass to survive as a conscious, independent adult. Saturn gives us the grade we've earned—so, if we have studied and prepared for our tests, we needn't be afraid of the "big bad wolf." Saturn in Capricorn is comfortable with this sign's emphasis on structure and respect for authority. In Cancer, however, it suggests both that feeling must become responsible and that authority cannot operate effectively without concern for the heart.

Your Saturn position can illuminate your fears, your hang-ups, your important lessons in life. Remember that Saturn is concerned with your maturity, what you need to know to survive in the world. Be sure to look it up in the Saturn chart in this book.

THE OUTER PLANETS

The three outer planets, Uranus, Neptune, and Pluto are slow-moving but powerful forces in your life. Since they stay in a sign at least seven years, you'll share the sign placement with everyone you went to school with and probably your brothers and sisters. However, the specific place (house) in the horoscope where each one operates is yours alone, and depends on your "moment in time" —the exact time you were born. That's why it is important to have an accurate birth chart.

URANUS

Uranus shakes us out of a rut and propels us forward. When Uranus hits a critical area of your life, such as when it passes another planet, or moves into a new area of your chart, nothing is ever the same again. Uranus strikes hardest at the fixed signs, where a shakeup is sometimes desperately needed. Uranus is right at home in the fixed air sign of Aquarius, where brilliant ideas have universal applications, but in the fixed fire sign of Leo, Uranus breaks up rigid patterns and seems to thumb its nose at proud, sometimes pompous Leo. In Scorpio, its insights lead to transformation, but in Taurus, Uranus becomes focused on revolutionizing earthly affairs, turning daily life topsy-turvy.

NEPTUNE

With Neptune, what you see is not what you get. Neptune is the planet of glamour, dissolution (it dissolves hard reality), illusion, makeup! Neptune is not interested in the world at face value—it dons tinted glasses or blurs the facts with the haze of an intoxicating substance. Where Neptune is, you don't see things quite clearly. This planet's function is to express our visions, and it is most at home in Pisces. In Virgo, Neptune can put visions to practical service. In Cancer, Neptune blends personal feelings and sensitivity on an elevated level, but in the opposite sign of Capricorn, where it is passing through this year, Neptunian glamour fogs over the impersonal structures of society and the workplace. Since Neptune has been in Capricorn for several years, we can witness this in the dissolution of Capricorn areas—big business and government scandals. Neptune can work for some of us while in Capricorn by bringing great creativity to the workplace as well.

PLUTO

Pluto deals with the underside of our personality, digging out our secrets to effect a total transformation. Pluto brings our deep subconscious feelings to the surface through painful probing. Nothing escapes—or is sacred—with Pluto. Because Pluto was discovered only recently, the signs of its exaltation and fall are still debated. But in Scorpio, which Pluto rules, we have been able to witness its effect in the past several years. Pluto symbolizes death and rebirth, violence, elimination, and renewal. Those with strong Scorpio influences in their chart—such as a Scorpio ascendant, sun, or other planets—have probably experienced a transformation in their life in some area.

Planets in Aries

In Aries, each planet will show its most assertive and powerful form.

Moon in Aries—Emotionally, you are independent and ardent. You love the challenge of an emotional pursuit and difficult situations in love only intensify your excitement. But once you attain your goal or conquer your pursuit, your ardor cools. To avoid continuous "treat 'em rough" situations, work on developing patience and tolerance.

Mercury in Aries—You say what you think, even if it provokes confrontation, and you have an active, assertive nature. Your mind is sharp, alert, impatient, though you may not think things through. You may need to develop thoroughness in your analytical processes.

Venus in Aries—You love the sense of challenge that adds spice to life, and might even pick a fight now and then to charge the atmosphere. Since a good chase revs up your romantic motor, you could abandon a romance if the going becomes too smooth. You're first on the block with the newest styles. And first out the door if you're bored or ordered around.

Mars in Aries—You run in high gear, showing the full force of Mars energy. You have a fiery explosive disposition, but are also very courageous, with enormous drive. You'll tackle problems head on and mow down anything that stands in your way. Though you're supercharged and can jump-start others, you are short on perseverance, especially when the situation requires diplomacy, patience, and tolerance.

Jupiter in Aries—You have big ambitions and won't settle for second place. You are luckiest when you are pioneering an innovative project, when you are pushing to be "first." You can break new ground with this placement, but watch a tendency to be pushy and arrogant.

You'll also need to learn patience and perseverance in the house where Jupiter falls in your horoscope.

Saturn in Aries—There's no pushing you around! Saturn puts the brakes on Aries' natural drive and enthusism. You'll have to learn to cooperate, tone down self-centeredness.

Uranus in Aries—With a powerful mixture of fire and electricity powering your generation, you were creative pioneers, developing the airplane, the computer, the cyclotron. You never let anything hold you back from exploring the unknown. You have a surprise in store for everyone, and your life can be jolted by sudden, unpredictable changes.

NEPTUNE and PLUTO were not in ARIES in this century.

Planets in Taurus

Planets in Taurus add stability and practicality to your chart.

Moon in Taurus—Solid, secure, comfortable situations and relationships appeal to you. You need displays of affection and gravitate to those who provide you with material comforts and sensual pleasures. Your emotions are steady and nurturing in this strong moon sign, but you could lean toward stubbornness when pushed. You could miss out on some of life's excitement by sticking to the safe straight and narrow road.

Mercury in Taurus—You are deliberate, thorough, with good concentration. You'll take the slow, methodical approach and leave no stone unturned. You'll see a problem through to the end, stick with a subject until you become an expert. You may talk very slowly, with a melodious or very distinctive voice.

Venus in Taurus—Venus is literally "at home" in Taurus. It's a terrific placement for a "Material Girl" or boy, an interior designer, or a musician. You love to surround yourself with the very finest smells, tastes, sounds, visuals, textures. You'd run from an austere lifestyle or uncomfortable surroundings. Creature comforts turn you on. And so does a beautiful, secure nest—and nest egg. Not one to rush about, you take time to enjoy your pleasures and treasures.

Mars in Taurus—Persistence is a great advantage of those with Mars in Taurus. Gifted with stamina and focus, this Mars may not be first out of the gate, but you're sure to finish. You tend to wear away or outlast your foes rather than bowl them over. This Mars is super-sensual sexually—you take your time and enjoy yourself all the way.

Jupiter in Taurus—You have expensive tastes and like to surround yourself with the luxuries money can buy, acquire beauty and comfort in all its forms. You could tend to expand physically—from overindulgence in good tastes! Dieting could be a major challenge. Land and real estate are especially lucky for you.

Saturn in Taurus—"How am I going to pay the rent?" You'll have to weather some lean periods, get control of your material life. Learn to use your talents to their fullest potential. In the same boat, Ben Franklin had the right idea: "A penny saved is a penny earned."

Uranus in Taurus—Your generation were the hippies who rejected the establishment values. You who were intent on doing your own thing are natural entrepreneurs —you'd probably like to be self-employed if you are not already on your own. However, it's likely that you've also had many sudden financial shake-ups. This is one of Uranus' most unstable positions.

NEPTUNE and PLUTO were not in TAURUS in this century.

Planets in Gemini

Planets in Gemini add a versatile, intellectual dimension to your chart.

Moon in Gemini—You need constant emotional stimulation and enjoy an outgoing, diversified lifestyle. You could have difficulty with commitment, and therefore marry more than once or have a love life of changing partners. An outgoing, interesting, talented partner could merit your attention, however. Don't spread yourself too thin to accomplish major goals—and watch a tendency to be emotionally fragmented. Find a creative way to express the range of your feelings.

Mercury in Gemini—This phase is a quick study. You can handle many subjects at once, jumping from one to the other with ease. You may, however, spread yourself too thin. You express yourself well both verbally and in writing. You are a "people person" who enjoys communicating with a large audience.

Venus in Gemini—You're a sparkler who "Loves the Night Life," with constant variety, a frequent change of scenes—and loves. You like lots of stimulation, a varied social life, and are better at light flirtations than serious romances. You may be attracted to younger playful lovers who have the pep and energy to keep up with you.

Mars in Gemini—"Two loves are better than one" is a philosophy that could get this Mars in trouble. Your restless nature searches out stimulation and will switch rather than fight. Your life gets complicated—but that only makes it more interesting for you. You have a way with words and can "talk" with your hands. Since you tend to go all over the lot in your interests, you may have to work hard to develop focus and concentration.

Jupiter in Gemini—You love to be in the center of a whirlwind of activity, talking a blue streak, with all phone lines busy. You have great facility in expressing yourself verbally or in writing. Work that involves communicating or manual dexterity is especially lucky for you. Watch a tendency to be too restless—slow down from time to time. Try not to spread yourself too thin.

Saturn in Gemini—You're a deep thinker, with lofty ideals—a good position for scientific studies. You may be quite shy, speak slowly, or have fears or difficulty communicating. You'll take shelter in abstract ideas when dealing with emotional issues.

Uranus in Gemini—You are the first generation of the information era. Electronic mass communication developed at breakneck speed in your lifetime. You were watching TV since childhood, and now stock up on fax machines, modems, car telephones, not to mention the most sophisticated home telephone systems. You are the generation that popularized the talk show—you are forever reaching out in new ways.

NEPTUNE was not in GEMINI in this century.

Pluto in Gemini—A time of mass suggestion and breakthroughs in communication. Many brilliant writers, such as Ernest Hemingway and F. Scott Fitzgerald, were born in this phase. Henry Miller, James Joyce, and D. H. Lawrence scandalized the world with explicit sex in literature. Muckraking journalism and psychoanalysis (talk therapy) transformed both journalism and mental health fields.

Planets in Cancer

These planets are more nurturing, sensitive, and emotionally self-protective.

Moon in Cancer—The moon is strongest here, making you the zodiac nurturer—one who needs to be needed. You have an excellent memory and an intuitive understanding of the needs of others. You are happiest at home and may work in a home office or turn your corner of the company into a home away from home. Work that supplies food and shelter, occult studies, and psychology could take advantage of this lunar position.

Mercury in Cancer—You have empathy for others—can read their feelings. You are intuitive, rather than logical. And your thoughts are always colored by your emotions. You have an excellent memory and imagination.

Venus in Cancer—You can be "Daddy's girl" or "Mama's boy," like the late Liberace. You love to be babied, coddled, and protected in a cozy, secure home. Men with this position are attracted to old-fashioned femininity, Victorian lace fantasies. Women are attracted to those who make you feel secure, well provided for. You could also have a secret love life or clandestine arrangement with a sugar daddy. You love to mother others as well.

Mars in Cancer—You are given to moods and can be quite crabby. This may be due to a fragile sense of security. You are quite self-protective and secretive about your life, which might make you appear untrustworthy or manipulative to others. Try not to take things so much to heart—cultivate a sense of impersonality or detachment. Sexually, you are tender and sensitive, a very protective lover.

Jupiter in Cancer—This Jupiter has a big safe-deposit box, an attic piled to overflowing with boxes of treasures. You may still have your christening dress or your beloved high school sweater. This Jupiter loves to accumulate things, to save for a rainy day, or gather collections. Negatively, you could be a hoarder with closets full of things you'll never use. This protective, nurturing Jupiter often has many mouths to feed— human or animal. Naturally, this placement produces great restaurateurs and hotel managers. The shipping business is also a good bet.

Saturn in Cancer—Some very basic fears could center on your early home environment, overcoming a negative childhood influence to establish a sense of security. You may fear being mothered or smothered—and be tested in your female relationships. You may have to learn to be objective and distance yourself emotionally when threatened or when dealing with negative feelings such as jealousy or guilt.

Uranus in Cancer—Your generation grew up at a time when women's roles were being redefined and the concept of the tight-knit nuclear family was changing. This was also the time of the family shows on electronic media, such as "I Love Lucy," "I Remember Mama," "Father Knows Best." Since divorce became commonplace with your generation, you probably have some unusual ideas about marriage and family. Your generation matured at the time of New Age movements, renewed interest in dreams, psychic phenomena.

Neptune in Cancer—Those with this placement were born in the first quarter of the century. This was a time when family ties extended to the nation—motherhood, the homeland, flag-waving patriotism characterizes this Neptune. Many of you, such as Julia Child and Dr. Spock, have found ways to glamorize and profit from homemaking and child rearing.

Pluto in Cancer—A time of mass manipulation by emotional appeals. Dictators pushed patriotism to extremes. Women's rights legislation transformed the role of women. You who have this placement are deeply sentimental, place great value on emotional and financial security, because this was the time of the Great Depression.

Planets in Leo

These planets show their boldest, most flamboyant show-biz side.

Moon in Leo—You need to be treated like royalty! Strong support, loyalty, and loud applause win your heart. You

29

rule over your territory, and resent anyone who intrudes on your turf. Your attraction to the finer things in people and in your lifestyle could give you a snobbish outlook. But basically you have a warm, passionate, loyal, emotional nature that gives generously to those you deem worthy.

Mercury in Leo—You express yourself dramatically and hold the attention of others. You think "big"—and prefer to skip the details. You are a good salesperson and public speaker.

Venus in Leo—You're an "Uptown Girl" or boy who loves "Putting on the Ritz," where you can consort with elegant people, dress extravagantly, and be the center of attention. Think of Coco Chanel, who piled on the jewelry and decorated tweed suits with gold braid. You dress and act like a star, but you may be attracted to hangers-on and flatterers rather than relationships with solid value.

Mars in Leo—This phase fills you with self-confidence and charisma. You come on strong, with show-biz flair. In fact you'll head right for the spotlight. Sexually, you're a giver—but you do demand the royal treatment in return. You enjoy giving orders and can create quite a scene if you're disobeyed. At some point, you may have to learn some lessons in humility.

Jupiter in Leo—Naturally warm, romantic, and playful, you can't get too much attention or applause. Politics or show business—anywhere you can perform for an audience —are lucky for you. You love the good life and are happy to share your wealth with others. Negatively, you could be extravagant and tend to hog center stage. Let others take a bow from time to time. Also, be careful not to overdo or overspend.

Saturn in Leo—This phase can bring ego problems. Because you have not received the love you crave, you could be an overly strict, dictatorial parent. You may demand respect and a position of leadership at any cost. You may have to watch a tendency toward rigidity and withholding affection. Learn to relax, have fun, lighten up!

Uranus in Leo—This period coincided with the rise of rock and roll and the heydey of Hollywood. Self-expression (Leo) led to the exhibitionism of the sixties. Electronic media was used skillfully for self-promotion. This "thirty-something" generation may have a very eccentric kind of charisma and a life sparked by unusual love affairs. Your children also may be out of the ordinary in some way. Where this planet falls in your chart, you'll show the full force of your personality in a unique way, like tennis great Martina Navratilova.

Neptune in Leo—Here was the glamour of the twenties, the beginning of the "star system" in Hollywood. Lavish spending blurred the harsh realities of the day. When Neptune left Leo in 1929, this coincided with the stock market crash. Those born with this placement have a flair for drama but may idealize fame without realizing there's a price to pay.

Pluto in Leo—This is the do-your-own-thing generation—who place extreme emphasis on self-expression. Flamboyant performers swayed the masses and those born during this time—such as Mick Jagger and John Lennon and the rock-and-roll stars—transformed the entertainment business. You born in this generation reflect this powerful Pluto's star quality, creativity, and self-centeredness.

Planets in Virgo

These planets show their most practical analytical side.

Moon in Virgo—This moon often draws you to situations in which you play the role of healer, teacher, or critic. You may find it difficult to accept others as they are or enjoy what you have. The Virgo moon, negatively, can be hard on others and yourself—you may have impossible standards and be constantly judging others to see if they "measure up." Take it easy!

Mercury in Virgo—You are a natural critic. You pay attention to details and have a talent for thorough analysis, although you tend to focus on the practical side of things. Teaching and editing come naturally to you.

Venus in Virgo—This Venus is attracted to perfect order, but underneath your pristine white dress is some naughty black lace! You fall for those who you can "make over" or improve in some way. You may also like those in the medical profession. Here Venus may express itself best through some kind of service—giving loving support. You may find it difficult to show your true feelings, to really let go in intimate moments.

Mars in Virgo—You are a worker bee, a "Felix Unger" character who notices every detail. This is a thorough, painstaking Mars who worries a great deal about making mistakes—this "worrier" tendency may lead to very tightly strung nerves under your controlled facade. Your energy can be expressed positively in a field such as teaching or editing; however, your tendency to find fault could make you a hard-to-please lover. Learning to delegate and praise, rather than do everything perfectly yourself, could make you easier to live with. You enjoy a good mental companionship, with less emphasis on sex and no emotional turmoil.

Jupiter in Virgo—You like to work! In fact, work can be more interesting than play for you. You have a sharp eye for details and notice every flaw! Be careful not to get caught up in nitpicking. You expect nothing short of perfection from others. Finding practical solutions to problems and helping others make the most of themselves are better uses for this Jupiter. Consider some form of health work, nutrition, medicine, or education.

Saturn in Virgo—You can be very hard on yourself, making yourself sick by worrying about every little detail. You must learn to set priorities, discriminate, and laugh!

Uranus in Virgo—Your generation came at a time of student rebellions, the civil rights movement, and mass acceptance of health foods. You'll be concerned with pollution and cleaning up the environment. You could revolutionize the healing arts, making nontraditional methods acceptable. This generation has also campaigned against the use of dangerous pesticides and cigarette smoking.

Neptune in Virgo—This Neptune glamorizes health and fitness (e.g., Jane Fonda). This generation invented fitness videos, marathon running, television sports. You may include psychotherapy as part of your mental health regime. You glamorized the workplace, and your devotion to working overtime and weekends inspired the term *workaholics*.

Pluto in Virgo—This is the "Yuppie" generation that sparked a mass movement toward fitness, health, career. During this generation, machines were invented to process the detail work efficiently. Inventions took a practical turn: answering machines, sophisticated telephones, office copiers, which helped transform the workplace.

Planets in Libra

These planets are concerned with relationships, aesthetics, and ideals.

Moon in Libra—Your emotional role is partnership-oriented. You may find it difficult to do things alone. You need the emotional balance of a strong "other." You thrive in an elegant, harmonious atmosphere, where you get attention and flattery. This moon needs to keep it light. Heavy emotions cause your Libran moon's scales to swing precariously. So does an overly possessive or demanding partner.

Mercury in Libra—You are a smooth talker, with a graceful gift of gab. Though skilled in diplomacy and debate, you may vacillate in making decisions, forever juggling the pros and cons. You speak in elegant, well-modulated tones.

Venus in Libra—"I Feel Pretty" sings this Venus. You love a beautiful, harmonious, luxurious atmosphere. Many artists and musicians thrive with this Venus, with its natural feeling for the balance of colors and sounds. In love, you make a very compatible partner in a supportive relationship where there are few confrontations. You can't stand arguments or argumentative people. The good looks of your partner may also be a deciding factor.

Mars in Libra—You are a passive aggressor who avoids confrontations and charms people into doing what you want. You do best in a position where you can exercise your great diplomatic skills. Mars is in its detriment in Libra, and expends much energy deciding which course of action to take. However, setting a solid goal in life, perhaps one that expresses your passion for beauty, justice, or art, could give you the vantage point you need to achieve success. In love, like Michael Douglas, you'll seek beauty in your partner and surroundings.

Jupiter in Libra—You function best when you have a stimulating partner. You also need harmonious, beautiful surroundings. Chances are, you have closets full of fashionable clothes. The serious side of this Jupiter has an excellent sense of fair play, and often plays the diplomat or judge. Careers in law, the arts, or fashion are favored.

Saturn in Libra—You may have your most successful marriage (or your first) later in life, because you must learn to stand on your own first. How to relate to others is one of your major lessons. Your great sense of fairness makes you a good judge or lawyer, or a prominent diplomat like former Secretary of State Henry Kissinger.

Uranus in Libra—Born at a time when the divorce rate soared and the women's lib movement gained ground, this generation will have some revolutionary ideas about marriage and partnerships. You may have an on-again, off-again relationship, choose unusual partners, or prefer to stay uncommitted. You'll also pioneer concepts in justice and revolutionize the arts.

Neptune in Libra—Born at a time when "Ozzie and Harriet" was the marital ideal, this generation went on to glamorize "relating" in ways that idealized equality and is still trying to find its balance in marriage. There have been many divorces as this generation tries to adapt traditional marriage concepts to modern times—and allow both sexes free expression.

Pluto in Libra—As this generation now begins to assert itself, we will see the reflection of the time of their birth—the 1970s and early 1980s. Attitudes toward relationships were transformed during this time from an emphasis on open relationships to more committed and safe partnerships. Landmark legislation on gay rights, euthanasia, and the ERA took place. Marital partnerships emphasized equal sharing.

Planets in Scorpio

These planets function in a very intense, focused, emotional way.

Moon in Scorpio—You take disappointments very hard and are often drawn to extreme situations, dealing with issues of power and control. You need a stable, secure emotional life, because you are especially vulnerable to jealousy. Meaningful work could provide a healthy outlet to diffuse your intense needs. Medicine, occult work, police work, and psychology are good possibilities.

Mercury in Scorpio—You have a sharp mind and can be sarcastic and prone to making cutting remarks. You have a penetrating insight and will stop at nothing to get to the heart of matters. You are an excellent and thorough researcher or detective. You enjoy problems that challenge your investigative skills.

Venus in Scorpio—Here, Venus wants "Body and Soul." Your attraction to the dark and mysterious could involve you with the wrong people—just to figure them out. You know how to keep a secret and have quite a few of your own. This is a very intense placement, where you can be preoccupied with sex and power. Living dangerously adds spice to your life, but don't get burned. All that's intense appeals to you—heady perfume, deep rich colors, dark woods, spicy foods.

Mars in Scorpio—You have a powerful drive (relax, sometimes!) that could become an obsession. So learn to use this energy wisely and well. For Mars in Scorpio hates to compromise, loves with "all or nothing" fever (while it lasts), and can become jealous or manipulative if you don't get your way! But your powerful concentration and nonstop stamina is an asset in challenging fields like medicine or scientific research. You're the Master Planner, a super-strategist who, when well-directed, can achieve important goals.

Jupiter in Scorpio—This phase loves the power of handling other people's money—or lives! Others see you as having nerves of steel. You have luck in detective work, sex-related ventures, psychotherapy, research, the occult, or tax matters—anything that involves a mystery. At least one great master spy has this placement. You're always going to extremes, testing the limits gives you a thrill. Your timing is excellent—you'll wait for the perfect moment to make your moves. Negatively this Jupiter could use power to achieve selfish ends.

Saturn in Scorpio—Your tests arise when you handle situations involving the control of others. You could fear depending on others financially or sexually—or there could be a blurring of the lines between sex and money. Sexual tests, periods of celibacy (resulting from fear of "merging" with another), sex for money are some ways this could manifest itself.

Uranus in Scorpio—Uranus here shook up our sexual ideas, and this generation (now adults) will have unorthodox sex lives, will delve beneath the surface to explore life after death, mediumship, transformation of any sort. This time signaled public awareness of the New Age. Body and mind control will be an issue with this generation—and they may explore innovative high-tech methods to do it, making breakthroughs in medicine and scientific research.

Neptune in Scorpio—Because of their healing, regenerative powers, this generation will be involved in rescuing the planet from the effects of the abuse of power. Born at a time that glamorized sex and drugs, this generation matured at a time when the price was paid in sexually transmitted diseases and abuses of drugs like cocaine. The emphasis on transformative spiritual power is especially heightened in their lives.

Pluto in Scorpio—Since August 1984, Pluto has been moving through its ruling sign of Scorpio, coming as close to the earth as its orbit will allow, and giving us the full force of its transformative power. Devastating, sexually transmitted diseases such as AIDS, nuclear power controversies, extreme turnabouts in international politics are signs of this tiny planet's force. It may be helpful to remember that Pluto clears the decks in order to start anew. It's the phoenix rising from the ashes that should hearten those of you who are undergoing Pluto transformations in your life. Babies born now will reflect Scorpio concerns such as sex, birth and death (and transcending death), nuclear power.

Planets in Sagittarius

Planets here expand personal freedom and elevate their energies.

Moon in Sagittarius—This moon needs freedom—you can't stand to be possessed by anyone. You have emotional wanderlust and may need a constant dose of mental and spiritual stimulation. But you cope with the fluctuations of life with good humor and a spirit of adventure. You may find great satisfaction in exotic situations, foreign travels, and spiritual studies, rather than in intense relationships.

Mercury in Sagittarius—You have a great sense of humor but a tendency toward tactlessness. You enjoy telling others what you see as the truth "for their own good." You can be dogmatic when you feel you're in the right, and you can expound endlessly on your own ideas. Watch a tendency to puff up ideas unrealistically (however, this talent could serve you well in sales positions).

Venus in Sagittarius—Travel, athletics, New Age philosophies, and a casual and carefree lifestyle appeal to you. You are attracted to exciting idealistic types who give you plenty of space. Large animals, especially horses, are part of your life. You probably have a four-wheel-drive vehicle—or a motorized skateboard—anything to keep moving.

Mars in Sagittarius—In Sagittarius, the "conquering hero" sets off on a crusade. You're great at getting things off the ground! Your challenge is to consider the consequences of your actions. In love with freedom, you don't always make the best marriage partner. Love 'em and leave 'em could be your motto. You may also gravitate toward risk and adventure and may have great athletic skill. You're best off in a situation where you can express your love of adventure, philosophy, and travel or where you can use artistic talents to elevate the lives of others, like Johann Sebastian Bach.

Jupiter in Sagittarius—In its natural place, Jupiter compels you to expand your mind, travel far from home, collect college degrees. This is the placement of the philosopher, the gambler, the animal trainer, the publisher. You have an excellent sense of humor and a cheerful disposition. This placement often works with animals, especially horses.

Saturn in Sagittarius—This phase accepts nothing at face value. You are the opposite of the "happy-go-lucky" Sagittarius. With Saturn here, your beliefs must be fully examined and tested. Firsthand experience, without the guidance of dogma, gurus, or teachers is your best education. This Saturn has little tolerance for another authority. You won't follow a "dream" unless you understand the idea behind it.

Uranus in Sagittarius—Those born in the 1980s could be the first generation to travel in outer space! Uranus (electronic innovation) in Sagittarius (long trips) tempts us to make speculations like this. Earlier in this century, the Wright brothers and Charles Lindberg began to fly during this transit. It's for sure that this generation will make some unusual modes of religion, philosophy, and higher education as well as long-distance travel.

Neptune in Sagittarius—In the 1970s and early 1980s, the New Age was born and astronaut travel became a reality. The Neptune influence glamorized mysticism, meditation, new approaches to religion—with gurus, and mind expansion via drugs. This generation will take a creative and imaginative approach to spiritual and philosophical life, with emphasis on mysticism, clairvoyance. Perhaps they will develop new spiritually oriented schools. They will also redefine the use of petroleum (Neptune-ruled) in travel.

Pluto in Sagittarius—Pluto moves into Sagittarius on January 17, 1995, a day to mark on your calendar! This should signal a time of great expansion and transformation physically, mentally, and spiritually. Perhaps Pluto, the planet of extremes, will make space travel (or space visitors) a reality. There will be new emphasis on publishing, higher education, religion, animal rights. And we'll be concerned with elevating our lives with a higher sense of purpose—something to look forward to at the close of the century!

Planets in Capricorn

Planets here function in their most organized, result-oriented way.

Moon in Capricorn—In its detriment, the moon here is cool and calculating. You get serious about matters of prestige and position, rather than romance. Although you are dutiful toward those you love, you expend most of your emotion on your climb to the top of the business or social ladder. Improving your position in life gives you the most satisfaction.

Mercury in Capricorn—This phase has excellent mental discipline. You take a serious, orderly approach and play by the rules. You have a super-organized mind that grasps structures easily, though you may lack originality. You have a dry sense of humor.

Venus in Capricorn—This ambitious Venus may seem calculating, but underneath you're insecure and want a substantial relationship you can count on. However, it wouldn't hurt if your beloved could help you up the ladder professionally. This Venus is often attracted to objects and people of a different generation (you could marry someone much older—or younger)—antiques, traditional clothing (sometimes worn in a very "today" way), and dignified conservative behavior are trademarks.

Mars in Capricorn—Mars is exalted in Capricorn, a "chief executive" placement that gives you a drive for success and the discipline to achieve it. You deliberately aim for status and a high position in life, and you'll keep climbing, despite the odds. This Mars will work for what you get. You are well organized and persistent—a winning combination. Sexually, you have a strong, earthy drive—but may prefer someone who can be useful to you rather than someone flashy or superficially fascinating.

Jupiter in Capricorn—You are luckiest working in an established situation, within a traditional structure. In the sign of caution and restraint, Jupiter is thrifty rather than a big spender. You accumulate duties and responsibilities, which is fine for business leadership. You'll expand in those areas where you can achieve respect, prestige, or social position. People with this position are especially concerned that nothing be wasted. You might have great success in a recycling or renovation business.

Saturn in Capricorn—You are sensitive to public opinion and achieving a high-status image. You are not a big risk taker, because you do not want to compromise your position. In its most powerful place, Saturn is the teacher par excellence, giving structure and form to your life. Your persistence will assure you a continual climb to the top.

Uranus in Capricorn—Passing through Capricorn since 1988, Uranus will be shaking up our lives in this area until 1996. During this time expect the foundations of traditional structures to rattle, if not crumble like the Berlin Wall. High-tech (Uranus) practical gadgets are revolutionizing our daily lives. Home and portable computers and fax machines bring new independence to the workplace. Increasing numbers of us will be working on our own. Those born with this placement will take an independent, innovative approach to their careers. They'll also have the task of reconciling tradition with change.

Neptune in Capricorn—Beginning in 1984 and continuing until 1998, this has been a time when material values are first glamorized, then dashed on the rocks of reality. As first Saturn, then Uranus, pass by, Neptune performs its dissolving magic on Capricorn's walls of tradition and structure everywhere. In the marketplace, we should see some especially disillusioned management as Neptune dissolves traditional corporate structures.

PLUTO will not be in CAPRICORN in this century.

Planets in Aquarius

Planets here show their most independent, original, and humanitarian functions.

Moon in Aquarius—This is a gregarious moon, happiest when surrounded by people. You're everybody's buddy—as long as no one gets too close. You'd rather stay pals. You make your own rules in emotional situations, may have a radically different life or love-style. Intimate relationships may feel too confining—and you need plenty of space.

Mercury in Aquarius—This phase has a highly original point of view, combined with good mental focus. You are an independent thinker, who would break the rules to make your point. You are, however, fixed mentally, and are reluctant to change your mind once it is made up—and you could come across as a know-it-all.

Venus in Aquarius—You love to be surrounded by people, but are uncomfortable with intense emotions (steer clear of Venus in Scorpio!). You like a spontaneous lifestyle, full of surprises. You make your own rules in everything you do, including love. The avant garde, high technology, and possible unusual sexual experiences attract you.

Mars in Aquarius—This phase is a visionary and often a revolutionary who stands out from the crowd. You are innovative and highly original in your methods. Sexually, you could go for out-of-the-ordinary relationships. You have a rebellious streak and like to shake people up a bit. Intimacy can be a problem—you may keep lots of people around you or isolate yourself to prevent others from getting too close.

Jupiter in Aquarius—This phase is lucky when doing good in the world. You are extremely idealistic and think in the most expansive terms about improving society at large—an excellent position for a politician or labor leader.

You're "everybody's buddy" who can relate to people of diverse backgrounds. You are luckiest when you can operate away from rigid rules and conservative organizations.

Saturn in Aquarius—Saturn here can make you feel like an outsider, one who doesn't fit into the group. There may be a lack of trust in others, a kind of defensiveness that could engender defensiveness in return. Not a superficial social butterfly, your commitment to groups must have depth and humanitarian meaning.

Uranus in Aquarius—At home in its own sign, Uranus produced great innovative minds such as Orson Welles and Leonard Bernstein, plus many breakthroughs in science and technology. It will once again enter Aquarius in 1995–2002, when we can expect the unexpected, because this planet will be at its most revolutionary, eccentric, and brilliant. This generation will be much concerned with global issues that unite humanity, and with experimentation on every level.

NEPTUNE and PLUTO will not be in AQUARIUS in this century.

Planets in Pisces

These planets show their most sensitive, emotional side.

Moon in Pisces—This watery moon needs an emotional anchor to help you keep grounded in reality. Otherwise, you tend to escape through fantasies or intoxicating substances. Creative work could give you a far more productive way to express yourself and get away from it all. Working in a healing or helping profession is also good for you because you get satisfaction from helping the underdog. You naturally attract people with sob stories, but you should also cultivate friends with a positive, upbeat point of view.

Mercury in Pisces—This phase has a poetic mind that is receptive to psychic, intuitive influences. You may be vague and forgetful of details and find it difficult to work within a structure, but you are strong on creative expression. You'll express yourself in a very sympathetic, caring way. You should find work that uses your imaginative talents.

Venus in Pisces—"Why not take all of me," sings this exalted Venus, who loves to give. You may have a collection of stray animals, lost souls, the underprivileged, the lonely. Try to assess their motives in a clear light. You're a natural for theater, film, anything involving fantasy. Psychic or spiritual life also fascinates you, as does selfless service for a needy cause.

Mars in Pisces—You like to play different roles. Your ability to tune in and project others' emotions makes you a natural actor—many film and television personalities have this placement, such as Mary Tyler Moore, Jane Seymour, Cybill Shepherd, Burt Reynolds, and Jane Fonda. You understand how to use glamour and illusion for your own benefit. You can switch emotions on and off quickly, and you're especially good at getting sympathy. You'll go for romance, though real-life relationships never quite live up to your fantasies.

Jupiter in Pisces—You work best in a creative field or in one where you are helping the downtrodden. You exude sympathy and gravitate toward the underdog. Beware a tendency to be too self-sacrificing and overly emotional. You should also be careful not to overindulge in alcohol or drugs. Some lucky work areas: oil, fragrances, dance, footwear, alcohol, pharmaceuticals, and the arts, especially film.

Saturn in Pisces—This phase generates a sense of helplessness, of vulnerability, of feeling like a victim of circumstances. You could underestimate yourself or subordinate yourself to a powerful institution. This placement can give great wisdom, however, if you can manage to look inward to contemplation and meditation—like

Edgar Cayce—rather than outward, for solutions. You have the ability to cope!

Uranus in Pisces—Many of the early well-known TV personalities were born with this placement, because this generation was the first to exploit the electronic media. This was the time of Prohibition (Pisces rules alcohol) and the development of the film industry (also Pisces ruled). The next go-round, in the early 2000s, could bring on the Hollywood of the twenty-first century!

NEPTUNE and PLUTO will not be in PISCES in this century.

3

Look Up Your Planets

The following tables are provided so that you can look up the signs of seven major planets—Venus, Mars, Saturn, Jupiter, Uranus, Neptune, and Pluto. We do not have room for tables for the moon and Mercury, which change signs often.

How to Use the Venus Table

Find the year of your birth in the vertical column on the left, then follow across the page until you find the correct date. The Venus sign is at the top of that column.

How to Use the Mars, Saturn, and Jupiter Tables

Find the year of your birth date on the left side of each column. The dates the planet entered each sign are listed on the right side of each column. (Signs are abbreviated to the first three letters.) Your birthday should fall on or between each date listed, and your planetary placement should correspond to the earlier sign of that period.

How to Use the Uranus, Neptune, and Pluto Tables

Find your birthday in the list following each sign.

LOOK UP YOUR URANUS PLACEMENT by finding your birthday on the following lists:

URANUS IN ARIES BIRTH DATES:

March 31–November 4, 1927
January 13, 1928–June 6, 1934
October 10, 1934–March 28, 1935

URANUS IN TAURUS BIRTH DATES:

June 6, 1934–October 10, 1935
March 28, 1935–August 7, 1941
October 5, 1941–May 15, 1942

URANUS IN GEMINI BIRTH DATES:

August 7–October 5, 1941
May 15, 1942–August 30, 1948
November 12, 1948–June 10, 1949

URANUS IN CANCER BIRTH DATES:

August 30–November 12, 1948
June 10, 1949–August 24, 1955
January 28–June 10, 1956

URANUS IN LEO BIRTH DATES:

August 24, 1955–January 28, 1956
June 10, 1956–November 1, 1961
January 10–August 10, 1962

VENUS SIGNS 1901–2000

	Aries	Taurus	Gemini	Cancer	Leo	Virgo
1901	3/29-4/22	4/22-5/17	5/17-6/10	6/10-7/5	7/5-7/29	7/29-8/23
1902	5/7-6/3	6/3-6/30	6/30-7/25	7/25-8/19	8/19-9/13	9/13-10/7
1903	2/28-3/24	3/24-4/18	4/18-5/13	5/13-6/9	6/9-7/7	7/7-8/17 9/6-11/8
1904	3/13-5/7	5/7-6/1	6/1-6/25	6/25-7/19	7/19-8/13	8/13-9/6
1905	2/3-3/6 4/9-5/28	3/6-4/9 5/28-7/8	7/8-8/6	8/6-9/1	9/1-9/27	9/27-10/21
1906	3/1-4/7	4/7-5/2	5/2-5/26	5/26-6/20	6/20-7/16	7/16-8/11
1907	4/27-5/22	5/22-6/16	6/16-7/11	7/11-8/4	8/4-8/29	8/29-9/22
1908	2/14-3/10	3/10-4/5	4/5-5/5	5/5-9/8	9/8-10/8	10/8-11/3
1909	3/29-4/22	4/22-5/16	5/16-6/10	6/10-7/4	7/4-7/29	7/29-8/23
1910	5/7-6/3	6/4-6/29	6/30-7/24	7/25-8/18	8/19-9/12	9/13-10/6
1911	2/28-3/23	3/24-4/17	4/18-5/12	5/13-6/8	6/9-7/7	7/8-11/8
1912	4/13-5/6	5/7-5/31	6/1-6/24	6/24-7/18	7/19-8/12	8/13-9/5
1913	2/3-3/6 5/2-5/30	3/7-5/1 5/31-7/7	7/8-8/5	8/6-8/31	9/1-9/26	9/27-10/20
1914	3/14-4/6	4/7-5/1	5/2-5/25	5/26-6/19	6/20-7/15	7/16-8/10
1915	4/27-5/21	5/22-6/15	6/16-7/10	7/11-8/3	8/4-8/28	8/29-9/21
1916	2/14-3/9	3/10-4/5	4/6-5/5	5/6-9/8	9/9-10/7	10/8-11/2
1917	3/29-4/21	4/22-5/15	5/16-6/9	6/10-7/3	7/4-7/28	7/29-8/21
1918	5/7-6/2	6/3-6/28	6/29-7/24	7/25-8/18	8/19-9/11	9/12-10/5
1919	2/27-3/22	3/23-4/16	4/17-5/12	5/13-6/7	6/8-7/7	7/8-11/8
1920	4/12-5/6	5/7-5/30	5/31-6/23	6/24-7/18	7/19-8/11	8/12-9/4
1921	2/3-3/6 4/26-6/1	3/7-4/25 6/2-7/7	7/8-8/5	8/6-8/31	9/1-9/25	9/26-10/20
1922	3/13-4/6	4/7-4/30	5/1-5/25	5/26-6/19	6/20-7/14	7/15-8/9
1923	4/27-5/21	5/22-6/14	6/15-7/9	7/10-8/3	8/4-8/27	8/28-9/20
1924	2/13-3/8	3/9-4/4	4/5-5/5	5/6-9/8	9/9-10/7	10/8-11/12
1925	3/28-4/20	4/21-5/15	5/16-6/8	6/9-7/3	7/4-7/27	7/28-8/21

Libra	Scorpio	Sagittarius	Capricorn	Aquarius	Pisces
8/23-9/17	9/17-10/12	10/12-1/16	1/16-2/9	2/9	3/5-3/29
			11/7-12/5	12/5-1/11	
10/7-10/31	10/31-11/24	11/24-12/18	12/18-1/11	2/6-4/4	1/11-2/6
					4/4-5/7
8/17-9/6	12/9-1/5			1/11-2/4	2/4-2/28
11/8-12/9					
9/6-9/30	9/30-10/25	1/5-1/30	1/30-2/24	2/24-3/19	3/19-4/13
		10/25-11/18	11/18-12/13	12/13-1/7	
10/21-11/14	11/14-12/8	12/8-1/1/06			1/7-2/3
8/11-9/7	9/7-10/9	10/9-12/15	1/1-1/25	1/25-2/18	2/18-3/14
	12/15-12/25	12/25-2/6			
9/22-10/16	10/16-11/9	11/9-12/3	2/6-3/6	3/6-4/2	4/2-4/27
			12/3-12/27	12/27-1/20	
11/3-11/28	11/28-12/22	12/22-1/15			1/20-2/14
8/23-9/17	9/17-10/12	10/12-11/17	1/15-2/9	2/9-3/5	3/5-3/29
			11/17-12/5	12/5-1/15	
10/7-10/30	10/31-11/23	11/24-12/17	12/18-12/31	1/1-1/15	1/16-1/28
				1/29-4/4	4/5-5/6
11/19-12/8	12/9-12/31		1/1-1/10	1/11-2/2	2/3-2/27
9/6-9/30	1/1-1/4	1/5-1/29	1/30-2/23	2/24-3/18	3/19-4/12
	10/1-10/24	10/25-11/17	11/18-12/12	12/13-12/31	
10/21-11/13	11/14-12/7	12/8-12/31		1/1-1/6	1/7-2/2
8/11-9/6	9/7-10/9	10/10-12/5	1/1-1/24	1/25-2/17	2/18-3/13
	12/6-12/30	12/31			
9/22-10/15	10/16-11/8	1/1-2/6	2/7-3/6	3/7-4/1	4/2-4/26
		11/9-12/2	12/3-12/26	12/27-12/31	
11/3-11/27	11/28-12/21	12/22-12/31		1/1-1/19	1/20-2/13
8/22-9/16	9/17-10/11	1/1-1/14	1/15-2/7	2/8-3/4	3/5-3/28
		10/12-11/6	11/7-12/5	12/6-12/31	
10/6-10/29	10/30-11/22	11/23-12/16	12/17-12/31	1/1-4/5	4/6-5/6
11/9-12/8	12/9-12/31		1/1-1/9	1/10-2/2	2/3-2/26
9/5-9/30	1/1-1/3	1/4-1/28	1/29-2/22	2/23-3/18	3/19-4/11
	9/31-10/23	10/24-11/17	11/18-12/11	12/12-12/31	
10/21-11/13	11/14-12/7	12/8-12/31		1/1-1/6	1/7-2/2
8/10-9/6	9/7-10/10	10/11-11/28	1/1-1/24	1/25-2/16	2/17-3/12
	11/29-12/31				
9/21-10/14	1/1	1/2-2/6	2/7-3/5	3/6-3/31	4/1-4/26
	10/15-11/7	11/8-12/1	12/2-12/25	12/26-12/31	
11/3-11/26	11/27-12/21	12/22-12/31		1/1-1/19	1/20-2/12
8/22-9/15	9/16-10/11	1/1-1/14	1/15-2/7	2/8-3/3	3/4-3/27
		10-12/11-6	11/7-12/5	12/6-12/31	

VENUS SIGNS 1901–2000

	Aries	Taurus	Gemini	Cancer	Leo	Virgo
1926	5/7-6/2	6/3-6/28	6/29-7/23	7/24-8/17	8/18-9/11	9/12-10/5
1927	2/27-3/22	3/23-4/16	4/17-5/11	5/12-6/7	6/8-7/7	7/8-11/9
1928	4/12-5/5	5/6-5/29	5/30-6/23	6/24-7/17	7/18-8/11	8/12-9/4
1929	2/3-3/7 4/20-6/2	3/8-4/19 6/3-7/7	7/8-8/4	8/5-8/30	8/31-9/25	9/26-10/19
1930	3/13-4/5	4/6-4/30	5/1-5/24	5/25-6/18	6/19-7/14	7/15-8/9
1931	4/26-5/20	5/21-6/13	6/14-7/8	7/9-8/2	8/3-8/26	8/27-9/19
1932	2/12-3/8	3/9-4/3	4/4-5/6 7/13-7/27	5/6-7/12 7/28-9/8	9/9-10/6	10/7-11/1
1933	3/27-4/19	4/20-5/28	5/29-6/8	6/9-7/2	7/3-7/26	7/27-8/20
1934	5/6-6/1	6/2-6/27	6/28-7/22	7/23-8/16	8/17-9/10	9/11-10/4
1935	2/26-3/21	3/22-4/15	4/16-5/10	5/11-6/6	6/7-7/6	7/7-11/8
1936	4/11-5/4	5/5-5/28	5/29-6/22	6/23-7/16	7/17-8/10	8/11-9/4
1937	2/2-3/8 4/14-6/3	3/9-4/17 6/4-7/6	7/7-8/3	8/4-8/29	8/30-9/24	9/25-10/18
1938	3/12-4/4	4/5-4/28	4/29-5/23	5/24-6/18	6/19-7/13	7/14-8/8
1939	4-25/5/19	5/20-6/13	6/14-7/8	7/9-8/1	8/2-8/25	8/26-9/19
1940	2/12-3/7	3/8-4/3	4/4-5/5 7/5-7/31	5/6-7/4 8/1-9/8	9/9-10/5	10/6-10/31
1941	3/27-4/19	4/20-5/13	5/14-6/6	6/7-7/1	7/2-7/26	7/27-8/20
1942	5/6-6/1	6/2-6/26	6/27-7/22	7/23-8/16	8/17-9/9	9/10-10/3
1943	2/25-3/20	3/21-4/14	4/15-5/10	5/11-6/6	6/7-7/6	7/7-11/8
1944	4/10-5/3	5/4-5/28	5/29-6/21	6/22-7/16	7/17-8/9	8/10-9/2
1945	2/2-3/10 4/7-6/3	3/11-4/6 6/4-7/6	7/7-8/3	8/4-8/29	8/30-9/23	9/24-10/18
1946	3/11-4/4	4/5-4/28	4/29-5/23	5/24-6/17	6/18-7/12	7/13-8/8
1947	4/25-5/19	5/20-6/12	6/13-7/7	7/8-8/1	8/2-8/25	8/26-9/18
1948	2/11-3/7	3/8-4/3	4/4-5/6 6/29-8/2	5/7-6/28 8/3-9/7	9/8-10/5	10/6-10/31
1949	3/26-4/19	4/20-5/13	5/14-6/6	6/7-6/30	7/1-7/25	7/26-8/19
1950	5/5-5/31	6/1-6/26	6/27-7/21	7/22-8/15	8/16-9/9	9/10-10/3
1951	2/25-3/21	3/22-4/15	4/16-5/10	5/11-6/6	6/7-7/7	7/8-11/9

Libra	Scorpio	Sagittarius	Capricorn	Aquarius	Pisces
10/6-10/29	10/30-11/22	11/23-12/16	12/17-12/31	1/1-4/5	4/6-5/6
11/10-12/8	12/9-12/31	1/1-1/7	1/8	1/9-2/1	2/2-2/26
9/5-9/28	1/1-1/3	1/4-1/28	1/29-2/22	2/23-3/17	3/18-4/11
	9/29-10/23	10/24-11/16	11/17-12/11	12/12-12/31	
10/20-11/12	11/13-12/6	12/7-12/30	12/31	1/1-1/5	1/6-2/2
8/10-9/6	9/7-10/11	10/12-11/21	1/1-1/23	1/24-2/16	2/17-3/12
	11/22-12/31				
9/20-10/13	1/1-1/3	1/4-2/6	2/7-3/4	3/5-3/31	4/1-4/25
	10/14-11/6	11/7-11/30	12/1-12/24	12/25-12/31	
11/2-11/25	11/26-12/20	12/21-12/31		1/1-1/18	1/19-2/11
8/21-9/14	9/15-10/10	1/1-1/13	1/14-2/6	2/7-3/2	3/3-3/26
		10/11-11/5	11/6-12/4	12/5-12/31	
10/5-10/28	10/29-11/21	11/22-12/15	12/16-12/31	1/1-4/5	4/6-5/5
11/9-12/7	12/8-12/31		1/1-1/7	1/8-1/31	2/1-2/25
9/5-9/27	1/1-1/2	1/3-1/27	1/28-2/21	2/22-3/16	3/17-4/10
	9/28-10/22	10/23-11/15	11/16-12/10	12/11-12/31	
10/19-11/11	11/12-12/5	12/6-12/29	12/30-12/31	1/1-1/5	1/6-2/1
8/9-9/6	9/7-10/13	10/14-11/14	1/1-1/22	1/23-2/15	2/16-3/11
	11/15-12/31				
9/20-10/13	1/1-1/3	1/4-2/5	2/6-3/4	3/5-3/30	3/31-4/24
	10/14-11/6	11/7-11/30	12/1-12/24	12/25-12/31	
11/1-11/25	11/26-12/19	12/20-12/31		1/1-1/18	1/19-2/11
8/21-9/14	9/15-10/9	1/1-1/12	1/13-2/5	2/6-3/1	3/2-3/26
		10/10-11/5	11/6-12/4	12/5-12/31	
10/4-10/27	10/28-11/20	11/21-12/14	12/15-12/31	1/1-4/4	4/6-5/5
11/9-12/7	12/8-12/31		1/1-1/7	1/8-1/31	2/1-2/24
9/3-9/27	1/1-1/2	1/3-1/27	1/28-2/20	2/21-3/16	3/17-4/9
	9/28-10/21	10/22-11/15	11/16-12/10	12/11-12/31	
10/19-11/11	11/12-12/5	12/6-12/29	12/30-12/31	1/1-1/4	1/5-2/1
8/9-9/6	9/7-10/15	10/16-11/7	1/1-1/21	1/22-2/14	2/15-3/10
	11/8-12/31				
9/19-10/12	1/1-1/4	1/5-2/5	2/6-3/4	3/5-3/29	3/30-4/24
	10/13-11/5	11/6-11/29	11/30-12/23	12/24-12/31	
11/1-1/25	11/26-12/19	12/20-12/31		1/1-1/17	1/18-2/10
8/20-9/14	9/15-10/9	1/1-1/12	1/13-2/5	2/6-3/1	3/2-3/25
		10/10-11/5	11/6-12/5	12/6-12/31	
10/4-10/27	10/28-11/20	11/21-12/13	12/14-12/31	1/1-4/5	4/6-5/4
11/10-12/7	12/8-12/31		1/1-1/7	1/8-1/31	2/1-2/24

VENUS SIGNS 1901–2000

	Aries	Taurus	Gemini	Cancer	Leo	Virgo
1952	4/10-5/4	5/5-5/28	5/29-6/21	6/22-7/16	7/17-8/9	8/10-9/3
1953	2/2-3/13	3/4-3/31	7/8-8/3	8/4-8/29	8/30-9/24	9/25-10/18
	4/1-6/5	6/6-7/7				
1954	3/12-4/4	4/5-4/28	4/29-5/23	5/24-6/17	6/18-7/13	7/14-8/8
1955	4/25-5/19	5/20-6/13	6/14-7/7	7/8-8/1	8/2-8/25	8/26-9/18
1956	2/12-3/7	3/8-4/4	4/5-5/7	5/8-6/23	9/9-10/5	10/6-10/31
			6/24-8/4	8/5-9/8		
1957	3/26-4/19	4/20-5/13	5/14-6/6	6/7-7/1	7/2-7/26	7/7-8/19
1958	5/6-5/31	6/1-6/26	6/27-7/22	7/23-8/15	8/16-9/9	9/10-10/3
1959	2/25-3/20	3/21-4/14	4/15-5/10	5/11-6/6	6/7-7/8	7/9-9/20
					9/21-9/24	9/25-11/9
1960	4/10-5/3	5/4-5/28	5/29-6/21	6/22-7/15	7/16-8/9	8/10-9/2
1961	2/3-6/5	6/6-7/7	7/8-8/3	8/4-8/29	8/30-9/23	9/24-10/17
1962	3/11-4/3	4/4-4/28	4/29-5/22	5/23-6/17	6/18-7/12	7/13-8/8
1963	4/24-5/18	5/19-6/12	6/13-7/7	7/8-7/31	8/1-8/25	8/26-9/18
1964	2/11-3/7	3/8-4/4	4/5-5/9	5/10-6/17	9/9-10/5	10/6-10/31
			6/18-8/5	8/6-9/8		
1965	3/26-4/18	4/19-5/12	5/13-6/6	6/7-6/30	7/1-7/25	7/26-8/19
1966	5/6-6/31	6/1-6/26	6/27-7/21	7/22-8/15	8/16-9/8	9/9-10/2
1967	2/24-3/20	3/21-4/14	4/15-5/10	5/11-6/6	6/7-7/8	7/9-9/9
					9/10-10/1	10/2-11/9
1968	4/9-5/3	5/4-5/27	5/28-6/20	6/21-7/15	7/16-8/8	8/9-9/2
1969	2/3-6/6	6/7-7/6	7/7-8/3	8/4-8/28	8/29-9/22	9/23-10/17
1970	3/11-4/3	4/4-4/27	4/28-5/22	5/23-6/16	6/17-7/12	7/13-8/8
1971	4/24-5/18	5/19-6/12	6/13-7/6	7/7-7/31	8/1-8/24	8/25-9/17
1972	2/11-3/7	3/8-4/3	4/4-5/10	5/11-6/11		
			6/12-8/6	8/7-9/8	9/9-10/5	10/6-10/30
1973	3/25-4/18	4/18-5/12	5/13-6/5	6/6-6/29	7/1-7/25	7/26-8/19
1974						
	55-5/31	6/1-6/25	6/26-7/21	7/22-8/14	8/15-9/8	9/9-10/2
1975	2/24-3/20	3/21-4/13	4/14-5/9	5/10-6/6	6/7-7/9	7/10-9/2
					9/3-10/4	10/5-11/9

Libra	Scorpio	Sagittarius	Capricorn	Aquarius	Pisces
9/4-9/27	1/1-1/2	1/3-1/27	1/28-2/20	2/21-3/16	3/17-4/9
	9/28-10/21	10/22-11/15	11/16-12/10	12/11-12/31	
10/19-11/11	11/12-12/5	12/6-12/29	12/30-12/31	1/1-1/5	1/6-2/1
8/9-9/6	9/7-10/22	10/23-10/27	1/1-1/22	1/23-2/15	2/16-3/11
	10/28-12/31				
9/19-10/13	1/1-1/6	1/7-2/5	2/6-3/4	3/5-3/30	3/31-4/24
	10/14-11/5	11/6-11/30	12/1-12/24	12/25-12/31	
11/1-11/25	11/26-12/19	12/20-12/31		1/1-1/17	1/18-2/11

Libra	Scorpio	Sagittarius	Capricorn	Aquarius	Pisces
8/20-9/14	9/15-10/9	1/1-1/12	1/13-2/5	2/6-3/1	3/2-3/25
		10/10-11/5	11/6-12/16	12/7-12/31	
10/4-10/27	10/28-11/20	11/21-12/14	12/15-12/31	1/1-4/6	4/7-5/5
11/10-12/7	12/8-12/31		1/1-1/7	1/8-1/31	2/1-2/24

Libra	Scorpio	Sagittarius	Capricorn	Aquarius	Pisces
9/3-9/26	1/1-1/2	1/3-1/27	1/28-2/20	2/21-3/15	3/16-4/9
	9/27-10/21	10/22-11/15	11/16-12/10	12/11-12/31	
10/18-11/11	11/12-12/4	12/5-12/28	12/29-12/31	1/1-1/5	1/6-2/2
8/9-9/6	9/7-12/31		1/1-1/21	1/22-2/14	2/15-3/10
9/19-10/12	1/1-1/6	1/7-2/5	2/6-3/4	3/5-3/29	3/30-4/23
	10/13-11/5	11/6-11/29	11/30-12/23	12/24-12/31	
11/1-11/24	11/25-12/19	12/20-12/31		1/1-1/16	1/17-2/10

Libra	Scorpio	Sagittarius	Capricorn	Aquarius	Pisces
8/20-9/13	9/14-10/9	1/1-1/12	1/13-2/5	2/6-3/1	3/2-3/25
		10/10-11/5	11/6-12/7	12/8-12/31	
10/3-10/26	10/27-11/19	11/20-12/13	2/7-2/25	1/1-2/6	4/7-5/5
			12/14-12/31	2/26-4/6	
11/10-12/7	12/8-12/23		1/1-1/6	1/7-1/30	1/31-2/23

Libra	Scorpio	Sagittarius	Capricorn	Aquarius	Pisces
9/3-9/26	1/1	1/2-1/26	1/27-2/20	2/21-3/15	3/16-4/8
	9/27-10/21	10/22-11/14	11/15-12/9	12/10-12/31	
10/18-11/10	11/11-12/4	12/5-12/28	12/29-12/31	1/1-1/4	1/5-2/2
8/9-9/7	9/8-12/31		1/1-1/21	1/22-2/14	2/15-3/10
9/18-10/11	1/1-1/7	1/8-2/5	2/6-3/4	3/5-3/29	3/30-4/23
	10/12-11/5	11/6-11/29	11/30-12/23	12/24-12/31	
	11/25-12/18	12/19-12/31		1/1-1/16	1/17-2/10
10/31-11/24					
8/20-9/13		1/1-1/12	1/13-2/4	2/5-2/28	3/1-3/24
		10/9-11/5	11/6-12/7	12/8-12/31	
			1/30-2/28	1/1-1/29	
10/3-10/26	10/27-11/19	11/20-12/13	12/14-12/31	3/1-4/6	4/7-5/4
			1/1-1/6	1/7-1/30	1/31-2/23
11/10-12/7	12/8-12/31				

VENUS SIGNS 1901–2000

	Aries	Taurus	Gemini	Cancer	Leo	Virgo
1976	4/8-5/2	5/2-5/27	5/27-6/20	6/20-7/14	7/14-8/8	8/8-9/1
1977	2/2-6/6	6/6-7/6	7/6-8/2	8/2-8/28	8/28-9/22	9/22-10/17
1978	3/9-4/2	4/2-4/27	4/27-5/22	5/22-6/16	6/16-7/12	7/12-8/6
1979	4/23-5/18	5/18-6/11	6/11-7/6	7/6-7/30	7/30-8/24	8/24-9/17
1980	2/9-3/6	3/6-4/3	4/3-5/12	5/12-6/5	9/7-10/4	10/4-10/30
			6/5-8/6	8/6-9/7		
1981	3/24-4/17	4/17-5/11	5/11-6/5	6/5-6/29	6/29-7/24	7/24-8/18
1982	5/4-5/30	5/30-6/25	6/25-7/20	7/20-8/14	8/14-9/7	9/7-10/2
1983	2/22-3/19	3/19-4/13	4/13-5/9	5/9-6/6	6/6-7/10	7/10-8/27
					8/27-10/5	10/5-11/9
1984	4/7-5/2	5/2-5/26	5/26-6/20	6/20-7/14	7/14-8/7	8/7-9/1
1985	2/2-6/6	6/8-7/6	7/6-8/2	8/2-8/28	8/28-9/22	9/22-10/16
1986	3/9-4/2	4/2-4/26	4/26-5/21	5/21-6/15	6/15-7/11	7/11-8/7
1987	4/22-5/17	5/17-6/11	6/11-7/5	7/5-7/30	7/30-8/23	8/23-9/16
1988	2/9-3/6	3/6-4/3	4/3-5/17	5/17-5/27	9/7-10/4	10/4-10/29
			5/27-8/6	8/6-9/7		
1989	3/23-4/16	4/16-5/11	5/11-6/4	6/4-6/29	6/29-7/24	7/24-8/18
1990	5/4-5/30	5/30-6/25	6/25-7/20	7/20-8/13	8/13-9/7	9/7-10/1
1991	2/22-3/18	3/18-4/13	4/13-5/9	5/9-6/6	6/6-7/11	7/11-8/21
					8/21-10/6	10/6-11/9
1992	4/7-5/1	5/1-5/26	5/26-6/19	6/19-7/13	7/13-8/7	8/7-8/31
1993	2/2-6/6	6/6-7/6	7/6-8/1	8/1-8/27	8/27-9/21	9/21-10/16
1994	3/8-4/1	4/1-4/26	4/26-5/21	5/21-6/15	6/15-7/11	7/11-8/7
1995	4/22-5/16	5/16-6/10	6/10-7/5	7/5-7/29	7/29-8/23	8/23-9/16
1996	2/9-3/6	3/6-4/3	4/3-8/7	8/7-9/7	9/7-10/4	10/4-10/29
1997	3/23-4/16	4/16-5/10	5/10-6/4	6/4-6/28	6/28-7/23	7/23-8/17
1998	5/3-5/29	5/29-6/24	6/24-7/19	7/19-8/13	8/13-9/6	9/6-9/30
1999	2/21-3/18	3/18-4/12	4/12-5/8	5/8-6/5	6/5-7/12	7/12-8/15
					8/15-10/7	10/7-11/9
2000	4/6-5/1	5/1-5/25	5/25-6/13	6/13-7/13	7/13-8/6	8/6-8/31

Libra	Scorpio	Sagittarius	Capricorn	Aquarius	Pisces
9/1-9/26	9/26-10/20	1/1-1/26	1/26-2/19	2/19-3/15	3/15-4/8
		10/20-11/14	11/14-12/6	12/9-1/4	
10/17-11/10	11/10-12/4	12/4-12/27	12/27-1/20		1/4-2/2
8/6-9/7	9/7-1/7			1/20-2/13	2/13-3/9
9/17-10/11	10/11-11/4	1/7-2/5	2/5-3/3	3/3-3/29	3/29-4/23
		11/4-11/28	11/28-12/22	12/22-1/16	
10/30-11/24	11/24-12/18	12/18-1/11			1/16-2/9
8/18-9/12	9/12-10/9	10/9-11/5	1/11-2/4	2/4-2/28	2/28-3/24
			11/5-12/8	12/8-1/23	
10/2-10/26	10/26-11/18	11/18-12/12	1/23-3/2	3/2-4/6	4/6-5/4
			12/12-1/5		
11/9-12/6	12/6-1/1			1/5-1/29	1/29-2/22
9/1-9/25	9/25-10/20	1/1-1/25	1/25-2/19	2/19-3/14	3/14-4/7
		10/20-11/13	11/13-12/9		
10/16-11/9	11/9-12/3	12/3-12/27			1/4-2/2
8/7-9/7	9/7-1/7			1/20-3/13	2/13-3/9
9/16-10/10	10/10-11/3	1/7-2/5	2/5-3/3	3/3-3/28	3/28-4/22
		11/3-11/28	11/28-12/22	12/22-1/15	
10/29-11/23	11/23-12/17	12/17-1/10			1/15-2/9
8/18-9/12	9/12-10/8	10/8-11/5	1/10-2/3	2/3-2/27	2/27-3/23
			11/5-12/10	12/10-1/16	
10/1-10/25	10/25-11/18	11/18-12/12	1/16-3/3	3/3-4/6	4/6-5/4
			12/12-1/5		
8/21-12/6	12/6-12/31	12/21-1/25/92		1/5-1/29	1/29-2/22
8/31-9/25	9/25-10/19	10/19-11/13	1/25-2/18	2/18-3/13	3/13-4/7
			11/13-12/8	12/8-1/3	
10/16-11/9	11/9-12/2	12/2-12/26	12/26-1/19		1/3-2/2
8/7-9/7	9/7-1/7			1/19-2/12	2/12-3/8
9/16-10/10	10/10-11/13	1/7-2/4	2/4-3/2	3/2-3/28	3/28-4/22
		11/3-11/27	11/27-12/21	12/21-1/15	
10/29-11/23	11/23-12/17	12/17-1/10/97			1/15-2/9
8/17-9/12	9/12-10/8	10/8-11/5	1/10-2/3	2/3-2/27	2/27-3/23
			11/5-12/12	12/12-1/9	
9/30-10/24	10/24-11/17	11/17-12/11	1/9-3/4	3/4-4/6	4/6-5/3
11/9-12/5	12/5-12/31	12/31-1/24		1/4-1/28	1/28-2/21
8/31-9/24	9/24-10/19	10/19-11/13	1/24-2/18	2/18-3/12	3/13-4/6
			11/13-12/8	12/8	

1901	MAR	1	Leo		APR	28	Gem
	May	11	Vir		JUN	11	Can
	JUL	13	Lib		JUL	27	Leo
	AUG	31	Scp		SEP	12	Vir
	OCT	14	Sag		OCT	30	Lib
	NOV	24	Cap		DEC	17	Scp
1902	JAN	1	Aqu	1907	FEB	5	Sag
	FEB	8	Pic		APR	1	Cap
	MAR	19	Ari		OCT	13	Aqu
	APR	27	Tau		NOV	29	Pic
	JUN	7	Gem	1908	JAN	11	Ari
	JUL	20	Can		FEB	23	Tau
	SEP	4	Leo		APR	7	Gem
	OCT	23	Vir		MAY	22	Can
	DEC	20	Lib		JUL	8	Leo
1903	APR	19	Vir		AUG	24	Vir
	MAY	30	Lib		OCT	10	Lib
	AUG	6	Scp		NOV	25	Scp
	SEP	22	Sag	1909	JAN	10	Sag
	NOV	3	Cap		FEB	24	Cap
	DEC	12	Aqu		APR	9	Aqu
1904	JAN	19	Pic		MAY	25	Pic
	FEB	27	Ari		JUL	21	Ari
	APR	6	Tau		SEP	26	Pic
	MAY	18	Gem		NOV	20	Ari
	JUN	30	Can	1910	JAN	23	Tau
	AUG	15	Leo		MAR	14	Gem
	OCT	1	Vir		MAY	1	Can
	NOV	20	Lib		JUN	19	Leo
1905	JAN	13	Scp		AUG	6	Vir
	AUG	21	Sag		SEP	22	Lib
	OCT	8	Cap		NOV	6	Scp
	NOV	18	Aqu		DEC	20	Sag
	DEC	27	Pic	1911	JAN	31	Cap
1906	FEB	4	Ari		MAR	14	Aqu
	MAR	17	Tau		APR	23	Pic

	JUN	2	Ari		MAY	4	Tau
	JUL	15	Tau		JUN	14	Gem
	SEP	5	Gem		JUL	28	Can
	NOV	30	Tau		SEP	12	Leo
1912	JAN	30	Gem		NOV	2	Vir
	APR	5	Can	1918	JAN	11	Lib
	MAY	28	Leo		FEB	25	Vir
	JUL	17	Vir		JUN	23	Lib
	SEP	2	Lib		AUG	17	Scp
	OCT	18	Scp		OCT	1	Sag
	NOV	30	Sag		NOV	11	Cap
1913	JAN	10	Cap		DEC	20	Aqu
	FEB	19	Aqu	1919	JAN	27	Pic
	MAR	30	Pic		MAR	6	Ari
	MAY	8	Ari		APR	15	Tau
	JUN	17	Tau		MAY	26	Gem
	JUL	29	Gem		JUL	8	Can
	SEP	15	Can		AUG	23	Leo
1914	MAY	1	Leo		OCT	10	Vir
	JUN	26	Vir		NOV	30	Lib
	AUG	14	Lib	1920	JAN	31	Scp
	SEP	29	Scp		APR	23	Lib
	NOV	11	Sag		JUL	10	Scp
	DEC	22	Cap		SEP	4	Sag
1915	JAN	30	Aqu		OCT	18	Cap
	MAR	9	Pic		NOV	27	Aqu
	APR	16	Ari	1921	JAN	5	Pic
	MAY	26	Tau		FEB	13	Ari
	JUL	6	Gem		MAR	25	Tau
	AUG	19	Can		MAY	6	Gem
	OCT	7	Leo		JUN	18	Can
1916	MAY	28	Vir		AUG	3	Leo
	JUL	23	Lib		SEP	19	Vir
	SEP	8	Scp		NOV	6	Lib
	OCT	22	Sag		DEC	26	Scp
	DEC	1	Cap	1922	FEB	18	Sag
1917	JAN	9	Aqu		SEP	13	Cap
	FEB	16	Pic		OCT	30	Aqu
	MAR	26	Ari		DEC	11	Pic

1923	JAN	21	Ari	JUN	26	Tau
	MAR	4	Tau	AUG	9	Gem
	APR	16	Gem	OCT	3	Can
	MAY	30	Can	DEC	20	Gem
	JUL	16	Leo	1929 MAR	10	Can
	SEP	1	Vir	MAY	13	Leo
	OCT	18	Lib	JUL	4	Vir
	DEC	4	Scp	AUG	21	Lib
1924	JAN	19	Sag	OCT	6	Scp
	MAR	6	Cap	NOV	18	Sag
	APR	24	Aqu	DEC	29	Cap
	JUN	24	Pic	1930 FEB	6	Aqu
	AUG	24	Aqu	MAR	17	Pic
	OCT	19	Pic	APR	24	Ari
	DEC	19	Ari	JUN	3	Tau
1925	FEB	5	Tau	JUL	14	Gem
	MAR	24	Gem	AUG	28	Can
	MAY	9	Can	OCT	20	Leo
	JUN	26	Leo	1931 FEB	16	Can
	AUG	12	Vir	MAR	30	Leo
	SEP	28	Lib	JUN	10	Vir
	NOV	13	Scp	AUG	1	Lib
	DEC	28	Sag	SEP	17	Scp
1926	FEB	9	Cap	OCT	30	Sag
	MAR	23	Aqu	DEC	10	Cap
	MAY	3	Pic	1932 JAN	18	Aqu
	JUN	15	Ari	FEB	25	Pic
	AUG	1	Tau	APR	3	Ari
1927	FEB	22	Gem	MAY	12	Tau
	APR	17	Can	JUN	22	Gem
	JUN	6	Leo	AUG	4	Can
	JUL	25	Vir	SEP	20	Leo
	SEP	10	Lib	NOV	13	Vir
	OCT	26	Scp	1933 JUL	6	Lib
	DEC	8	Sag	AUG	26	Scp
1928	JAN	19	Cap	OCT	9	Sag
	FEB	28	Aqu	NOV	19	Cap
	APR	7	Pic	DEC	28	Aqu
	MAY	16	Ari	1934 FEB	4	Pic

	MAR	14	Ari			NOV	19	Pic
	APR	22	Tau		1940	JAN	4	Ari
	JUN	2	Gem			FEB	17	Tau
	JUL	15	Can			APR	1	Gem
	AUG	30	Leo			MAY	17	Can
	OCT	18	Vir			JUL	3	Leo
	DEC	11	Lib			AUG	19	Vir
1935	JUL	29	Scp			OCT	5	Lib
	SEP	16	Sag			NOV	20	Scp
	OCT	28	Cap		1941	JAN	4	Sag
	DEC	7	Aqu			FEB	17	Cap
1936	JAN	14	Pic			APR	2	Aqu
	FEB	22	Ari			MAY	16	Pic
	APR	1	Tau			JUL	2	Ari
	MAY	13	Gem		1942	JAN	11	Tau
	JUN	25	Can			MAR	7	Gem
	AUG	10	Leo			APR	26	Can
	SEP	26	Vir			JUN	14	Leo
	NOV	14	Lib			AUG	1	Vir
1937	JAN	5	Scp			SEP	17	Lib
	MAR	13	Sag			NOV	1	Scp
	MAY	14	Scp			DEC	15	Sag
	AUG	8	Sag		1943	JAN	26	Cap
	SEP	30	Cap			MAR	8	Aqu
	NOV	11	Aqu			APR	17	Pic
	DEC	21	Pic			MAY	27	Ari
1938	JAN	30	Ari			JUL	7	Tau
	MAR	12	Tau			AUG	23	Gem
	APR	23	Gem		1944	MAR	28	Can
	JUN	7	Can			MAY	22	Leo
	JUL	22	Leo			JUL	12	Vir
	SEP	7	Vir			AUG	29	Lib
	OCT	25	Lib			OCT	13	Scp
	DEC	11	Scp			NOV	25	Sag
1939	JAN	29	Sag		1945	JAN	5	Cap
	MAR	21	Cap			FEB	14	Aqu
	MAY	25	Aqu			MAR	25	Pic
	JUL	21	Cap			MAY	2	Ari
	SEP	24	Aqu			JUN	11	Tau

	JUL	23	Gem	1951	JAN	22	Pic
	SEP	7	Can		MAR	1	Ari
	NOV	11	Leo		APR	10	Tau
	DEC	26	Can		MAY	21	Gem
1946	APR	22	Leo		JUL	3	Can
	JUN	20	Vir		AUG	18	Leo
	AUG	9	Lib		OCT	5	Vir
	SEP	24	Scp		NOV	24	Lib
	NOV	6	Sag	1952	JAN	20	Scp
	DEC	17	Cap		AUG	27	Sag
1947	JAN	25	Aqu		OCT	12	Cap
	MAR	4	Pic		NOV	21	Aqu
	APR	11	Ari		DEC	30	Pic
	MAY	21	Tau	1953	FEB	8	Ari
	JUL	1	Gem		MAR	20	Tau
	AUG	13	Can		MAY	1	Gem
	OCT	1	Leo		JUN	14	Can
	DEC	1	Vir		JUL	29	Leo
1948	FEB	12	Leo		SEP	14	Vir
	MAY	18	Vir		NOV	1	Lib
	JUL	17	Lib		DEC	20	Scp
	SEP	3	Scp	1954	FEB	9	Sag
	OCT	17	Sag		APR	12	Cap
	NOV	26	Cap		JUL	3	Sag
1949	JAN	4	Aqu		AUG	24	Cap
	FEB	11	Pic		OCT	21	Aqu
	MAR	21	Ari		DEC	4	Pic
	APR	30	Tau	1955	JAN	15	Ari
	JUN	10	Gem		FEB	26	Tau
	JUL	23	Can		APR	10	Gem
	SEP	7	Leo		MAY	26	Can
	OCT	27	Vir		JUL	11	Leo
	DEC	26	Lib		AUG	27	Vir
1950	MAR	28	Vir		OCT	13	Lib
	JUN	11	Lib		NOV	29	Scp
	AUG	10	Scp	1956	JAN	14	Sag
	SEP	25	Sag		FEB	28	Cap
	NOV	6	Cap		APR	14	Aqu
	DEC	15	Aqu		JUN	3	Pic

	DEC	6	Ari		MAR	12	Pic
1957	JAN	28	Tau		APR	19	Ari
	MAR	17	Gem		MAY	28	Tau
	MAY	4	Can		JUL	9	Gem
	JUN	21	Leo		AUG	22	Can
	AUG	8	Vir		OCT	11	Leo
	SEP	24	Lib	1963	JUN	3	Vir
	NOV	8	Scp		JUL	27	Lib
	DEC	23	Sag		SEP	12	Scp
1958	FEB	3	Cap		OCT	25	Sag
	MAR	17	Aqu		DEC	5	Cap
	APR	27	Pic	1964	JAN	13	Aqu
	JUN	7	Ari		FEB	20	Pic
	JUL	21	Tau		MAR	29	Ari
	SEP	21	Gem		MAY	7	Tau
	OCT	29	Tau		JUN	17	Gem
1959	FEB	10	Gem		JUL	30	Can
	APR	10	Can		SEP	15	Leo
	JUN	1	Leo		NOV	6	Vir
	JUL	20	Vir	1965	JUN	29	Lib
	SEP	5	Lib		AUG	20	Scp
	OCT	21	Scp		OCT	4	Sag
	DEC	3	Sag		NOV	14	Cap
1960	JAN	14	Cap		DEC	23	Aqu
	FEB	23	Aqu	1966	JAN	30	Pic
	APR	2	Pic		MAR	9	Ari
	MAY	11	Ari		APR	17	Tau
	JUN	20	Tau		MAY	28	Gem
	AUG	2	Gem		JUL	11	Can
	SEP	21	Can		AUG	25	Leo
1961	FEB	5	Gem		OCT	12	Vir
	FEB	7	Can		DEC	4	Lib
	MAY	6	Leo	1967	FEB	12	Scp
	JUN	28	Vir		MAR	31	Lib
	AUG	17	Lib		JUL	19	Scp
	OCT	1	Scp		SEP	10	Sag
	NOV	13	Sag		OCT	23	Cap
	DEC	24	Cap		DEC	1	Aqu
1962	FEB	1	Aqu	1968	JAN	9	Pic

	FEB 17 Ari		DEC 24 Tau
	MAR 27 Tau	1974	FEB 27 Gem
	MAY 8 Gem		APR 20 Can
	JUN 21 Can		JUN 9 Leo
	AUG 5 Leo		JUL 27 Vir
	SEP 21 Vir		SEP 12 Lib
	NOV 9 Lib		OCT 28 Scp
	DEC 29 Scp		DEC 10 Sag
1969	FEB 25 Sag	1975	JAN 21 Cap
	SEP 21 Cap		MAR 3 Aqu
	NOV 4 Aqu		APR 11 Pic
	DEC 15 Pic		MAY 21 Ari
1970	JAN 24 Ari		JUL 1 Tau
	MAR 7 Tau		AUG 14 Gem
	APR 18 Gem		OCT 17 Can
	JUN 2 Can		NOV 25 Gem
	JUL 18 Leo	1976	MAR 18 Can
	SEP 3 Vir		MAY 16 Leo
	OCT 20 Lib		JUL 6 Vir
	DEC 6 Scp		AUG 24 Lib
1971	JAN 23 Sag		OCT 8 Scp
	MAR 12 Cap		NOV 20 Sag
	MAY 3 Aqu	1977	JAN 1 Cap
	NOV 6 Pic		FEB 9 Aqu
	DEC 26 Ari		MAR 20 Pic
1972	FEB 10 Tau		APR 27 Ari
	MAR 27 Gem		JUN 6 Tau
	MAY 12 Can		JUL 17 Gem
	JUN 28 Leo		SEP 1 Can
	AUG 15 Vir		OCT 26 Leo
	SEP 30 Lib	1978	JAN 26 Can
	NOV 15 Scp		APR 10 Leo
	DEC 30 Sag		JUN 14 Vir
1973	FEB 12 Cap		AUG 4 Lib
	MAR 26 Aqu		SEP 19 Scp
	MAY 8 Pic		NOV 2 Sag
	JUN 20 Ari		DEC 12 Cap
	AUG 12 Tau	1979	JAN 20 Aqu
	OCT 29 Ari		FEB 27 Pic

	APR	7	Ari			MAR	15	Tau
	MAY	16	Tau			APR	26	Gem
	JUN	26	Gem			JUN	9	Can
	AUG	8	Can			JUL	25	Leo
	SEP	24	Leo			SEP	10	Vir
	NOV	19	Vir			OCT	27	Lib
1980	MAR	11	Leo			DEC	14	Scp
	MAY	4	Vir		1986	FEB	2	Sag
	JUL	10	Lib			MAR	28	Cap
	AUG	29	Scp			OCT	9	Aqu
	OCT	12	Sag			NOV	26	Pic
	NOV	22	Cap		1987	JAN	8	Ari
	DEC	30	Aqu			FEB	20	Tau
1981	FEB	6	Pic			APR	5	Gem
	MAR	17	Ari			MAY	21	Can
	APR	25	Tau			JUL	6	Leo
	JUN	5	Gem			AUG	22	Vir
	JUL	18	Can			OCT	8	Lib
	SEP	2	Leo			NOV	24	Scp
	OCT	21	Vir		1988	JAN	8	Sag
	DEC	16	Lib			FEB	22	Cap
1982	AUG	3	Scp			APR	6	Aqu
	SEP	20	Sag			MAY	22	Pic
	OCT	31	Cap			JUL	13	Ari
	DEC	10	Aqu			OCT	23	Pic
1983	JAN	17	Pic			NOV	1	Ari
	FEB	25	Ari		1989	JAN	19	Tau
	APR	5	Tau			MAR	11	Gem
	MAY	16	Gem			APR	29	Can
	JUN	29	Can			JUN	16	Leo
	AUG	13	Leo			AUG	3	Vir
	SEP	30	Vir			SEP	19	Lib
	NOV	18	Lib			NOV	4	Scp
1984	JAN	11	Scp			DEC	18	Sag
	AUG	17	Sag		1990	JAN	29	Cap
	OCT	5	Cap			MAR	11	Aqu
	NOV	15	Aqu			APR	20	Pic
	DEC	25	Pic			MAY	31	Ari
1985	FEB	2	Ari			JUL	12	Tau

	AUG	31	Gem		FEB	15	Pic
	DEC	14	Tau		MAR	24	Ari
1991	JAN	21	Gem		MAY	2	Tau
	APR	3	Can		JUN	12	Gem
	MAY	26	Leo		JUL	25	Can
	JUL	15	Vir		SEP	9	Leo
	SEP	1	Lib		OCT	30	Vir
	OCT	16	Scp	1997	JAN	3	Lib
	NOV	29	Sag		MAR	8	Vir
1992	JAN	9	Cap		JUN	19	Lib
	FEB	18	Aqu		AUG	14	Scp
	MAR	28	Pic		SEP	28	Sag
	MAY	5	Ari		NOV	9	Cap
	JUN	14	Tau		DEC	18	Aqu
	JUL	26	Gem	1998	JAN	25	Pic
	SEP	12	Can		MAR	4	Ari
1993	APR	27	Leo		APR	13	Tau
	JUN	23	Vir		MAY	24	Gem
	AUG	12	Lib		JUL	6	Can
	SEP	27	Scp		AUG	20	Leo
	NOV	9	Sag		OCT	7	Vir
	DEC	20	Cap		NOV	27	Lib
1994	JAN	28	Aqu	1999	JAN	26	Scp
	MAR	7	Pic		MAY	5	Lib
	APR	14	Ari		JUL	5	Scp
	MAY	23	Tau		SEP	2	Sag
	JUL	3	Gem		OCT	17	Cap
	AUG	16	Can		NOV	26	Aqu
	OCT	4	Leo	2000	JAN	4	Pic
	DEC	12	Vir		FEB	12	Ari
1995	JAN	22	Leo		MAR	23	Tau
	MAY	25	Vir		MAY	3	Gem
	JUL	21	Lib		JUN	16	Can
	SEP	7	Scp		AUG	1	Leo
	OCT	20	Sag		SEP	17	Vir
	NOV	30	Cap		NOV	4	Lib
1996	JAN	8	Aqu		DEC	23	Scp

JUPITER SIGN 1901–2000

1901	JAN	19	Cap		1930	JUN	26	Can
1902	FEB	6	Aqu		1931	JUL	17	Leo
1903	FEB	20	Pic		1932	AUG	11	Vir
1904	MAR	1	Ari		1933	SEP	10	Lib
	AUG	8	Tau		1934	OCT	11	Scp
	AUG	31	Ari		1935	NOV	9	Sag
1905	MAR	7	Tau		1936	DEC	2	Cap
	JUL	21	Gem		1937	DEC	20	Aqu
	DEC	4	Tau		1938	MAY	14	Pic
1906	MAR	9	Gem			JUL	30	Aqu
	JUL	30	Can			DEC	29	Pic
1907	AUG	18	Leo		1939	MAY	11	Ari
1908	SEP	12	Vir			OCT	30	Pic
1909	OCT	11	Lib			DEC	20	Ari
1910	NOV	11	Scp		1940	MAY	16	Tau
1911	DEC	10	Sag		1941	MAY	26	Gem
1913	JAN	2	Cap		1942	JUN	10	Can
1914	JAN	21	Aqu		1943	JUN	30	Leo
1915	FEB	4	Pic		1944	JUL	26	Vir
1916	FEB	12	Ari		1945	AUG	25	Lib
	JUN	26	Tau		1946	SEP	25	Scp
	OCT	26	Ari		1947	OCT	24	Sag
1917	FEB	12	Tau		1948	NOV	15	Cap
	JUN	29	Gem		1949	APR	12	Aqu
1918	JUL	13	Can			JUN	27	Cap
1919	AUG	2	Leo			NOV	30	Aqu
1920	AUG	27	Vir		1950	APR	15	Pic
1921	SEP	25	Lib			SEP	15	Aqu
1922	OCT	26	Scp			DEC	1	Pic
1923	NOV	24	Sag		1951	APR	21	Ari
1924	DEC	18	Cap		1952	APR	28	Tau
1926	JAN	6	Aqu		1953	MAY	9	Gem
1927	JAN	18	Pic		1954	MAY	24	Can
	JUN	6	Ari		1955	JUN	13	Leo
	SEP	11	Pic			NOV	17	Vir
1928	JAN	23	Ari		1956	JAN	18	Leo
	JUN	4	Tau			JUL	7	Vir
1929	JUN	12	Gem			DEC	13	Lib

1957	FEB	19	Vir
	AUG	7	Lib
1958	JAN	13	Scp
	MAR	20	Lib
	SEP	7	Scp
1959	FEB	10	Sag
	APR	24	Scp
	OCT	5	Sag
1960	MAR	1	Cap
	JUN	10	Sag
	OCT	26	Cap
1961	MAR	15	Aqu
	AUG	12	Cap
	NOV	4	Aqu
1962	MAR	25	Pic
1963	APR	4	Ari
1964	APR	12	Tau
1965	APR	22	Gem
	SEP	21	Can
	NOV	17	Gem
1966	MAY	5	Can
	SEP	27	Leo
1967	JAN	16	Can
	MAY	23	Leo
	OCT	19	Vir
1968	FEB	27	Leo
	JUN	15	Vir
	NOV	15	Lib
1969	MAR	30	Vir
	JUL	15	Lib
	DEC	16	Scp
1970	APR	30	Lib
	AUG	15	Scp
1971	JAN	14	Sag
	JUN	5	Scp
	SEP	11	Sag
1972	FEB	6	Cap
	JUL	24	Sag
	SEP	25	Cap

1973	FEB	23	Aqu
1974	MAR	8	Pic
1975	MAR	18	Ari
1976	MAR	26	Tau
	AUG	23	Gem
	OCT	16	Tau
1977	APR	3	Gem
	AUG	20	Can
	DEC	30	Gem
1978	APR	12	Can
	SEP	5	Leo
1979	FEB	28	Can
	APR	20	Leo
	SEP	29	Vir
1980	OCT	27	Lib
1981	Nov	27	Scp
1982	DEC	26	Sag
1984	JAN	19	Cap
1985	FEB	6	Aqu
1986	FEB	20	Pic
1987	MAR	2	Ari
1988	MAR	8	Tau
	JUL	22	Gem
	NOV	30	Tau
1989	MAR	11	Gem
	JUL	30	Can
1990	AUG	18	Leo
1991	SEP	12	Vir
1992	OCT	10	Lib
1993	NOV	10	Scp
1994	DEC	9	Sag
1996	JAN	3	Cap
1997	JAN	21	Aqu
1998	FEB	4	Pic
1999	FEB	13	Ari
	JUN	28	Tau
	OCT	23	Ari
2000	FEB	14	Tau
	JUN	30	Gem

SATURN SIGN 1903–2000

1903	JAN	19	Aqu		1942	MAY	8	Gem
1905	APR	13	Pic		1944	JUN	20	Can
	AUG	17	Aqu		1946	AUG	2	Leo
1906	JAN	8	Pic		1948	SEP	19	Vir
1908	MAR	19	Ari		1949	APR	3	Leo
1910	MAY	17	Tau			MAY	29	Vir
	DEC	14	Ari		1950	NOV	20	Lib
1911	JAN	20	Tau		1951	MAR	7	Vir
1912	JUL	7	Gem			AUG	13	Lib
	NOV	30	Tau		1953	OCT	22	Scp
1913	MAR	26	Gem		1956	JAN	12	Sag
1914	AUG	24	Can			MAY	14	Scp
	DEC	7	Gem			OCT	10	Sag
1915	MAY	11	Can		1959	JAN	5	Cap
1916	OCT	17	Leo		1962	JAN	3	Aqu
	DEC	7	Can		1964	MAR	24	Pic
1917	JUN	24	Leo			SEP	16	Aqu
1919	AUG	12	Vir			DEC	16	Pic
1921	OCT	7	Lib		1967	MAR	3	Ari
1923	DEC	20	Scp		1969	APR	29	Tau
1924	APR	6	Lib		1971	JUN	18	Gem
	SEP	13	Scp		1972	JAN	10	Tau
1926	DEC	2	Sag			FEB	21	Gem
1929	MAR	15	Cap		1973	AUG	1	Can
	MAY	5	Sag		1974	JAN	7	Gem
	NOV	30	Cap			APR	18	Can
1932	FEB	24	Aqu		1975	SEP	17	Leo
	AUG	13	Cap		1976	JAN	14	Can
	NOV	20	Aqu			JUN	5	Leo
1935	FEB	14	Pic		1977	NOV	17	Vir
1937	APR	25	Ari		1978	JAN	5	Leo
	OCT	18	Pic			JUL	26	Vir
1938	JAN	14	Ari		1980	SEP	21	Lib
1939	JUL	6	Tau		1982	NOV	29	Scp
	SEP	22	Ari		1983	MAY	6	Lib
1940	MAR	20	Tau			AUG	24	Scp

1985	NOV	17	Sag	1994	JAN	28	Pic
1988	FEB	13	Cap	1996	APR	7	Ari
	JUN	10	Sag	1998	JUN	9	Tau
	NOV	12	Cap		OCT	25	Ari
1991	FEB	6	Aqu	1999	MAR	1	Tau
1993	MAY	21	Pic	2000	AUG	10	Gem
	JUN	30	Aqu		OCT	16	Tau

URANUS IN VIRGO BIRTH DATES:

November 1, 1961–January 10, 1962
August 10, 1962–September 28, 1968
May 20, 1969–June 24, 1969

URANUS IN LIBRA BIRTH DATES:

September 28, 1968–May 20, 1969
June 24, 1969–November 21, 1974
May 1–September 8, 1975

URANUS IN SCORPIO BIRTH DATES:

November 21, 1974–May 1, 1975
September 8, 1975–February 17, 1981
March 20–November 16, 1981

URANUS IN SAGITTARIUS BIRTH DATES:

February 17–March 20, 1981
November 16, 1981–February 15, 1988
May 27, 1988–December 2, 1988

URANUS IN CAPRICORN BIRTH DATES:

December 20, 1904–January 30, 1912
September 4–November 12, 1912
February 15–May 27, 1988
December 2, 1988–April 1, 1995
June 9, 1995–January 12, 1996

URANUS IN AQUARIUS BIRTH DATES:

January 30–September 4, 1912
November 12, 1912–April 1, 1919
August 16, 1919–January 22, 1920

URANUS IN PISCES BIRTH DATES:

April 1–August 16, 1919
January 22, 1920–March 31, 1927
November 4, 1927–January 13, 1928

LOOK UP YOUR NEPTUNE PLACEMENT by finding your birthday on the following lists:

NEPTUNE IN CANCER BIRTH DATES:

July 19–December 25, 1901
May 21, 1902–September 23, 1914
December 14, 1914–July 19, 1915
March 19–May 2, 1916

NEPTUNE IN LEO BIRTH DATES:

September 23–December 14, 1914
July 19, 1915–March 19, 1916
May 2, 1916–September 21, 1928
February 19, 1929–July 24, 1929

NEPTUNE IN VIRGO BIRTH DATES:

September 21, 1928–February 19, 1929
July 24, 1929–October 3, 1942
April 17–August 2, 1943

NEPTUNE IN LIBRA BIRTH DATES:

October 2, 1942–April 17, 1943
August 2, 1943–December 24, 1955
March 12–October 9, 1956
June 15–August 6, 1957

NEPTUNE IN SCORPIO BIRTH DATES:

August 6, 1957–January 4, 1970
May 3–November 6, 1970

NEPTUNE IN SAGITTARIUS BIRTH DATES:

January 4–May 3, 1970
November 6, 1970–January 19, 1984
June 23–November 21, 1984

NEPTUNE IN CAPRICORN BIRTH DATES:

January 19, 1984–June 23, 1984
November 21, 1984–January 29, 1998

FIND YOUR PLUTO PLACEMENT in the following list:

Pluto in Gemini—Late 1800s until May 28, 1914
Pluto in Cancer—May 28, 1914–June 16, 1939
Pluto in Leo—July 16, 1939–August 19, 1957
Pluto in Virgo—August 19, 1957–October 5, 1971
               April 17, 1972–July 30, 1972
Pluto in Libra—October 5, 1971–April 17, 1972
               July 30, 1972–August 28, 1984
Pluto in Scorpio—August 28, 1984–January 17, 1995
Pluto in Sagittarius–starting January 17, 1995

4

Find Your Power Planets

Certain planets in your horoscope can play especially important roles in determining your success and happiness. These are your personal power planets, which at times can even be more decisive in your life than the sun! Here is how to locate them and what they could mean to you.

Many factors determine how powerful a planet can be. First, there is the planet's sign. Each planet rules a special sign where it is most comfortably at home. But it also excels in another sign, called its "exaltation," where it functions more like a special guest.

Then consider the planet's position in your chart. Situated on the horizontal or vertical axes of the horoscope wheel, a planet can be the driving force of your chart, especially if it's at the top of your chart or on the ascendant (rising sign). It is also powerful when isolated from other planets. It then becomes a center of attention—your chart could "swing" on the happenings of that lone planet!

Sometimes the planet that rules a sign packs an extra wallop. For example, if there are three or more planets in one sign, then the planetary ruler of that sign assumes high priority, even if it is located elsewhere, because it "disposes" of (or masterminds) the energy in that heavily populated sign. The planet that rules your rising sign is very high status because it colors your outward identity. This planet can guide you to a successful career choice, one that reflects its sign and house placement. Yet other important planets to reckon with are the rulers of your sun and moon signs, which influence how your personality and emotions operate.

* * *

Check the chart in this chapter to find out how your planets rate!

A Planet in the Sign It Rules ("dignity")

Each sign is ruled by a planet, so naturally, any planet in your chart located in the sign it rules is sure to be one of the most important. There it is most at home and can work most effectively. Because you'll express the clear energy of the planet, astrologers call this placement the planet's "dignity" for it is here the planet shows off its best qualities. For example, the moon can express its nature most strongly through the watery sign of Cancer. So those with this placement will be strongly emotional, have all the lunar qualities of good memory, insight, psychic abilities, interest in nurturing. Venus expresses itself most easily in Taurus, the earthy, sensual side of Venus emerges or in Libra, where Venus is more abstract, aesthetic, concerned with the ideals of beauty.

When a Planet Is in Its Detriment

The sign opposite (six signs away) from the one it rules is a planet's detriment. Here it is considered to be at a disadvantage—the dreamy nature of the moon is not as easily expressed through the "here and now" matter-of-fact sign of Capricorn. Venus goes to extremes in Scorpio (the opposite of Taurus) and is self-centered in Aries (the opposite of Libra).

When a Planet Is Exalted

The qualities of a planet also function especially well in the sign that is called its exaltation—here it is able to express its highest purpose—the moon in Taurus promotes emotional steadiness and growth. The nurturing qualities of the moon can "bear fruit" in this fixed earth sign. Venus in Pisces expresses the sensitive, loving, giving, elevated side of the planet.

If Your Planet Is in Its Fall . . .

Opposite its exaltation is the sign of a planet's fall, often considered a disadvantage. Mars, which expresses its goal-directed energy most forcefully in Capricorn, could be diverted by emotional concerns in Cancer, its fall. Venus, which functions well in the accepting, unjudgmental sign of Pisces, is ill at ease in critical Virgo. But, cheer up if you have one or more planets in this situation—you'll have many opportunities to develop and expand that planet's energy in this lifetime.

Power Planet Chart:

Planet	Sign Ruled	Detriment	Exaltation	Fall
The Sun	Leo	Aquarius	Aries	Libra
The Moon	Cancer	Capricorn	Taurus	Scorpio
Mercury	Gemini/ Virgo	Sagittarius	Virgo	Pisces
Venus	Taurus/ Libra	Scorpio/Aries	Pisces	Virgo
Mars	Aries/ Scorpio	Libra/Taurus	Capricorn	Cancer
Saturn	Capricorn/ Aquarius	Cancer/Leo	Libra	Aries

Planet	Sign Ruled	Detriment	Exaltation	Fall
Jupiter	Sagittarius/ Pisces	Gemini/Virgo	Cancer	Capricorn
Uranus	Aquarius	Leo	Scorpio	Taurus
Neptune	Pisces	Virgo	Gemini	Sagittarius
Pluto	Scorpio	Taurus	Leo	Aquarius

A Powerful Sun: This gives you a desire to put your stamp on the world, to be "somebody." You'll have a forceful personality, love to be noticed, and need recognition for your work. You head for leadership positions, where you command the spotlight. Negatively, you can be quite self-centered and occasionally arrogant.

EXAMPLE: Rock star Mick Jagger, who has the sun and three planets in Leo with Leo rising, was bound to make his presence felt. Although his looks are not particularly impressive, he has dramatized himself to the hilt to make himself the "king" of any stage on which he performs.

A Powerful Moon: You have an expressive emotional nature, with sharp perceptions and an excellent memory. Your personality may be more reflective, changeable according to mood. Family life is especially important to you. You have a talent for intimacy—may prefer one-on-one relationships to a crowded social life.

EXAMPLE: Romantic singer Julio Iglésias, with a powerful moon in Cancer, its ruling sign, started out as a soccer player but made his fortune as a singer of tender, emotional ballads. Linda Ronstadt, whose sun sign is moon-ruled Cancer, yet her moon stands alone in Aquarius, is an interesting lunar type who favors ballads and love songs but with an unpredictable "Aquarian" individualistic twist; her musical mood shifts from country music, to rock, to mariachi, to classic ballads of the forties.

A Powerful Mercury: Your special gifts are an analytical mind and talent for communicating via the written or spoken word. Your thought processes work quickly, helping you to handle a variety of interests, several projects or careers efficiently.

EXAMPLE: Joan Collins, with five planets in Mercury-ruled Gemini and Virgo, has managed dual careers as an actress and a writer of best-selling gossipy novels, true to her Gemini sun sign nature.

A Powerful Venus: You excel in relationships and express yourself artistically with grace and charm. You may have highly developed senses, and could be prone to overindulge them. You love to surround yourself with beauty, present an image that helps you relate to others, have a beautiful smile.

EXAMPLE: Singer Willie Nelson, whose sun and Venus are in Venus-ruled Taurus, adopted hippie garb, which won him legions of free-thinking fans.

A Powerful Mars: This gives you a dynamic drive to achieve goals; a competitive spirit; vigorous energy; a direct, assertive, aggressive manner.

EXAMPLE: Rock star/entrepreneur Prince, with Mars in Aries, its ruling sign, pioneered his own hard-driving music genre and founded a successful state-of-the-art recording studio and film production center in Minneapolis, which could change the image of that conservative city.

A Powerful Jupiter: You have an optimistic personality with a joyous sense of humor, a love and rapport with animals and the outdoors, and athletic ability. You place much emphasis on faith and luck. You could be a big risk taker, a gambler, or you could embody Jupiter's philosophical, spiritual side.

EXAMPLE: Robert Redford, with Jupiter in Sagittarius standing alone at the top of his chart, has gambled successfully with acting, directing, and ski resort development, and has backed environmental concerns.

A Powerful Saturn: This emphasizes function, order, structure. You keep your eye on the bottom line. Saturn gives you discipline, a strong sense of family duty, of following the rules to the letter. You'll be concerned with things that last. You'll never let up on pursuing your goals and may become more successful as you grow older.

EXAMPLE: Actor Paul Newman, with conservative Saturn standing alone at the top of his chart, is a very serious actor who exercises great self-discipline in his work. Shunning Hollywood, he prefers quiet family life in Connecticut. His career has expanded into business ventures, and he has become even more popular as he has aged.

A Powerful Uranus: You possess brilliant insights, an unconventional approach, a touch of eccentricity, a charisma that appeals to the masses. You challenge the establishment with original but sometimes rebellious ideas. You have an unpredictable streak. You love to experiment and could be especially successful in fields that use electronic media.

EXAMPLE: Outrageous comedienne Phyllis Diller has a Cancer sun sign, but her offbeat charisma is revealed by Uranus in its ruler Aquarius, standing alone at the top of her chart, which emphasizes the unconventional, eccentric, zany side of Aquarius and her major career success on television (Uranus ruled).

A Powerful Neptune: This gives you creativity, especially in the world of illusion, glamour, film, and theater. You have a need to get "high" (and may choose drugs or alcohol to get there), but you could also satisfy this need by developing your spiritual and creative gifts to express the one-ness of life.

EXAMPLE: David Bowie, with magical Neptune on the ascendant, is a master of illusion, with a quick-change personality who has become a film star (Neptune ruled) as well as a singer.

A Powerful Pluto: You have personal magnetism, sex appeal, an inner power. You'll probe beneath the surface of life for deep meaning, and transform others in some way. You are intense and can be manipulative.

EXAMPLE: Michael Jackson, with Pluto in Virgo on the ascendant, has, since childhood, been able to sway the masses; he has also totally transformed his own physical appearance (ruled by his Pluto ascendant).

5

When to Make
Your Moves in 1992

It's no secret that some of the most powerful and famous people, from Julius Caesar to financier J. P. Morgan, from Ronald Reagan to Cher, have consulted astrologers before they made their moves. If it works for the rich and famous, why not learn how to put astrology to work for you?

You can get control of your life and set it on its most successful course by letting astrology help you coordinate your activities. For instance, if you know the dates that the tricky planet Mercury will be creating havoc with communications, you'll back up that vital fax with a duplicate by Express Mail, you'll read between the lines of contracts and put off closing that deal until you have double-checked all the information. When Venus is on your side, you'll revamp your image or ask someone special to dinner. A retrograde Mars period would not be the best time to launch an aggressive campaign.

To find out for yourself if there's truth to the saying "timing is everything," mark your own calendar for love, career moves, vacations, and important events, using the following information and the tables in this chapter and the one titled "Look Up Your Planets," as well as the moon sign listings under your daily forecast. Here are the happenings to note on your agenda:

- Dates of your astrological sun sign (high-energy period)
- The month previous (low-energy period)
- Dates of planets in your sun sign (see "Look Up Your Planets")
- Full and new moons (with special attention to those falling in your sun sign)
- Eclipses (mark off eclipse period)

- Moon in your sun sign every month as well as moon in opposite sign (listed in daily forecast)
- Mercury retrogrades
- Other retrograde periods

With your astrological agenda, you have a tool for making the most of your personal best days this year and taking advantage of the "down times" to relax, reevaluate, and reorganize.

YOUR PERSONAL POWER TIME

Every birthday starts a cycle of solar energy for you. You should feel a new surge of vitality as the powerful sun enters your sign. This is the time when predominant energies are most favorable to you. So go for it! Start new projects, make your big moves. You'll get the recognition you deserve now when everyone is attuned to your sun sign. Look in the tables in this book to see if other planets will be passing through your sun sign at this time. Venus (love, beauty), Mars (energy, drive), or Mercury (communication, mental sharpness) reinforce the sun and give an extra boost to your life in the areas they affect. Venus will rev up your social and love life, making you seem especially attractive. Mars gives you extra energy and drive. Mercury fuels your brain power and helps you communicate. Jupiter signals an especially lucky period of expansion.

There are two "down" times related to the sun. During the month before your birthday period, when you are winding up your annual cycle, you could be feeling especially vulnerable and depleted so get extra rest, watch your diet, don't overstress yourself. Use this time to gear up for a big "push" when the sun enters your sign.

Another "down" time is when the sun in the opposite sign (six months from your birthday)—and the prevailing energies are very different from yours. You may feel at odds with the world, and things might not come easily. You'll have to work harder for recognition, because people are not on your wavelength. However, this could be a good time to work on a team, in cooperation with others or behind the scenes.

How to Use the Moon's Phase and Sign

Working with the PHASES of the moon is as easy as looking up at the night sky. At the new moon, when both sun and moon are in the same sign, it's the best time to begin new ventures, especially the activities that are favored by that sign. You'll have powerful energies pulling you in the same direction. You'll be focused outward, toward action, doing. Postpone breaking off, terminating, deliberating, or reflecting, activities that require introspection and passive work.

Get your project under way during the first quarter, then go public at the full moon, a time of high intensity, when feelings come out into the open. This is your time to shine—to express yourself. Be aware however, that because pressures are being released, other people are also letting off steam and confrontations are possible. So try to avoid arguments. Traditionally, astrologers often advise against surgery at this time, which could produce heavier bleeding.

During the last quarter of the new moon, you'll be most controlled. This is a winding-down phase, a time to cut off unproductive relationships, do serious thinking, and inward-directed activities.

You'll feel some new and full moons more strongly than others, especially those new moons that fall in your sun sign and full moons in your opposite sign. Because that full moon happens at your low-energy time of year, it is likely to be an especially stressful time in a relationship, when any hidden problems or unexpressed emotions could surface.

1992 FULL AND NEW MOONS

	DATE:	SIGN:
NEW MOON	January 4	Capricorn*
FULL MOON	January 19	Cancer
NEW MOON	February 3	Aquarius
FULL MOON	February 18	Leo

	DATE:	SIGN:
NEW MOON	March 4	Pisces
FULL MOON	March 18	Virgo
NEW MOON	April 3	Aries
FULL MOON	April 17	Libra
NEW MOON	May 2	Taurus
FULL MOON	May 16	Scorpio
NEW MOON	June 1	Gemini
FULL MOON	June 15	Sagittarius*
NEW MOON	June 30	Cancer*
FULL MOON	July 14	Capricorn
NEW MOON	July 29	Leo
FULL MOON	August 13	Aquarius
NEW MOON	August 28	Virgo
FULL MOON	September 12	Pisces
NEW MOON	September 26	Libra
FULL MOON	October 11	Aries
NEW MOON	October 25	Scorpio
FULL MOON	November 10	Taurus
NEW MOON	November 24	Sagittarius
FULL MOON	December 9	Gemini*
NEW MOON	December 24	Capricorn*

* Take special note: there are eclipses at these times.

HOW TO HANDLE ECLIPSES

One of the most amazing phenomena in the cosmos, which many of us take for granted, is the spatial relationship between the sun and the moon. How many of us have ever noticed or marveled that, relative to our viewpoint here on earth (the physically largest source of energy), the sun, and the smallest, the moon, appear to be the same size! This is most evident to us at the time of the solar eclipse, when the moon is directly aligned with the sun and so nearly covers it that scientists use the moment of eclipse to study solar flares.

When the two most powerful forces in astrology—the sun and moon—are lined up, we're sure to feel the effects, both in world events and in our personal lives. So it might help us to learn how best to cope with the periods around eclipses, especially because there are five coming up in 1992.

Both solar and lunar eclipses are times when our natural rhythms are changed, depending on where the eclipse falls in your horoscope. If it falls on or close to your sign—Capricorn, Sagittarius, Cancer, and Gemini this year—you're going to have important changes in your life, perhaps a turning point. The other cardinal (Aries and Libra) and mutable (Pisces and Virgo) signs may experience this year's eclipse effects to a lesser degree.

Lunar eclipses happen at times when the earth is on a level plane with the sun and moon and moves between them at the time of the full moon, breaking the powerful monthly opposition cycle of these two forces. Normally the full moon is the time when emotions come to a head and are released. During an eclipse, however, this rhythmic process is temporarily short-circuited. The effect can be either confusion or clarity—as our subconscious energies that normally feel the "pull" of the opposing sun and moon are turned off. Freed from subconscious attachments, we might have objective insights that could help us change any destructive emotional patterns, such as addictions, which normally occur at this time. This momentary "turn-off" could help us turn our lives around. On the other hand, this break in the cycle could cause a bewildering disorientation that intensifies insecurities.

The solar eclipse occurs at the new moon, when the moon comes between the earth and the sun, blocking the sun's energies. This time the objective, conscious force in our life will be temporarily darkened, because the "pull" between the earth and sun is cut off by the moon. The subconscious lunar forces then dominate, putting us in a highly subjective state. Emotional truths can be revealed—or emotions can run wild, as our objectivity is cut off and hidden patterns surface. If your sun sign is affected, you may find yourself beginning a period of work on a deep inner level, you may have psychic experiences or a surfacing of deep emotional truths.

You'll start feeling the energies of an upcoming eclipse a few days after the previous new or full moon. The energy continues to intensify until the actual eclipse, then disperses for three or four days. So plan ahead at least a week or more before an eclipse and allow several days after, for the natural rhythms to return. Try not to make major moves during this period (it's not a great time to get married, change jobs, or buy a home).

ECLIPSES IN 1992

	DATE		SIGN
SOLAR ECLIPSE	January 4	in	Capricorn
LUNAR ECLIPSE	June 15	in	Sagittarius
SOLAR ECLIPSE	June 30	in	Cancer
LUNAR ECLIPSE	December 9	in	Gemini
SOLAR ECLIPSE	December 24	in	Capricorn

VOID OF COURSE MOON

Approximately every two days, just before the moon changes into another sign, is the period known as the "void of course," which refers to the time between the last contact or aspect a moon makes with another planet and the time when it changes signs. This is a kind of twilight zone—a time for inner activity such as meditation, spiritual work, sleep, reading—basically passive experiences. This time can last for a few minutes or for almost a day, so it is worth noting if you have many important activities to plan. If you do not have an astrological ephemeris, as the detailed book of planetary tables is called, you can find astrological calendars that show the void of course in your local metaphysical bookstore. The key for the void of course is to put major projects on hold—there will be lots of talk but little follow-through. Don't look for results now. You might, however, negatively, work on projects where you *don't* want action. If you want nothing to happen, choose the void of course moon.

Moon Sign Timing

For the daily emotional "weather" for your monthly high and low days and to synchronize your activities with the cycle and the sign of the moon, take note of the moon's SIGN under your daily forecast at the end of the book. Here are some of the activities favored and moods you are likely to encounter under each sign.

MOON IN ARIES

Get moving! The new moon in Aries is an ideal time to start new projects. Everyone is pushy, raring to go, rather impatient, and short-tempered. Leave details and follow-up for later. Competitive sports or martial arts are great ways to let off steam. Quiet types could use some assertiveness training, but it's a great day for dynamos!

MOON IN TAURUS

It's time to do solid, methodical tasks. This is the time to tackle follow-through or backup work. Lay the foundations for success. Make investments, buy real estate, do appraisals, do some hard bargaining. Enjoy creature comforts, music, a good dinner, sensual lovemaking.

MOON IN GEMINI

Talk means action today. Telephone, write letters, fax! Make new contacts, stay in touch with steady customers. You can handle lots of tasks at once. A great day for mental activity of any kind. Don't try to pin people down—they too are feeling restless. Keep it light. Flirtations and socializing are good. Watch gossip—and don't give away secrets.

MOON IN CANCER

This is a moody, sensitive, emotional time. People respond to personal attention, mothering. Stay at home, have a family dinner, call your mother. Nostalgia, memories, psychic powers are heightened. You'll want to hang on to people and things (don't clean out your closets now). You could have some shrewd insights into what others really need and want now. Pay attention to your dreams, intuition, gut reactions.

MOON IN LEO

Everybody is in a much more confident, warm, generous mood. It's a good day to ask for a raise, show what you can do, dress like a star. People will respond to flattery, enjoy a bit of drama and theater. You may be extravagant, treat yourself royally, and show off a bit (but don't break the bank!). Be careful that you don't promise more than you can deliver!

MOON IN VIRGO

Do solid down-to-earth work. Review your budget. Make repairs. Be an efficiency expert. *Not* a day to ask for a raise. Have a health checkup. Revamp your diet. Buy vitamins or health food. Take care of details, piled-up chores. Reorganize your work and life so they run more smoothly and efficiently. Save money. Be prepared for others to be in a critical, fault-finding mood.

MOON IN LIBRA

Attend to legal matters. Negotiate contracts. Arbitrate. Do things with your favorite partner. Socialize. Be romantic. Buy a special gift, a beautiful object. Decorate yourself or your surroundings. Buy new clothes. Throw a party. Have an elegant, romantic evening. Smooth over any ruffled feathers. Avoid confrontations, stick to civilized discussions.

MOON IN SCORPIO

This is a day to do things with passion. You'll have excellent concentration and focus. Try not to get too intense emotionally, however, and avoid sharp exchanges with loved ones. Others may tend to go to extremes, get jealous, overreact. Great for troubleshooting, problem-solving, research, scientific work—and making love. Pay attention to psychic vibes.

MOON IN SAGITTARIUS

A great time for travel. Have philosophical discussions. Set long-range career goals. Work out, do sports, or buy athletic equipment. Others will be feeling upbeat, exuberant, and adventurous. Risk taking is high—you may feel like taking a gamble, betting on the horses. Teaching, writing, and spiritual activities also get the green light. Relax outdoors. Take care of animals.

MOON IN CAPRICORN

You can accomplish a lot today, so get on the ball! Issues concerning your basic responsibilities, duties, family, and parents could crop up. You'll be expected to deliver on promises now. Weed out the dead wood from your life. Get a dental checkup. The moon passing over Neptune and Uranus will illuminate your dreams and imagination—and could stir up some fantasies. Write down those creative ideas and listen to your intuition.

MOON IN AQUARIUS

A great day for doing things with groups—clubs, meetings, outings, politics, parties. Campaign for your candidate. Work for a worthy cause. Deal with larger issues that affect humanity: the environment, metaphysical questions. Buy a computer or electronic gadget. Watch TV. Wear something outrageous. Try something you've never done before. Present an original idea. Don't stick to a rigid schedule—go with the flow. Take a class in meditation, mind control, yoga.

MOON IN PISCES

This can be a very creative day, so let your imagination work overtime. Film, theater, music, ballet could inspire you. Spend some time alone, resting and reflecting, reading or writing poetry. Daydreams can be profitable. Help those less fortunate or lend a listening ear to someone who may be feeling blue. Don't overindulge in self-pity or escapism, however—people are especially vulnerable to substance abuse now. Turn your thoughts to romance and someone special.

When the Planets Go Backward

All the planets except for the sun and moon have times when they seem to move backward—or retrograde—in the sky from our point of view on earth. At these times, planets do not work as they usually do, leading us to "take a break" from that planet's energies in our life and do some work on an inner level.

MERCURY RETROGRADE

Mercury goes retrograde most often and its effects can be especially irritating. When it reaches a short distance ahead of the sun three times a year, it seems to move backward from our point of view. Astrologers often compare retrograde motion to the optical illusion that occurs when we ride on a train that passes another train traveling at a different speed—the second train appears to be moving in reverse.

What this means to you is that the Mercury-ruled areas of your life—analytical thought processes, communications, scheduling, and such—are subject to all kinds of snafus. Be prepared. People will change their minds, renege on commitments. Communications equipment can break down. Schedules must be changed on short notice. People are late for appointments or don't show up at all. Traffic is terrible. Major purchases malfunction, don't work out, or get delivered in the wrong color. Letters don't arrive or are delivered to the wrong address. Coworkers will make errors that have to be corrected later. Contracts don't work out or must be renegotiated.

Since most of us can't put our lives on "hold" for nine weeks every year, we should learn to tame the trickster and make it work for us. The key is in the prefix "re." This is the time to go back over things in your life— REflect on what you've done during the previous months. Look for deeper insights, spot errors you've missed, take time to review and reevaluate what has happened. This time is very good for inner spiritual work and meditation. REst and REward yourself—it's a good time to take a vacation, especially if you revisit a favorite place. REorganize your work and finish up projects that have been hanging around. Clean out your desk and closets. If you must sign contracts or agreements, do so with a contingency clause that lets you reevaluate the terms later.

Postpone major purchases or commitments. Don't get married. Try not to rely on other people keeping appointments, contracts, or agreements to the letter—have several alternatives. Double-check and read between the lines. Don't buy anything connected with communications or transportation (if you must, be sure to cover yourself). Mercury retrograding through your sun sign will intensify its effect on your life.

If Mercury was retrograde when you were born, you may be one of the lucky people who don't suffer the frustrations of this period. If so, your mind probably works in a very intuitive, insightful way.

The sign Mercury is retrograding through can give you an idea of what's in store—as well as the sun signs that will be especially challenged. This year, it's the fire signs—so look before you leap, and don't make promises you can't keep.

MERCURY RETROGRADE PERIODS IN 1992

March 17–April 9 in Aries
July 20–August 13 in Leo
November 11–December 1 in Sagittarius

MARS RETROGRADE

Mars retrograde times are fascinating periods when drive, arrogance, aggressive maneuvers, and fast action are sure to trip you up. If there is ever a time when passive, reactive, peaceful action will get you farther ahead, this is it! People who are normally that way will make surprising gains, whereas the go-getters will be stalled or become losers. So watch the so-called wimps for some surprising moves! If you have planned to go full speed ahead on anything, first check out Mars. If it's retrograde, put your plans on the back burner. Flight COULD get you farther than fight, now!

Fortunately Mars only turns retrograde every 2½ years;

however, we will be hit this December, just in time for the holidays! Try to avoid buying mechanical gifts—they often malfunction. This is a time to take extra care of your health—your energy may be low. So, even though you may be raring to go after the Mercury retrograde ends on December 1, be patient a while longer.

Those who aggressively initiate at this time will be at a disadvantage (you could, of course, profit from this if your competition launches a new venture). Let others fire first! Arrogance is a particular danger now. Avoid it! And never underestimate the underdog at this time. Remember the last game of the 1990 World Series? A stunning surprise upset by the underdog Cincinnati Reds over the cocksure Oakland Athletics occurred on the very day Mars turned retrograde. So don't bet on a "sure thing" during a Mars retrograde, and keep your eye on the dark horse! Fortunately this period occurs after this year's Presidential elections, so it should not adversely affect the candidates as it did Mars-ruled Michael Dukakis' campaign during the Mars retrograde that preceded the 1988 Presidential elections!

Rather than bottle up anger or aggressive feelings during this time, try to find nondestructive ways to let off steam. Physical exercise is a good idea, particularly low-risk, noncompetitive exercise such as cross-country skiing, swimming, jogging, or bike riding.

Mars-ruled signs of Scorpio and Aries, normally quite strong-willed and forceful, may seem unusually slow-moving and reflective now. Aries may seem especially out of character in a more introspective mode. Since Mars will be transiting the emotionally sensitive sign of Cancer this year, watch for any tendency to take things too personally, especially family disputes or well-meaning criticism.

Mars turns retrograde November 28 and remains so through February 16, 1993. Cancers and Capricorns will experience this passage most acutely.

VENUS RETROGRADE

Fortunately, there is no Venus retrograde in 1992. You will have to deal with it next year, however. A Venus retrograde can cause trouble in relationships, causing you to be extravagant and impractical. Not a good time to redecorate—you'll hate the color of the walls later—to try a new hairstyle, or to fall in love. But if you wish to make amends in an already troubled relationship, make peaceful overtures then.

WHEN OTHER PLANETS RETROGRADE

Planets retrograding at the same time indicate a period of readjustment on many levels. Luckily this will be happening during the summer months of 1992; it's an excellent idea to take time off for a vacation! During this July, five planets will be retrograde: Mercury, which we've discussed, will have the most dramatic effects. So double-check travel plans, reservations, and maps. Plan several alternatives in case of foul-ups, and be patient with delays.

The other, slower-moving planets, stay retrograde for months at a time—Saturn, Neptune, Uranus, and Pluto. Saturn is retrograde almost five months in Aquarius (May 28–October 16), a time when you may feel more like hanging out at the beach than getting things done. It's an uphill battle with self-discipline at this time. In Capricorn, Neptune retrograde (April 20–September 27) promotes a dreamy escapism from reality, whereas Uranus retrograde (April 21–September 22) may mean setbacks in areas where there have been sudden changes and a general lack of originality and inspiration. Think of this as an adjustment period. Pluto retrograde in Scorpio (February 24–July 30) is not a good time for extreme military action or dramatic transformations. This is a better time to work on establishing proportion, balance.

When the planets start moving forward again, there's a shift in the atmosphere. Activities connected with each planet start moving ahead, plans that were stalled get rolling. Make a special note of those days on your calendar and proceed accordingly.

WILL THIS BE YOUR LUCKY YEAR?

Look to Jupiter for the lucky times of your life. When Jupiter is passing through your sun sign, you're due for a period of expansion as you begin a new twelve-year cycle. This is the time to expose yourself to new things, take risks, get higher education, travel, meet new people. This is true to a lesser degree for those born in sun signs of the same element (earth, air, fire, water signs). Jupiter retrogrades in Virgo until April 30, however, so postpone risk-taking ventures until that date. Virgo and other earth signs (Taurus, Capricorn) should have many new opportunities coming their way for the rest of the summer. When Jupiter enters Libra, October 10, this air sign (plus Aquarius and Gemini) should get set for beneficial rays through the remainder of 1992.

WHO WILL BE TIGHTENING THEIR BELTS?

Saturn moving through your sun sign signals a period of self-discipline—the very opposite of a Jupiter period! This year Aquarians will have to buckle down and put nose to the grindstone. With your ruler, Uranus, helping out in no-nonsense Capricorn, this can be a time when you'll achieve much on a practical level, giving those far-out ideas a solid foundation. Saturn periods aren't easy, but there is some consolation in that the work you do now will have lasting results. Leo, the opposite sign of Aquarius, will also feel Saturn's restrictions. We'll be seeing more of the hard-working side of Leo and less of his flamboyant show-biz side this year.

The Merger of the 1990s— Uranus and Neptune

No discussion of when to make your moves would be complete without dealing with this year's major planetary happening, the alignment of Uranus and Neptune in Capricorn. This alignment will be exact (and have the most dramatic effects) next year—but the forces have been in effect since April 1991, and will continue until December 1995. They're sure to be affecting the overall focus of your life and determining the prevailing trends of the 1990s.

Alignments of the slow-moving outer planets (Uranus, Neptune, and Pluto) are rare, but when they do occur, there is a global change in consciousness that alters the course of history. The last time was a Pluto-Uranus merger in the radical 1960s (in Virgo) and in the last century, the same conjunction in Aries preceded the Civil War. Those of you born from September 1964–September 1968, at the time of the 1960s alignment, will be especially energized on a personal and collective level by the happenings of the 1990s.

Uranus (revolution, social reform, sudden changes, electricity, high tech) and Neptune (imagination, creativity, dissolution, escapism, film, drugs, oil!), two mysterious planets, together in Capricorn (tradition, structure, organizations, corporations, status) suggest both spiritual and sociological revolutions. Possibilities include the dissolving of established structures—anything with an "ism" attached, including rigid fundamentalist systems of belief. On a positive note, this could be a time of creative renaissance—revolutionary medicines, imaginative spiritual high-tech ventures, the blending of spiritual and social concerns, the expanded use of electronic media such as global satellite entertainment networks, revolutionary changes in energy use, which could positively affect oil-producing countries—this is another potential face of a decade when these two creative planetary forces, working in tandem, bring us together in new ways.

Look for more futuristic, imaginative structures in the creative arts, imaginative yet practical inventions, a structured space-age look in fashions reminiscent of the 1960s, a more creative and expanded use of computers. In Capricorn, the sign of traditions and institutions, the establishment as we know it is due for sweeping changes. Take note of these changes on a personal level (especially if you have planets in Capricorn or Capricorn rising) to plan how you can maximize your role in the drama of the decade.

6

How to Pick
the Big Day

You may have wondered what a difference a day could make when planning a party, timing your big event, signing a lease or contract. Twenty-four little hours can make a big difference, most astrologers would agree. You can give your event the luckiest send-off possible by choosing the time according to the techniques of electional astrology, which astrologers use to find the optimum time for a specific action.

When you set a date for an event, whether it's something as routine as a business meeting or as momentous as a wedding, you are giving that event a "birthday." Therefore, that moment has a horoscope, with the planets and aspects to be interpreted just like the horoscope of a person. Astrologers, who believe that each moment reveals potential for success or failure, have developed a technique called electional astrology for finding the best time for a given event.

Electional astrology is routinely practiced in the Far East, where the governments of India, Sri Lanka, Thailand, and Nepal regularly consult astrologers before setting important dates. Closer to home, Thomas Jefferson is thought to have set the signing of the Declaration of Independence by consulting astrological tables. The governor of California in 1967, Ronald Reagan, is believed to have timed his 12:16 A.M. inauguration by the stars and is known to have relied on astrological advice to time his later Presidential schedule. Tycoon J. P. Morgan and opera legend Enrico Caruso were among those who moved on the advice of astrologer Evangeline Adams. The most successful English monarch, Elizabeth I, had her personal court astrologer, John Dee, time her coronation for the most auspicious aspects of her horoscope.

Though the techniques for electional astrology are often quite complex for a neophyte astrologer, there are some basic guidelines that can be very helpful in planning your schedule. When choosing the right time for a special event such as a marriage, the launching of a product, starting a business, or signing an important document, you should realize that it is not always possible to find the "perfect" time, one that meets all the possible criteria for success. However, you can try to avoid the major problem times within the parameters of your schedule.

Here are a few general rules for choosing the right day for your event. First, consider the fast-moving planets, the moon and Mercury. A waxing moon is considered better for action than a waning moon. Avoid the period every two days known as the void of course moon (this is the time period between the last aspect of the moon and its entrance into a new sign). If you cannot find an astrological calendar that lists the void of course, try for a time period within the first ten hours after the moon changes signs, which are most often "safe" from the void of course. Moon sign changes are noted for Eastern Standard Time in the daily forecast section of this book. Also avoid the time period near an eclipse (this is known as the "shadow of the eclipse"—if possible, allow two weeks before the eclipse and a week after for good measure!).

The other major "no-no" is the Mercury retrograde period (explained in Chapter 5 "When to Make Your Moves in 1992"), which is a three-week time period. The best Mercury is directly AFTER the retrograde.

Since we will be referring to the element of signs, here is a handy reference list. In general, harmonious combinations are:

EARTH SIGNS (Taurus, Virgo, Capricorn) with WATER SIGNS (Cancer, Scorpio, Pisces)
AIR SIGNS (Gemini, Libra, Aquarius) with FIRE SIGNS (Aries, Leo, Sagittarius)
Bear these combinations in mind when you consider the relationship of any two planets on a given day.

When planning your date, you should also consider the nature of the event. If you're signing a contract, going for a job interview, giving a speech—anything where your ability to communicate in the written or spoken word is critical—pay attention to the sign of Mercury. It would be most helpful if Mercury was in an air sign, with the moon harmoniously placed in a fire or air sign.

Mars-related events are the aggressive moves in your life, daring competitive sports and launching new products. Make sure Mars is in direct motion, and preferably in a fire or earth sign such as Aries or Capricorn. However, make certain that Mars is not challenged by Saturn at this time, which can put a damper on your plans. Try to have Saturn in either the same or a complimentary element as Mars, if possible, but not in the same sign or six signs away.

When beginning any venture, time it for the period following a new moon, preferably if the moon is in a fire sign.

A strong Venus in the same sign or element as the sun or moon will enhance artistic projects. Venus also adds sparkle and beauty to parties and social affairs. Plan your party when the moon is in Libra, for an elegant social event. Moon in Cancer or Taurus is good for family gatherings. Moon in Leo or Sagittarius is great for a theatrical production—when you want to make a big splash. Jupiter in harmony with the moon will put everyone in a upbeat mood.

Retrograde periods of Mercury and Saturn are good for getaways, vacations, rest, and relaxation. Try to make your reservations before the retrograde period begins, however. The moon in adventure-loving Sagittarius or communicative Gemini is an excellent time for travel, meeting new people, getting a change of scene. (Avoid the moon in homebound Taurus and Cancer.)

HOW TO SET THE BEST WEDDING DATES

First set your time parameters, giving yourself ample leeway and avoiding Mercury retrograde periods (time it for after a retrograde if possible). Then consider each of the following prerequisites, trying to accomplish as many as possible:

1. First choose the sun sign of your wedding. It is helpful if this is in the same sun sign or element as your birth sign or that of your mate. Some signs, such as Venus-ruled Libra or Taurus are considered naturally favorable. June weddings, most often in Gemini (the "dual" sign of the "twins"), emphasize strong communications and would be best if Mercury is in an air or fire sign.
2. The moon sign should be in harmony with the sun sign in either an earth/water or air/fire element combination. It is also very helpful to have Venus and Jupiter in harmonious elements. Your best bet is a waxing moon, preferably the quarter before the full moon.
3. The ascendant or rising sign sets up the happenings of the marriage and also reveals the attitudes of both partners. Fixed signs (Taurus, Scorpio, Aquarius, Leo) are stable, enduring, steady. These are most preferable, so check the rising sign tables in this book. Active cardinal signs (Aries, Cancer, Capricorn, Libra) could signify striving or competition, rather than a nurturing atmosphere. Mutable signs (Gemini, Virgo, Sagittarius, Pisces) could bring restlessness, instability, infidelity. Try not to have the disruptive planet Uranus six signs away from the ascendant, which could indicate break-offs. Therefore be very careful of marriages with Cancer rising this year.

Helpful Tables in This Book

Mercury Retrograde Periods as well as New Moons, Full Moons, and Eclipses—"When to Make Your Moves in 1992"
Daily Moon Sign Changes—"Daily Forecasts"
Rising Sign Tables
Planetary Movements—"Look Up Your Planets"

A CHECKLIST FOR SCHEDULING BY THE STARS

Moon sign is _____
Moon phase is _____
Sun sign is _____
    (Are they in harmony?)

Is the date in an eclipse period?

Is Mercury retrograde?

Mars and Saturn signs for beginning a project, sports events _____

    (check if harmonious—should not be six signs apart or close together in the same sign)

For social events:

    Moon sign _____

    Venus sign _____

    Jupiter sign _____

For weddings:

    Sun sign _____

    Sun signs of bride and groom _____

    Moon sign _____

    Venus _____

    Jupiter _____

7

Understanding
Your Horoscope Chart

When you first see your chart you'll probably be bewildered by the page filled with mysterious symbols placed on a circle, which is divided into twelve sectors. It looks like another language—and not an easy one to read, at first. But as you get acquainted with your chart, you'll see how it makes common, cosmic sense.

What you are looking at is a picture of a moment in time as seen from a particular place on earth. The earth is the center of the chart, surrounded by the zodiac portion of the sky, divided into wedge-shaped segments. This is simply a graphic depiction of the energies happening at a given moment at a certain place.

Anything that happens can have a horoscope—a meeting, a person, a marriage—anything that can be pinned down to a time and a place. There are horoscopes for countries, cities, businesses and events as well as people.

Each wedge-shaped segment of the chart is called a "house" and deals with a specific area of life. The house reflects the character of two signs. First, the sign that rules the house, which has a natural affinity for it. You might think of this as the house's owner. The planet that rules this sign is also naturally at home in this house. The other important sign is the one that is passing over the house at the moment the chart is cast, which colors the house individually; this sign is what makes the house uniquely "yours" because it is passing over at your moment in time.

The houses rotate counterclockwise from the left center horizontal spoke (that would be the number 9 on a clock), which is the first house or ascendant. The signs were moving clockwise around the chart at the time they were "frozen" in place on the chart.

The houses progress around the chart, starting with the birth of the self in the first chart and evolving through the different areas of life, as the self becomes mature and finally "dissolves" in the twelfth house. It is somewhat like a "Hero's Journey"—a progression of growth and maturity. Here is what each house will tell you about your development.

THE FIRST HOUSE
natural place of Aries and Mars

How you assert yourself—what others see first.

This is the house of "firsts"—the first gasp of independence, the first impression you make, how you initiate matters, the image you choose to project. This is where you advertise yourself. Planets that fall here will intensify how you come across to others. Often the first house will project an entirely different type of personality than the sun sign. For instance a Capricorn with Leo in the first house will come across as much more flamboyant than the average Capricorn. The sign passing over this house is known as your ascendant or rising sign.

THE SECOND HOUSE
home of Taurus and Venus

How you experience the material world, what you value.

Here is your contact with the material world—your attitudes about money, possessions, finances, whatever belongs to you—what you own. Your earning and spending capacity. On a deeper level, this house reveals your sense of self-worth, the inner values that draw wealth in various forms.

THE THIRD HOUSE
home of Gemini and Mercury

How well you communicate with others—are you understood?

This house shows how you reach out to others nearby and interact with the immediate environment. Here is how your thinking process works, how you communicate, if you are misunderstood. It shows your first relationships, experiences with brothers and sisters, how you deal with people close to you, such as your neighbors or pals. It's where you take short trips, write letters, or use the telephone. It shows how your mind works in terms of left-brain logical and analytical functions.

THE FOURTH HOUSE
natural place of Cancer and the Moon

How you are nurtured and made to feel secure.

At the bottom of the chart, the fourth house, like the home, shows the foundation of life, the psychological underpinnings. Here is where you have the deepest confrontations with whom you are, how you make yourself feel secure. It shows your early home environment and the circumstances of the end of your life—your final "home"—as well as the place you call home now. Astrologers look here for information about the parental nurturers in your life.

THE FIFTH HOUSE
home of Leo and the Sun

How you express yourself creatively—your idea of play.

The Leo house is where creative potential develops. Here you express yourself and procreate (children), in the sense that children are outgrowths of your creative ability. But this house most represents your inner childlike self who delights in play. Assuming inner security has been established by the time you reach this house, you are now free to have fun, romance, love affairs, and to GIVE of yourself. This is also the place astrologers look for playful love affairs and brief romantic encounters (rather than long-term commitments).

THE SIXTH HOUSE
home of Virgo and Mercury

How you function in daily life.

The sixth house has been called the "repair and maintenance" department. Here is the shop where you get things done, how you look after others and fulfill responsibilities, such as taking care of pets. Here is your daily survival, your "job" (as opposed to your career, which is the domain of the tenth house), your diet, health, and fitness regimens. This house shows how you take care of your body and maintenance systems so you can perform efficiently in the world.

THE SEVENTH HOUSE
natural place of Libra and Venus

How you form a partnership.

Here is how you relate to others, your close, intimate one-on-one relationships. Your attitudes toward partners and those with whom you enter commitments, contracts, or agreements are here. Open hostilities, lawsuits, divorces as well as marriages happen here. If the first house is the "I"—the seventh or opposite house is the "Not-I"—the complementary partner you attract by the way you come across. If you are having trouble with partnerships, consider what you are attracting by the energies of your first and seventh houses.

THE EIGHTH HOUSE
home of Scorpio and Pluto (also Mars)

How you merge with something greater than yourself.

This is one of the most mysterious and powerful houses, where your energy transforms itself from "I" to "we." As you give up power and control, you unite with what is larger than yourself—two kinds of energies merge and become something greater—and lead to a regeneration of the self. Here are your attitudes toward sex, shared resources, taxes (you share with the government). Because this house involves what belongs to others, you face issues of control and power struggles, or undergo a deep psychological transformation as you bond with another. Here you transcend yourself with the occult, dreams, drugs, or psychic experiences that reflect the collective unconscious.

THE NINTH HOUSE
home of Sagittarius and Jupiter

How you search for wisdom and higher knowledge, your belief system.

As the third house represents the "Lower Mind," its opposite on the wheel, the ninth house, is the "Higher Mind," the abstract, intuitive, spiritual mind that asks "big" questions like why are we here. The ninth house shows what you believe in. After the third house explored what was close at hand, the ninth stretches out to explore more exotic territory, either by traveling, broadening mentally with higher education or stretching spiritually with religious activity. Here is where you write a book or extensive thesis, where you pontificate, philosophize, or preach.

THE TENTH HOUSE
natural place of Capricorn and Saturn

Your public image and how you handle authority.

This house is located directly overhead at the "high noon" position. This is the most "visible" house in the chart, the one where the world sees you. It deals with your public image, your career (but not your routine "job"), your reputation. Here is where you go public, take on responsibilities (as opposed to the fourth house, where you stay home). This will affect the career you choose and your "public relations." This house is also associated with the father figure or whoever else was the authority figure in your life.

THE ELEVENTH HOUSE
home of Aquarius and Uranus

Your support system, how you relate to society, your goals.

Here you extend yourself to a group, a goal, a belief system. This house is where you define what you really want, what kinds of friends you have, your political affiliations, what kind of groups you identify with as an equal. Here is where you could become a socially-conscious humanitarian—or a party-going social butterfly, where you look to others to stimulate you, where you discover your kinship to the rest of humanity. The sign on this house can help you understand what you gain and lose from friendships.

THE TWELFTH HOUSE
home of Pisces and Neptune

How you become selfless.

Here is where the boundaries between yourself and others are blurred. In your trip around the zodiac, you've gone from the "I" of self-assertion in the first house to the final house symbolizing the dissolution that happens before a rebirth, a place where the accumulated experiences are processed in the unconscious. Spiritually oriented astrologers look to this house for your past lives and karma. Places where we go to be alone and do spiritual or reparatory work belong here, such as retreats, religious institutions, hospitals. Here is also where we withdraw from society—or are forced to withdraw because of antisocial activity. Self-less giving through charitable acts is part of this house. In your daily life, the twelfth house reveals your deepest intimacies, your best-kept secrets—especially those you hide from yourself, repressed deep in the unconscious. It is where we surrender a sense of a separate self to a deep feeling of wholeness, such as selfless service in religion or any activity that involves merging with the greater whole. Many famous athletes have important planets in the twelfth house, which enable them to "go with the flow" of the game, to rise above competition and find an inner, almost mystical, strength that transcends their limits. Madonna, the rock star, has a strong twelfth-house emphasis in her horoscope and reflects this house's religious, psychological, and sexual concerns.

WHO'S HOME IN YOUR HOUSES?

Houses are stronger or weaker depending on how many planets are inhabiting them. If there are many planets in a given house, it follows that the activities of that house will be especially important in your life. If the planet that rules the house is also located there, this too adds power to the house.

ASTROLOGY'S SIGN LANGUAGE

Beginners are often baffled by the strange-looking symbols all over their charts. Actually, these symbols are universally recognized and make life easier for the astrologer, because they enable any astrologer of any nationality— from Indian to Russian to American—to read your chart with ease.

This international symbolic language is written in mysterious-looking hieroglyphics called "glyphs"—those are the odd-looking characters, which are actually sort of a cosmic shorthand, representing planets, signs, and aspects. Each character contains the code to its meaning, so once you learn the "code," it's full of clues to the sign, the planet, or relationship between the planets.

The glyphs for the planets are stylized representations of three basic cosmic symbols—the circle for the eternal spirit, the semicircle for the soul, and the cross for matter. The exception to this rule is Pluto, which can be represented either by a glyph that combines the preceding symbols or one that is a stylized version of the letters PL. The relative size and placement of the elements divulge the planet's meaning. For instance, the symbol for Neptune, which is often stylized into a trident, is actually the upturned semicircle of the soul penetrated by matter, revealing this planet's dynamics of bringing cosmic energy into material form and dissolving material form into cosmic energy, the union of the material with the divine.

The more recent discoveries of the asteroids and Chiron are often included on computer charts. These are also exceptions to the rule and have specific glyphs based on their individual personalities rather than the basic cosmic symbols.

Glyphs for the signs go back to ancient times, some as far as ancient Egypt or Chaldea. Some forms are abstractions of the animal symbol of the sign, such as a bull's head for Taurus and a ram's horns for Aries. The roman numeral for two hints at the Gemini twins; similarly the two curved lines joined at the center for Pisces fish. The Libra scales, Sagittarius arrow, and Aquarius waves are keys to the sign's meaning. Scorpio and Virgo's variation on the M shape hint at male and female genitalia. Cancer and Capricorn require you to stretch your imagination a bit more. Cancer's horizontal 69 figure could remind you of a crab's claws or female breasts. Capricorn's V shape, ending in a looped flourish, could be the horns and tail of the sea goat.

The preceding two kinds of glyphs are shown on most astrological charts. However, there are also symbols to describe the aspects or relationships between planets. These are shown by geometric forms, the most important of which are:

- The triangle for a "trine" (120-degree angle)
- A circle with a vertical line for a conjunction, or two planets in near-exact alignment
- Two vertically slanted circles for an opposition (180 degrees)
- A square for 90 degrees
- A six-pointed "asterisk" for a sextile (60 degrees)
- A horizontal K shape for a quincunx (150 degrees)

8

The Ultimate Compatibility Chart

"I've got your number!" is the old saying when you've finally figured out what makes someone tick. But, in astrology, this cliché takes on new meaning—getting someone's astrological number in relation to your sign can give you terrific clues, not only to *how* you'll relate to each other, but *why!*

Use this chart to get the "number" of those close to you and then read the explanation in this chapter. I've called it the "ultimate compatibility chart" because you can use it not only to compare sun signs, but to relate *any* two planets within your own horoscope chart or to compare your planets with those of another chart.

Use it to help you understand the dynamics between you and the people you interact with. You might find it the key to getting along better with your boss and co-workers. Or discover what the real dynamics are with your difficult relatives and your best friends.

What this chart *won't* do is tell you that there are signs you can't get along with. There are no two totally incompatible signs—there are many happy marriages between signs that succeed because of the stimulation and "chemistry" their differences provide. To understand your astrological connection with another person, you need to identify the spatial relationship between signs. The sign "next door" is something like your next-door neighbor, who loans you his lawn mower or feeds your cats—or disputes your property boundaries. Signs distant from yours also have attitudes based on their "neighborhood."

A sign by definition is a specific territory, a division of an energy belt called the zodiac, which circles the earth. Each division is distinguished by an element (earth, air, fire, water), a quality or modality (cardinal, fixed, mutable), and a polarity or "charge" (positive/negative). No two signs have the same combination. These variables alternate around the zodiac belt in an established order: first fire, next earth, air, and water. The qualities alternate first with cardinal (active), then fixed (growth), and last mutable (change) signs. It follows that the positive and negative signs also alternate, like the charge of a battery. As the energy flow progresses around the zodiac, starting with Aries, the signs become more complex, less self-oriented. So the place in line around the "belt" becomes a factor, too.

Since the zodiac is a circle, the signs also relate to each other according to the angle of the distance between them. Between signs of the same polarity (masculine/feminine, positive/negative, yin/yang), which are numbers 0, 2, and 4, energy flows most easily (with one exception: the sign opposite yours—number 6). Between signs of different polarity, which are numbered 1, 3, 5, you'll experience tension or challenge (and possibly a very sexy "charge!") Here's how it works out . . .

THE ULTIMATE COMPATIBILITY CHART

	AR	TA	GE	CAN	LEO	VIR	LIB	SC	SAG	CAP	AQ	PIS
Aries	0	1	2	3	4	5	6	5	4	3	2	1
Taurus	1	0	1	2	3	4	5	6	5	4	3	2
Gemini	2	1	0	1	2	3	4	5	6	5	4	3
Cancer	3	2	1	0	1	2	3	4	5	6	5	4
Leo	4	3	2	1	0	1	2	3	4	5	6	5
Virgo	5	4	3	2	1	0	1	2	3	4	5	6
Libra	6	5	4	3	2	1	0	1	2	3	4	5
Scorpio	5	6	5	4	3	2	1	0	1	2	3	4
Sagittarius	4	5	6	5	4	3	2	1	0	1	2	3
Capricorn	3	4	5	6	5	4	3	2	1	0	1	2
Aquarius	2	3	4	5	6	5	4	3	2	1	0	1
Pisces	1	2	3	4	5	6	5	4	3	2	1	0

Find your sign in the vertical list. Then read across the row until you come to the column under the sign of your partner, mate, lover, boss, and so on. Then read the description of the number in this chapter.

Your "0" Relationships

"0" relationships are with those of your own sign, so naturally you'll have much in common. This could be the soul mate you've been looking for—one who understands and sympathizes with you like no other sign can! One who understands your need for space, yet knows how and when to be "there" for you. There are many examples of long-term partnerships between sun sign twins—Roy Rogers and Dale Evans (both Scorpio), Abigail and John Adams (Scorpio), George and Barbara Bush (Gemini), Bob and Delores Hope (both Gemini). Working relationships fare especially well with sun signs in common, though you may have to delegate unwanted tasks to others. In a public lifestyle or one where there is much separation or stimulation, your similarities can hold you together—there is the feeling of "you and me against the world." The problem is when there is too much of a good thing with no stimulation or challenge—or when there is no "chemistry," which can often happen between signs that share so much—the same element, quality, and polarity. The solution is to bring plenty of outside excitement into your lives!

Your "1" Relationships

These signs are your next-door neighbors on the zodiac wheel. Your relationship is based on evolution—you've evolved out of the previous sign carrying energies that have been accumulating and developing through the zodiac cycle. The sign following yours is where your energy is headed, the next step. In a way, it's like sitting at a dinner table and passing the plate from left to right. You receive certain qualities from the previous sign and pass on those, plus your own, to the next.

This is also like a sibling relationship where the sign coming before yours is like a protective older brother or sister, who's "been there," and the next sign is your eager younger sibling. Every sign also has a compensating factor for its predecessor—this sign embodies lessons you should have learned (and which could trip you up if you've forgotten them).

But although both are in the same "family," sibling signs actually have little in common, because you have different basic values (elements), ways of operating (qualities), and types of energy (polarity). You probably won't feel sparks of chemistry or the deep rapport of a soul mate unless other planets in your horoscopes provide this bond. Instead, the emphasis is on pals, best friends, working partners, who are enhanced by the sibling sign position.

The sign ahead can inspire you—they're where you are heading, but you may be afraid to take the first brave step. For example, to Pisces, Aries embodies dynamic, forceful, self-oriented will—whereas Pisces is the formless, selfless, imaginative state where Aries originated. So Aries energizes Pisces, gets Pisces moving. The sign behind backs you up, supports you. This relationship often makes one of the most lasting and contented unions—several famous examples are the Duke and Duchess of Windsor (Cancer/Gemini), Paul Newman and Joanne Woodward (Aquarius/Pisces), and Jerry Hall/Mick Jagger (Cancer/Leo).

To reveal how you'll relate to your zodiac "sibling," here's how energy evolves through the twelve signs:

Aries, the first sign of the zodiac, is "born" from Pisces, the last. In Pisces, individual energy has dissolved into universal energy—to be reasserted again in Aries. Aries is the new "baby"—Pisces is the pre-birth gestation, full of spiritual energy. Pisces reminds self-oriented Aries that there is more to life than "me." Pisces teaches Aries compassion, and consciousness of others, whereas Aries infuses Pisces with new energy and gets Pisces to assert itself.

Taurus is the baby taking the first steps into the material world, feeling its way with the senses. Taurus stabilizes Aries, gives this sign direction and purpose, asks where all that energy and drive is going. Taurus also imposes boundaries and limits to Aries—pulls it down to earth and stubbornly insists "you can't have it your way all the time," or "what are you really getting done?" or "what will it cost?"

Gemini teaches Taurus (who is often stuck on its own turf) to communicate, to socialize, to reach out to others, paving the way for the first emotional water sign, Cancer, where feelings are top priority, so the energy becomes nurturing, self-protective. Cancer adds the dimension of caring to Gemini (who would rather not deal with emotions at all).

The nurturing qualities of Cancer burst forth in Leo. Leo's confidence and self-expression come out of the security Cancer provides. Leo, who needs this kind of caring to shine, can be quite insecure and demanding if good mothering has not been received. And that becomes a hallmark of the Cancer/Leo relationship: ideally, Cancer nurtures Leo (in a not-so-ideal relationship, Cancer's fearfulness holds Leo back) and Leo in turn brings this vulnerable sign out into public life. Virgo is concerned with making things work, with helping, and says, "Leo, this is all very impressive, but is it useful? Will it work? Here's how to improve it." Virgo edits Leo creativity (which Leo might resent, but which makes for a better end result). Leo's confidence rubs off on shyer Virgos.

Like Virgo, Libra is also concerned with measuring up. While Virgo is concerned with the practical, Libra is in love with beauty. When Virgo asks: What good is something beautiful if it doesn't work? Libra answers: Beauty is its own justification. Virgo stimulates and grounds Libra. Libra takes Virgo further into aesthetics.

Scorpio plunges into deep emotional territory that Libra might prefer not to enter. However, the balance of Libra is first necessary for Scorpio to reach its most positive, decisive expression. Scorpio's intensity challenges Libra to look deeper, not to be content with superficial beauty.

Sagittarius evolves from Scorpio's deeper understanding and projects this to higher levels. Sagittarius brings optimism, uplifting ideals and humor to counter Scorpio negativity. Sagittarius also gains direction from the following sign, Capricorn, who brings structure and order to Sagittarius, which can help achieve its aspirations.

Capricorn is inspired by Sagittarius, but this bottomline earth sign is concerned with getting concrete results. Aquarius, its neighbor, brings in higher principles, consideration for the elements of surprise, inventiveness, unpredictability. There is always a higher purpose with Aquarius.

Pisces, the final sign in the cycle, is the most sensitive to outside input (and as a result can be self-sacrificing or self-pitying) and shares a universal with Aquarius. However, Aquarius reminds Pisces of detachment, involvement with a group, and the need to keep perspective. Aries, which has no patience for self-pity, will dry out this watery sign with optimism and drive. Pisces, which represents the amorphous prenatal world, often brings the spiritual dimension into Aries life, which becomes an important part of their relationship.

Your "2" Relationships

With your "2" signs, you share the same electrical charge, so energy flows freely between you. You also are considered to have compatibility though different elements. For example, air and fire work well together—air makes fire burn brighter. But too much of either element can suffocate or blow out the flame. Earth and water signs can either make flowers—as the earth "contains" the water—or mud flats or a wasteland.

The "2's" line up as follows:

Combination A. The earth signs (Taurus, Virgo, Capricorn) with water signs (Cancer, Scorpio, Pisces).

These are usually very fertile nurturing combinations, each providing the emotional and material security the other sign needs to reach full potential. Problems arise when the earth sign's material orientation and "here-and-nowness" stifles the more cosmic water sign's creativity.

Combination B. The air signs (Gemini, Libra, Aquarius) with fire signs (Aries, Leo, Sagittarius).

These are very stimulating, energetic combinations. Both kinds of signs are positive, outgoing, active, and this usually describes their relationship as well. The problem with excess here is that the more objective, detached air sign's preference for reason over enthusiasm could cool the fire sign's ardor. The fire sign's enthusiastic but often egocentric and unreasonable approach could in turn exasperate reasoning, relationship-oriented air signs.

Your "3" Relationships

If you recognize that stress in a relationship often stimulates growth, and that sexual tension can be heightened by a challenge, you can succeed with a "3" relationship. These relationships between signs of a similar quality have lots of erotic energy, challenging sparks, and passion. Some of these thrive on difficulty. You can make peace with this sign, but the person probably won't be easy to be with. However, these will also be your least boring partners!

"3's" share the same modality; you're both either cardinal, fixed, or mutable signs. So you'll understand how the other operates, though you won't necessarily share the same basic values or type of energy. One of the things that often happens with this relationship is that you continually confront each other—here is a sign that is just as restless, just as stubborn, or just as driven as you are! This isn't going to be the partner who gives you security, who settles down, or backs you up. Will you compete, join forces, or forge an equal partnership?

Mutable signs, which are the most changeable, understand each other's restlessness and low tolerance for boredom. This is a couple that can easily fragment, however, going off in different directions. This union often falls apart under stress but challenges you mutables to make order out of chaos; in other words, get your act together.

Cardinal couples with equal drive and energy often are characterized by goal-driven intensity—they never sit still. Fixed signs can be the most stable partners or, negatively, they can wrestle for control, war over territory, or have a stubborn Mexican standoff.

Positively, this is one of the sexiest aspects—these two signs challenge each other, bring about growth. Here are some of the issues likely to arise between each "3" pair-up:

ARIES–CANCER

Aries is forced by Cancer to consider the consequences of actions, particularly those that threaten security and hurt feelings. However, introspection cramps Aries style—this sign wants perfect freedom to act as they please and has no patience for self-pity or self-protectiveness. Although Cancer admires Aries' courage, the interaction will have to confront the conflict between the Aries outward-directed desire to have their own way and Cancer's inward-turning drive to create safety and security.

CANCER–LIBRA

Cancer is most satisfied by symbiotic, intimate, emotionally dependent relationships. So when you meet someone you like who is very independent, you feel hurt, rejected and throw up a defensive shell or get moody and depressed. Unfortunately, you risk this happening with Libra, a romantic, but rather emotionally cool sign. Libras want an equal partner, tends to judge their partner on a detached idealistic level, by their looks, style, ideas, conversation. Libra recognizes that the best partnerships are between equals, but the issue here is what do you have to share? Libra won't be able to escape emotions through social activities or intellectual analysis here.

LIBRA–CAPRICORN

Both of you love the good life, but you may have conflicting ideas about how to get it. Capricorn is a very disciplined, goal-directed, ordered worker who requires concrete results. Libra is more about style, abstract principles, and can be quite self-indulgent. Libran indulgence versus Capricorn discipline could be the cruncher here. Another bone to pick would be differing ideas about what's fair and just. Capricorn often believes that the "ends justify the means." Libra upholds fairness over bottom-line concerns.

CAPRICORN–ARIES

Earth wants solidity, fire wants freedom. Both are survivors who love to win. But Capricorn works for status and material rewards—Aries works for glory, heroism, for the joy of being first. Capricorn wants to stay in control. Aries wants freedom. In a positive way, Aries must grow up with Capricorn, but gives this tradition-oriented sign a new young lease on life.

TAURUS–LEO

Leo has an insatiable appetite for admiration, Taurus for pleasure. Taurus sensuality can make Leo feel like a star. Leo's romantic gestures appeal to Taurus on a grand scale. Taurus will have to learn courtship and flattery to keep Leo happy—bring on the champagne and caviar! Leo will have to learn not to tease the bull, especially by withholding affection—and to enjoy simple meat-and-potatoes kinds of pleasures as well. Money can be an important issue here: Leo likes to spend royally, Taurus likes to accumulate.

SCORPIO–LEO

Scorpio wants adventure in the psychic underworld, Leo wants to stay in the throne room. Scorpio challenges Leo to experience life intensely, which can bring out the best in Leo. Leo burns away Scorpio negativity—with low tolerance for dark moods. Scorpio is content to work behind the scenes, giving Leo center stage. But Leo must never mistake a quiet Scorpio for a gentle pussycat. There will be plenty of action behind the scenes. Settle issues of control without playing power games.

SCORPIO–AQUARIUS

Aquarius' love of freedom and Scorpio's possessiveness could clash here. Scorpio wants to own you—Aquarius wants to remain friends. This is one unpredictable sign Scorpio can't figure out but has fun trying. Aquarius' flair for group dynamics could bring Scorpio out. However, too many outside interests could put a damper on this combination.

TAURUS–AQUARIUS

Taurus lives in the touchable realm of the earth, Aquarius in the electric, invisible realm of air, which can't be fenced in. It's anyone's guess if Taurus can ground Aquarius or if Aquarius can uplift Taurus. Taurus' talent as a realist could be the anchor this free spirit needs. Aquarian originality opens new territory to Taurus.

GEMINI–VIRGO

Nerves can be stimulated or frayed when these Mercury-ruled signs sound off. Both have much to say to each other—from different points of view. Gemini deals in abstractions, Virgo in down-to-earth facts. Common interests could keep this pair focused on each other.

VIRGO–SAGITTARIUS

Safety versus risk could be the hallmark of this relationship. Virgo plays it safe and cautious, Sagittarius operates on faith and enthusiasm. You're two natural teachers who have different philosophies and have much to learn from each other. When Virgo picks things apart or gets bogged down in details, Sag urges them to look for the TRUTH—the big picture. Sag's lack of organization or follow-through will either drive Virgo crazy or provide a job. Virgo pins Sagittarius down with facts, deflating overblown promises and sales pitches.

SAGITTARIUS–PISCES

There should be many philosophical and spiritual discussions and debates here. When Sagittarius says I'm right, Pisces says everything's relative. We're all right and wrong, so what? Sagittarius is about elevating the self and Pisces is about merging the self, losing the self. On a less cosmic level, these too high-flying signs may never get down to earth. Pisces' supersensitivity is easily wounded by Sagittarius' moments of truth. But Sag can help sell those creative Piscean ideas; that is, if you don't wander off in different directions.

PISCES–GEMINI

Gemini is always trying to understand, abstract, rationalize. Pisces wants to merge and flow, find a soul mate, go beyond the mind. Pisces' moods get on Gemini's nerves. Gemini runs away from emotional mergers, which really matter to Pisces. Yet Pisces' glamour can intrigue Gemini and Gemini's lightness and wit help Pisces laugh away the blues.

Your "4" Relationships

These are considered the easiest relationships possible, the most compatible partners. You share the same element and the same polarity, but sometimes there is too much of a good thing. These tend to lack the dynamism and sexy sparks of the "3" and "5" relationships. They can be too comfortable as you adjust very easily to each other. But what can you teach each other? If it's too easy, you might look for excitement elsewhere.

Relationships between the three earth signs (Taurus, Virgo, Capricorn) are mutually profitable, both professionally and personally. You won't find the other sign tampering with your financial security, frittering away hard-earned funds, or flirting with danger. You could fulfill your dreams of a comfortable life together. Too much comfort could leave you yawning, however—you need someone to shake you up once in a while.

Fire signs (Aries, Leo, Sagittarius) can ignite each other, but watch out for temper and jealousy. You both demand exclusive attention, are happiest when your ego is stroked and you feel like number one, so you may have to curb any tendency to flirt. Because you tend to be big risk takers and free spenders, you may have to delegate the financial caretaking carefully or find an expert adviser.

Water signs (Cancer, Scorpio, Pisces) have found partners who aren't afraid of emotional depths or heights. These are the ones who can understand and sympathize with your moods. This could be your soul mate who gives you the emotional security you need. When moods collide, however, you could find it difficult to get each other out of deep water.

Air signs (Gemini, Libra, Aquarius) communicate well together. There is no heavy emotionalism or messy ego or possessiveness to deal with. You both respect the need for freedom and personal space and can make your own rules for an open, equal partnership. Staying in touch is the problem here. You could be so involved in your own pursuits that you let romance fly by or are never there for each other. Be sure to cultivate things in common because, unless there are many shared interests, it is easy to float away.

Your "5" Relationships

This is the relationship that challenges your sign the most. You have to stretch yourself to make this work. You are totally different in basic values (element), way of acting (quality), kind of energy (polarity) and, unlike your next-door signs that also have those differences, you don't have the closeness of being next in line. Instead of being beside you, the other sign is off on the other side of the zodiac.

On the other hand, this very separateness can have an erotic quality, the attraction of the unknown (and unattainable). This is someone you'll never quite figure out.

And this sign also has many threatening traits—if you get into this relationship, there will be risks, you won't quite know what to expect. The "5" relationship is the proverbial square peg and round hole. Even though the stress of making this relationship work can be great, so can the stimulation and creativity that result from trying to find out what makes each other tick.

When positive and negative signs come together, lights go on, as you discover methods in dealing with situations and different ways of viewing the world, which can move you out of the doldrums. Here is how your sign relates to its "5" partners.

ARIES: SCORPIO/VIRGO

Scorpio, who tends to be secretive and manipulative, embodies everything that is foreign to Aries. Aries is clear-cut, openly demanding. If an Aries attacks, it will be swift and open. Scorpio will wait for the time when an opponent is most vulnerable—years, if necessary—to deal the lethal blow. Aries burns out much sooner. Yet your very strong differences only make the conquest more exciting.

Virgo thinks the way to solve problems is to get organized, think things through—steamrolling Aries wants fast action, quick results. Both Scorpio and Virgo will challenge Aries to go against the grain—be careful, organized, persevere, delve deeply, look at the long haul. Aries will have to tone down impulsiveness with these signs.

TAURUS: LIBRA/SAGITTARIUS

Libra, also Venus ruled, is involved with the abstract, idealistic side of the planet, whereas Taurus is involved with the sensual, materialistic, self-indulgent side. Libra challenges Taurus to abstract, to get into the mind as well as the body. Taurus will bring Libra down to earth and provide stability for this sign.

Sagittarius challenges Taurus to expand its territory. Taurus is the most rooted of signs, and can be immobile— Sagittarius is the happy wanderer. Taurus moves outside its turf with Sagittarius, who challenges it intellectually, spiritually, and physically.

GEMINI: SCORPIO/CAPRICORN

Here, playful, verbal, mental Gemini is confronted by the failure to probe, the failure to deal with passion, deep real emotional stuff with Scorpio. Contact with Scorpio often precipitates a crisis in Gemini's life as this sign realizes there is something powerful it's been missing. Scorpio challenges Gemini to delve deeply and make commitments rather than deals.

Capricorn makes Gemini develop discipline, set goals, and do practical bottom-line things the sign is not prepared to do. Capricorn has no tolerance for fragmented efforts and forces Gemini to focus and produce.

CANCER: SAGITTARIUS/AQUARIUS

Fearful, frugal Cancer must take risks to make a relationship work with Sagittarius, who loves to gamble, has faith in the Universe. Everyone's buddy, Aquarius makes Cancer give love with an open hand, placing less emphasis on personal security, property.

Cancer must give up possessiveness with both these signs, who actually enjoy the kind of insecurity that Cancer most fears. In these relationships, Cancer's expectations of what a relationship should be have to change. It gets no protection from either sign and its favorite sympathy-winning techniques (playing "poor little me," whining, clinging, or complaining) only alienate these signs further. In the process of coping with these distant signs, however, Cancer can eventually become more independent and truly secure within itself.

LEO: CAPRICORN/PISCES

Capricorn demands that Leo deliver on promises. With this down-to-earth sign, Leo can't coast for long on looks and star power. Capricorn wants results, pushes Leo to produce, and casts a cold eye on shows of ego and sees through bluffs. Conversely, both enjoy many of the same things, such as a high-profile lifestyle, if for different reasons.

Pisces is on another planet from solar Leo—the Neptunian embodies all that is not-self. This is a sign that devalues the ego. Pisces teaches Leo to be unselfish, to exercise compassion and empathy, to walk in others' shoes. Leo has to give up arrogance and false pride for a lasting relationship with Pisces.

VIRGO: AQUARIUS/ARIES

Aquarius sheds light on Virgo's problem with getting bogged down in details. Interaction with Aquarius expands Virgo, prepares this sign for the unpredictable, the sudden, the unexpected. Aquarius gets Virgo to broaden scope—to risk experimenting. Aries gives Virgo positive energy and gets Virgo away from self-criticism and out into the world.

LIBRA: PISCES/TAURUS

Looking for a decision-maker—Libra won't find it in Pisces! Pisces and Libra both share an artistic nature, but executed in a different way. Libra can't project its need for direction onto Pisces. Libra says, "What should I do?" Pisces says, "I know how you feel. It's tough not knowing what to do." Pisces challenges Libra to go within, to understand where others are coming from rather than expecting them to conform to an abstract ideal.

Taurus brings Libra into the practical material world and gives this sign grounding, but Taurus will also insist on material value. Taurus will ask, "How much does it cost?" Libra says, "I don't care, it's so pretty." Libra would rather not worry about function and operations, which become Taurus' task. Libra will either desperately need Taurus' practicality or find it a drag.

SCORPIO: ARIES/GEMINI

Listen for the clanking of iron shields as Mars-ruled Aries and Scorpio get together. Both of you thrive on challenge and find it in each other. The issue here: who's the conquerer when neither will give in or give up? You'll have to respect each other's courage and bravery, and enjoy the sparks, like the archetypal Aries/Scorpio couple, Spencer Tracy and Katharine Hepburn.

Gemini is the sign you can never pin down or possess—and this is super-fascinating for Scorpio. Their quicksilver wit and ability to juggle many people and things are talents not found in the Scorpio repertoire. Scorpios never stop trying to fathom the power of Gemini—just when they've almost got them pegged, Gemini's on to something or someone else! As long as you don't expect devotion, you won't be disappointed.

SAGITTARIUS: TAURUS/CANCER

This is a dialogue between the rooted and the rootless. Both Taurus and Cancer are the most home-loving signs of the zodiac, while Sagittarius is the eternal wanderer—mentally, physically, or both. Will they be content to keep the home fires burning for Sagittarius? Another sticky point: both signs are very careful with money. However, these two financially savvy signs could help Sagittarius achieve miracles instead of talking about them. Sag will have to learn patience with Taurus, who will inevitably try to tie Sag down. Cancer could dampen Sag's spirits with self-pity if they feel neglected in any way. Sag will have to learn sensitivity to feelings. If Sag can give up the position as teacher and become a student, these relationships might last.

CAPRICORN: GEMINI/LEO

Both of these signs are social charmers who need organization, which is Capricorn's forte. They can help Capricorn get a desired position with Gemini's deft charm or Leo's warmth and poise. The trade-off is that Capricorn will have to learn to take life less seriously, be as devoted to the partnership as to work. Otherwise these two signs will look for amusement elsewhere. Gemini should inspire Capricorn to diversify, communicate, and spread wings socially. Leo adds confidence, authority, status. They'll appreciate Capricorn's adding structure to their lives.

AQUARIUS: CANCER/VIRGO

Aquarius, the most freedom-loving sign, here encounters two different dimensions, both of which tend to bring this sign back to the realities of operating on a day-to-day level (Virgo) and honoring emotional attachments, the level of feeling (Cancer). Cancer is the home-loving sign who values security, family, emotional connections—an area often dismissed by Aquarians. Virgo is about organization, critical judgment, efficiency—which enhance Aquarius accomplishments.

PISCES: LEO/LIBRA

With Leo, Pisces learns to find and project itself. Leo enjoys Pisces talent and often profits by it. In return Leo gives this often-insecure sign confidence. With Leo, Pisces can't hide any longer, must come out from the depths—but Leo will not sympathize or indulge Pisces' blue moods or self-pity. Pisces has to give up negativity with Leo.

Libra's instinct is to separate and analyze. Pisces instinct is to merge. The more Pisces goes into emotions, the more Libra becomes cool and detached. But Pisces can gain objectivity from this relationship, which insists on seeing both sides of any matter equally. Libra can provide the balance that keeps Pisces out of the depths.

Your "6" Relationships

"6" relationships are with your opposite sign in the zodiac. This sign is your complement, your other half who manifests qualities that you think you don't have. There are many marriages between "opposite numbers," because one sign expresses what the other suppresses.

Because most lasting relationships are between equals, the attraction to your "opposite number" could backfire. What happens if you're an easygoing Aquarius married to a star-quality Leo and you decide it's time to show off your natural charisma on center stage? Or a disorganized Pisces with an efficient Virgo who goes on a clean-up, shape-up program and out-organizes the Virgo? No longer does the opposite partner have exclusive rights to certain talents or attitudes. If they can make adjustments to the new you, fine. Otherwise, someone could be out of a job.

It's an excellent idea to ask yourself, if you are attracting your opposite number in love or other relationships, what these signs are acting out for you. It could be a clue to what you need to develop. Sometimes, after the initial chemistry dies down, and two opposite signs actually begin living together, you'll be irritated by the same qualities that at first attracted you. That's because they reveal the part you are afraid of within yourself—the part you haven't really claimed for yourself, and you resent them from taking it over. Here's how it works out with opposite numbers: The more you learn to express "both sides of the same coin," the better chance your relationship with a "6" will have.

ARIES–LIBRA

Aries brings out Libra's placating, accommodating talents. And at first, Libra is happy to play the charmer in exchange for Aries' decisiveness. Aries revels in the chance to take charge and to be so openly needed. But in close quarters, Aries seems too pushy, too bossy. And when Libra decides to make its own decisions, Aries had better learn to charm.

VIRGO–PISCES

In Pisces, Virgo finds someone who apparently needs their services badly. Virgo in turn is attracted to Pisces because this sign can deal with the tricky side of life that can't be organized or made to run on schedule. Sensitive Pisces seems to need Virgo's clarity, orderliness, and practicality to keep together and in line. You can see how easy it is for this to become a bargain between the helper and the apparently helpless. When Pisces gets organized and Virgo gets in touch with their own irrational side, these two could form a more solid relationship.

TAURUS–SCORPIO

This is one of the most powerful attractions, which is often found in marriages and long-term relationships. Some of these couples manage to balance out their differences nicely; others are just too stubborn to give up or give in. The uncomplicated, earthy, sensual Taurus likes safety, comfort, and pleasurable physical things. Scorpio, who enjoys the challenge and dangers of intense feelings (and could live in a monk's cell) is often attracted to danger and risk. Scorpio wants a deep, powerful merger. Taurus likes to stay above ground, enjoying innocent pleasures. Both are possessive and jealous, with a need to control their own territory. Scorpio marvels at the uncomplicated basic drives of Taurus—couldn't they get into trouble together? Taurus enjoys teasing Scorpio with promises of innocent pleasure, but learns that Scorpios sting when teased. Settle issues of control early on—and never underestimate each other's strength.

GEMINI–SAGITTARIUS

Gemini is the eager student of the world; Sagittarius is the perfect guide, only too happy to teach, enlighten, and expound. This is a very stimulating combination. Sagittarius enjoys telling others what to believe, however, and Gemini can't be bossed. Gemini also turns off fiery confrontations and absolute declarations of truth, and may deflate Sagittarius with barbs of wit. On a positive note, this could be a wonderful combination both socially and professionally. Romantically it works best if they can be both student and teacher to each other.

CANCER–CAPRICORN

Both of these signs have strong defense mechanisms. Cancer's is a protective shell, Capricorn's is a cold stony wall. In a relationship, both of these defenses play off one other. Cancer shows weakness (complains, whines) as a means of getting protection, which dovetails nicely with Capricorn's need to play the authoritarian parental father figure (even if female) who takes responsibility for the vulnerable child (Cancer). But if Capricorn shows vulnerability, such as a fear of not being "right," Cancer panics, becomes insecure, and erects a self-protective shell. On the other hand, if Capricorn takes over Cancer's life, this active cardinal sign gets crabby. Learning to "parent" each other and reinforce strong traditional values could be the key to happiness here.

LEO–AQUARIUS

Here we have two stubborn fixed signs with opposite points of view. Leo is "me-oriented" and does not like to share. Aquarius is "them-oriented" and identifies with others. The Leo charisma comes from projecting the self—others are there for applause. Aquarius shines as the symbol of spokesperson of a group, which reflects self-importance. Leo stands apart, onstage; Aquarius stands with the crowd. Leo is not about to become one of the Aquarius crowd (especially if the crowd includes Aquarius' ex-lovers). Aquarius will not confine interests to Leo (become a Leo fan). If Leo can learn to share and Aquarius can give one-on-one attention, this could balance out.

9

Keeping Your
Lover Faithful

According to the last U.S. census report, marriage and committed relationships are on the upswing. But with women entering and staying in the workplace, generally leading more independent lives, and mingling with available men, extramarital affairs are also on the rise! Although the danger of sexually transmitted diseases has discouraged promiscuity, the actual statistics on marital success are not encouraging—almost four out of ten marriages fail before the fourth anniversary, according to a 1990 survey by Adweek's *Marketing Week*.

With so many temptations to stray, one of the biggest concerns in any long-term relationship is keeping your love life exciting and fulfilling—and your mate from wandering. Even though there is no "golden rule" for fidelity, astrology can help you to assess your lover's needs for freedom versus closeness and balance them with your own, for a more fulfilling and committed partnership.

To understand your partner's potential for fidelity, it's important to discover what an ideal relationship means to him or her—for some people, the major emphasis is on a safe, secure home; for others it's a soul mate; for still others, it's stimulating companionship. One of the easiest ways to get insights into your partner's expectations and turn-ons is by using their astrological element. Signs are grouped by four elements—fire, earth, air, and water; each element has certain characteristics that can give you valuable clues to your partner's basic romantic character.

THE FIRE SIGNS (Aries, Leo, Sagittarius)

Fire signs are the Don Juans of the zodiac who like the excitement of "playing with fire" but rarely consider the consequences of possibly being burned. Great romantics, they tend to fall head over heels in love—and while the fantasy lasts, it's a blazing passion. When disappointed, however, fire signs can burn out fast and fall out of love easily, which often happens when the responsibilities and realities of life close in. Fire sign women enjoy the excitement of a life outside the home and are rarely content with a wife/mother role. In love, they often have idealistic fantasies that are difficult for mates to sustain. They tend to "see what they want to see" and become very disillusioned when their lover's human frailties become obvious. Nevertheless, it is possible to have a lasting relationship—and not get burned—with these passionate lovers.

The Aries Lover—To keep your Aries mate red-hot, be sure to maintain your energy level. This is one sign that shows little sympathy for aches, pains, and physical complaints. Curb any tendency toward self-pity—whining is one sure Aries turn-off (water signs take note). This is an open, direct sign—don't expect your lover to probe your innermost needs. Intense psychological discussions that would thrill a Cancer or Scorpio only make Aries restless. Aries is not the stay-at-home type; this sign is sure to have plenty of activities going on at once. Share them (or they'll find someone else who will)!

Always be a bit of a challenge to your Aries mate—this sign loves the chase almost as much as the conquest. So don't be too easy or accommodating—let them feel a sense of accomplishment when they've won your heart.

Stay up-to-date in your interests and appearance. You can wear the latest style off the fashion-show runway with an Aries, especially if it's bright red. Aries is a pioneer, an adventurer, always ahead of the pack. Play up your frontier spirit. Present the image of the two of you as an unbeatable team, one that can conquer the world, and you'll keep this courageous sign at your side.

Since they tend to idealize their lovers, Aries is especially disillusioned when their mates flirt. Be sure they always feel like number one in your life.

The Leo Lover—Whether the Leo is a sunny upbeat partner or reveals catlike claws could depend on how you handle the royal Leo pride. A relationship is for TWO people—a fact that ego-centered Leo can forget. You must gently remind them. Be well-groomed and dressed, someone they're proud to show off.

Leo thinks big—so don't you be petty or miserly—and likes to live like a king. Remember special occasions with a beautifully wrapped gift or flowers. Make an extra effort to treat them royally. Keep a sense of fun and playfulness and loudly applaud Leo's creative efforts. React, respond, be a good audience! If Leo's ignored, this sign will seek a more appreciative audience—fast! Cheating Leos are almost always looking for an ego boost.

Be generous with compliments. You can't possibly overdo here. Always accentuate the positive. Make them feel important by asking for advice and consulting them often. Leo enjoys a charming, sociable companion, but be sure to make them the center of attention in your life.

The Sagittarius Lover—Be a mental and spiritual traveling companion. Sagittarius is a footloose adventurer whose ideas know no boundaries—so don't try to fence them in! Sagittarians resent restrictions of any kind. For a long-lasting relationship, be sure you are in harmony with Sagittarius' ideals and spiritual beliefs. They like to feel that their life is constantly being elevated, taken to a higher level. Since down-to-earth matters often get put aside in the Sagittarian's scheme of things, get finances under control (money matters upset more relationships with Sagittarians than any other problem), but try to avoid being the stern disciplinarian in this relationship (find a good accountant).

Sagittarius is not generally a homebody (unless there are several homes). Be ready and willing to take off on the spur of the moment, or they'll go without you. Sports, outdoor activities, and physical fitness are important—stay in shape with some of Sagittarian Jane Fonda's tapes. Dress with flair and style—it helps if you look especially good in sportswear. Sagittarian men like beautiful legs, so play up yours. And this is one of the great animal lovers so try and get along with the dog, cat, or horse.

THE EARTH SIGNS (Taurus, Virgo, Capricorn)

Earth signs tend to think long and hard before leaving a solid relationship. These signs naturally revere home life. However, if there is something lacking sensually in the relationship, or if outside activities seem too important to their mate, they can be shaken up and swept away by a very unlikely and surprisingly impractical affair. Earth sign infidelities are the stuff of scandals. In the 1950s, cool Virgo actress Ingrid Bergman stunned the nation by leaving her solid marriage for a volcanically passionate liaison with an Italian director. But your earthy lover will stay faithful if you focus on building a solid foundation; don't stint on affection, and emphasize the cozy comforts of home.

The Taurus Lover—Taurus is an extremely sensual, affectionate, nurturing lover, but can be quite possessive. Taurus likes to "own" you. Don't hold back with them or play power games. If you need more space in the relationship, be sure to set clear boundaries, letting them know exactly where they stand. When ambiguity in a relationship makes Taurus uneasy, they may go searching for someone more solid and substantial. A Taurus romance works best where the limits are clearly spelled out.

Taurus needs physical demonstrations of affection—don't hold back on hugs. Together, you should create an atmosphere of comfort, good food, and beautiful surroundings. In fact, Taurus is often seduced by surface physical beauty alone. Their five senses are highly susceptible so find ways to appeal to all of them! Your home should be a restful haven from the outside world. Get a great sound system, some comfortable furniture to sink into, and keep the refrigerator stocked with treats. Most Taureans would rather entertain on their own turf than gad about town, so it helps if you're a good host or hostess.

Taurus likes a calm, contented, committed relationship. This is not a sign to trifle with. Don't flirt or tease if you want to please. Don't rock the boat or try to make this sign jealous. Instead, create a steady, secure environment with lots of shared pleasures.

The Virgo Lover—Virgo may seem cool and conservative on the surface, but underneath you'll find a sensual romantic. Think of Raquel Welch, Sophia Loren, Jacqueline Bisset, Garbo! It's amazing how seductive this practical sign can be!

They are idealists, however, looking for someone who meets their high standards. If you've measured up, they'll do anything to serve and please you. Virgos love to feel needed, so give them a job to do in your life. They are great fixer-uppers. Take their criticism as a form of love and caring, of noticing what you do. Bring them out socially—they are often very shy. Calm their nerves with good food, a healthy environment, trips to the country.

Mental stimulation is a turn-on to this Mercury-ruled sign. An intellectual discussion could lead to romantic action, so stay on your toes and keep well-informed. This sign often mixes business with pleasure so it helps if you share the same professional interests—you'll get to see more of your busy mate. With Virgo, the couple who works as well as plays together, stays together.

The Capricorn Lover—These people are ambitious—even if they are the stay-at-home-partner in your relationship. They will be extremely active, have a strong sense of responsibility to their partner, and take commitments seriously. However, they might look elsewhere if the relationship becomes too dutiful. They also need romance, fun, lightness, humor, adventure!

Generation gaps are not unusual in Capricorn romances, where the older Capricorn partner works hard all through life and seeks pleasurable rewards with a young partner, or the young Capricorn gets a taste of luxury and instant status from an older lover. This is one sign that grows more interested in romance as they age! Younger Capricorns often tend to put business way ahead of pleasure.

Capricorn is impressed by those who entertain well, have "class," and can advance their status in life. Keep improving yourself and cultivate important people. Stay on the conservative side. Extravagant or frivolous loves don't last—Capricorn keeps an eye on the bottom line. Even the wildest Capricorns, such as Elvis Presley, Rod Stewart, or David Bowie, show a conservative streak in their personal lives. It's also important to demonstrate a strong sense of loyalty to your family, especially older members. This reassures Capricorn, who'll be happy to grow old along with you!

THE AIR SIGNS (Gemini, Libra, Aquarius)

Air sign lovers usually think their actions are justified and can rationalize any affair away, but they are least likely to get involved in an outside relationship if they communicate well with their partner. If they feel that their wings are clipped by commitment or if heavy emotional dramas weigh them down, they could fly away. They often tend to have accidental affairs, which happen on the spur of the moment, rather than deliberately planned and executed conquests. Sometimes relationships with friends become intimate sexually, because these are already people with whom they communicate. But they are unlikely to stray too far from the nest if they are given plenty of space and a stimulating atmosphere.

The Gemini Lover—Keeping Gemini faithful is like walking a tightrope. This sign needs stability and a strong home base to accomplish their goals. But they also require a great deal of personal freedom.

A great role model is Barbara Bush, a Gemini married to another Gemini. This is a sign that loves to communicate! Sit down and talk things over. Don't interfere: be interested in your partner's doings, but have a life of your own and ideas to contribute. Since this is a gad-about social sign, don't insist on quiet nights at home when your Gemini is in a party mood.

Gemini needs plenty of rope but a steady hand. Focus on common goals and abstract ideals. Gemini likes to share—be a twin soul, do things together. Keep up on their latest interests. Stay in touch mentally and physically, use both your mind and your hands to communicate.

Variety is the spice of life to this flirtatious sign. Guard

132

against jealousy—it is rarely justified. Provide a stimulating sex life—this is a very experimental sign—to keep them interested. Be a bit unpredictable. Don't let lovemaking become a routine. Most of all, sharing lots of laughs together can make Gemini take your relationship very seriously.

The Libra Lover—Libra enjoys life with a mate and needs the harmony of a steady relationship. Outside affairs can throw them off balance. However, members of this sign are natural charmers who love to surround themselves with admirers, and this can cause a very possessive partner to feel insecure. Most of the time, Librans, who love to be the belle of the ball, are only testing their allure with harmless flirtations and will rarely follow through, unless they are not getting enough attention or there is an unattractive atmosphere at home.

Mental compatibility is what keeps Libra in tune. Unfortunately this sign, like Taurus, often falls for physical beauty or someone who provides an elegant lifestyle, rather than someone who shares their ideals and activities, the kind of sharing that will keep you together in the long run.

Do not underestimate Libra's need for beauty and harmony. To keep them happy, avoid scenes. Opt for calm, impersonal discussion of problems (or a well-reasoned debate) over an elegant dinner. Pay attention to the niceties of life. Send little gifts like Valentines and don't forget birthdays and anniversaries. Play up the romance to the hilt—with all the lovely gestures and trimmings—but tone down intensity and emotional drama (Aries, Scorpio take note). Libra needs to be surrounded by a physically tasteful atmosphere—elegant, well-designed furnishings, calm colors, good manners, and good grooming at all times.

The Aquarius Lover—Aquarius is one of the most independent, least domestic signs. Finding time alone with this sign may be one of your greatest challenges. They are everybody's buddy, usually surrounded by people they collect, some of whom may be old lovers who are now "just friends." However, it is unlikely that old passions will be rekindled if you become Aquarius' number-one best friend as well as lover, and if you get actively involved in other important aspects of Aquarius' life, such as the political or charitable causes they believe in.

Aquarius needs a supportive backup person who encourages them, but is not overly possessive when their natural charisma attracts admirers by the dozen. Take a leaf from Joanne Woodward, whose marriage to perennial Aquarius heartthrob Paul Newman has lasted more than 30 years! Encourage them to develop their original ideas. Don't rain on their parade if they decided suddenly to market their spaghetti sauce and donate the proceeds to their favorite charity, or drive racing cars. Share their goals, be their fan, or you'll never see them otherwise.

You may be called on to give them grounding where needed. Aquarius needs someone who can keep track of their projects. But always remember, it's basic friendship—with the tolerance and common ideals that implies—that will hold you together.

THE WATER SIGNS (Cancer, Scorpio, Pisces)

The fidelity of these emotional signs is often determined by how secure they feel in a relationship. Always consider their feelings (this might be difficult for air and fire signs) because when their feelings are hurt or they are made to feel insecure, water signs head for consolation, solace, or escape elsewhere. Emotional manipulation and power trips are other negative manifestations of insecurity that could make water signs difficult to live with. But when they do feel secure and supported, they reveal their talent for true intimacy and make romantic, tender, and loving mates.

The Cancer Lover—This is probably the water sign that requires the most TLC. Cancers tend to be very private people who may take some time to open up. They are extremely self-protective and will rarely tell you what is truly bothering them. They operate indirectly, like the movements of the crab. You may have to divine their problem by following subtle clues. Draw them out gently and try to voice any criticisms in the most tactful, supportive way possible.

Family ties are especially strong for Cancer. They will rarely break a strong family bond. Create an intimate family atmosphere, with emphasis on food and family get-togethers. You can get valuable clues to Cancer appeal from their mothers and their early family situation. If their early life was unhappy, it is even more important that they feel they have found a close family with you.

Encouraging their creativity can counter Cancer's moodiness, which is also a sure sign of emotional insecurity. Find ways to distract them from negative moods. Calm them with a good meal or a trip to the seashore. Cancers are usually quite nostalgic and attached to the past. So be careful not to throw out their old treasures or photos.

The Scorpio Lover—Scorpios are often deceptively cool and remote on the outside, but don't be fooled: this sign always has a hidden agenda and feels very intensely about most things. The disguise is necessary because Scorpio does not trust easily; but when they do, they are devoted and loyal, will stick with you through the toughest times. You can lean on this very intense and focused sign. The secret is in first establishing that basic trust through mutual honesty and respect.

Mars-ruled Scorpio is fascinated by power and control in all its forms. They don't like to compromise—it's all or nothing. Therefore they don't trust or respect anything that comes too easily. Be a bit of a challenge, keep them guessing. Maintain your own personal identity, in spite of Scorpio's desire to probe your innermost secrets.

Sex is especially important to this sign, which will demand fidelity from you (though they may not plan to deliver it themselves), so communication on this level is critical. Explore Scorpio's fantasies together. Scorpio is a detective—watch your own flirtations—don't play with fire. This is a jealous and vengeful sign, so you'll live to regret it. Scorpio's rarely flirt for the fun of it themselves. There is usually a strong motive behind their actions.

Scorpio has a fascination with the dark, mysterious side of life. If unhappy, they are capable of carrying on a secret affair. So try to emphasize the positive, constructive side of life with them. Don't fret if they need time alone to sort out problems. They may also prefer time alone with you to socializing with others, so plan romantic getaways together to a private beach or a secluded wilderness spot.

The Pisces Lover—To keep a Pisces hooked, don't hold the string too tight! This is a sensitive, creative sign that may appear to need someone to manage their lives or point the direction out of their Neptunian fog; but if you fall into that role, expect your Pisces to rebel against any strong-arm tactics. Pisces is more susceptible to a play for sympathy than a play for power. They are suckers for a sob story, the most empathetic sign of the zodiac. More than one Pisces has been seduced and held by someone who plays the underdog role.

They are great fantasists, and extremely creative lovers, so use your imagination to add drama and spice to your times together. You can let your fantasies run wild with this sign—and they'll go you one better! They enjoy variety in lovemaking, so try never to let it become routine.

Long-term relationships work best if you can bring Pisces down to earth and, at the same time, encourage their creative fantasies. Deter them from escapism into alcohol or substance abuse by helping them to get counseling, if needed. Pisces will stay with the lover who gives positive energy, self-confidence, and a safe harbor as well as one who is their soul mate.

10

What Your Rising Sign Can Tell You About Your Luckiest Career Choice

Luck is often defined as being in the right place at the right time; that is, a place where you'll be noticed and where you'll make the best possible first impression. Both of these factors are strongly influenced by your rising sign, or ascendant, the sign coming over the horizon at the time you were born.

Your rising sign announces your presence in the world. It's your personal advertisement, casting an overlay or mask on your sun sign, which can make you appear like another sign entirely. Some people's sun signs are so difficult to guess because they have a rising sign with a much stronger public face—it is only after you get to know them that the personality of the sun shines through.

Rising signs change every two hours with the earth's rotation. Those born early in the morning, when the sun was on the horizon, will project the image of the sun sign most strongly. These people are often called a "double Cancer" or a "double Capricorn," because the two strong components of the sun and ascendant reinforce each other. There is usually no problem guessing their sun sign!

In your horoscope chart, the other signs follow the rising sign in sequence, rotating counterclockwise. The rising sign rules your first sector, or "house," which governs your physical impression—and also influences the way you choose to present yourself—your taste and style, as well as your preferred physical environment.

The tenth house around the horoscope circle governs the area of life where you are most visible to the public, where you get noticed and recognized. And this is also used as an indicator of your career, which reflects what you want to become in the public eye and the position you want to achieve in the world. By understanding this area of your chart you have an effective guide to choosing the position that's best for you.

Look up your rising sign in the chart in this book then read the following descriptions for an idea of the type of career criteria most fortunate for you and the way you come across to influential people—such as your job interviewer. These descriptions are based on the most likely mid-heaven position for each rising sign—yours may vary according to the time and latitude you were born. (Check the preceding and following rising signs, if your description doesn't seem to fit.)

ARIES RISING

Lucky Career Tips: You have a strong need to "make it" in spite of difficulties or disappointments. You'll do it the hard way, if necessary. The business world is a natural for you, and you're a born entrepreneur who can take all the "lumps" on the way to the top. Your career choice should be in a highly regarded prestige field. You might also win medals and stripes in the military. Select a job that rewards hard work and dedication, which offers you the chance to work toward executive responsibility. It'll be sure to pay off especially if you start the business yourself. You could take the proverbial shoestring and make a fortune.

Interview Personality: You'll be the most aggressive version of your sun sign. You'll come across as a go-getter, headed for the fast track, dynamic, energetic, aggressive. Billy Graham and Bette Midler show the sparkle and fire of this ascendant. But you can also be somewhat combative, so try to be more diplomatic or head for an area where your feistiness will be appreciated.

TAURUS RISING

Lucky Career Tips: You'll succeed by being an "original." You luckiest career is one in which you can stand out, break out of the mold. Highly creative professional work is fine, but by playing it safe, you could miss the boat. You'll also work well in an unusual group. Head for a futuristic area in the sciences, particularly electronics. You have excellent staying power, good concentration, and an analytical mind. The key is to cultivate and capitalize on the unusual—you may have a very distinctive voice—like Greta Garbo—and could talk your way to success via the electronic media.

Interview Personality: There is nothing lightweight about you. You come across as powerful, steady, thorough, not easily dismissed. You may have a very unusual and memorable voice, great concentration, and stamina.

GEMINI RISING

Lucky Career Tips: Make the most of your ability to sense and communicate the mood of the masses. Though you may not openly seek the spotlight, your strong imagination and vision could put you on center stage. You need a creative career that offers you variety and creative challenges (or you may tend to job-hop). You're a gadabout, so watch a tendency to scatter your energies. You may not be suited to a corporate job or anything too confining. Jobs that use your visionary talents are worth waiting for. Look in the more free-flowing imaginative areas of business, in publishing, literature, the creative or spiritual arts.

Interview Personality: You're a social, articulate, witty personality, a quick thinker and a quick study. You also could come across as nervous, undirected, too scattered, a jack-of-all-trades. Play up your analytical mind, your ability to communicate well and to adapt to different people and environments.

CANCER RISING

Lucky Career Tips: You're competitive and quite assertive in your career. You enjoy having goals to reach or promotions to win. Physical activity is also important: there are many athletes and dancers with this placement. John Travolta in *Saturday Night Fever* is a typical success story. But be careful of jobs that require too much physical risk! Some of you are attracted and challenged by danger. Find stimulation through pioneering career maneuvers. You'd be great at starting up your own business.

Interview Personality: You may come across as shy, sweet, sensitive, and caring. You'll be able to convince others that you are nurturing, protective, the "mother of the world." But you are also very astute business-wise, with a sharp sense of what will sell.

LEO RISING

When you feel worthwhile in your job, you have a remarkably stable career. You can stick firmly to a game plan. Some of you will strongly uphold your beliefs in public, sometimes against great odds, like Martin Luther or Jane Fonda. Many religious figures have this placement. You may work your way to the top slowly. But you may have great success at Venus-ruled occupations in the beauty, exercise, fashion, or art world. Or consider other Taurus-influenced careers of finance (like J. P. Morgan), agriculture, or mining.

Interview Personality: You project a regal air of authority, which instills confidence in your abilities. You come across as someone who can take charge. You are very poised in the spotlight and know how to present yourself to play up your special star quality, such as Ava Gardner or ballerina Cynthia Gregory and Marilyn Monroe. You attract attention, and tend to take center stage. In business you can be the epitome of executive style.

VIRGO RISING

Lucky Career Tips: Mental stimulation is a key for you. You have a talent for originating ideas, communicating with others, and will probably gravitate to people-oriented jobs where you are constantly dealing with many different personalities. You have the ability to juggle many tasks, details, and contacts, yet stay emotionally detached. Some of you may have two or more professions or a variety of clients.

*   *   *

Interview Personality: Your intelligence and analytical ability come across. You seem well-organized, with a no-nonsense air of knowing what you're doing. You're a hard worker who gets on with it. You're not one to slack off. Your manner may be a bit aloof, critical of others who don't share your sense of mastery of your craft, of doing it to perfection.

LIBRA RISING

Lucky Career Tips: You need to care deeply about your career and are most successful in areas that appeal to human needs, such as providing a home, child care, or serving your country. For example, entertainers such as Sally Field have been most successful in roles in which they play parents, nurturers, or patriots. Sally Struthers' success in "All in the Family" is another case in point. Food, architecture, the hotel business are several possibilities. You work especially well in a family business or as part of a supportive team, and your career may surge ahead after you've found the right partner. This is important because you may feel especially anxious and indecisive at times.

Interview Personality: You come across as charming, attractive, well-dressed, diplomatic. Your first impression is one of social ease, harmony. You enjoy working with others and it shows.

SCORPIO RISING

Lucky Career Tips: You need a career that allows you to assume authority. If you can't be the boss, many of you choose to work alone rather than as a team player. This is one of the most dramatic career positions, a natural for the public eye. Jacqueline Kennedy Onassis, Diana Ross, Joan Crawford, and Katharine Hepburn personify the type of command and control found with this placement— you usually aren't in the position of taking orders. You have great personal flair—a standout look, not one of the crowd. Your job should allow you to exercise creative ability, self-expression and provide a form of recognition.

Interview Personality: You come on strong, with a touch of mystery, even if you don't say a word. Intense, charismatic, you'll make your presence felt with a penetrating gaze. Be careful not to come on too strong. You might consider toning down your intensity, tempering it with a touch of humor.

SAGITTARIUS RISING

Lucky Career Tips: Intellectual and communications fields are natural for you. You excel at analytical problem-solving tasks and long to contribute something of lasting value to humanity. You often make excellent teachers or gravitate to fields where you can convey an example. Many of you choose careers in health care or professional sports. Publishing, as an editor or writer spreading the truth, appeals to many, like Candice Bergen, who has had careers as a writer, journalist, and TV actress (playing a journalist). Since you are extremely flexible, you may have several different careers in your lifetime. You often have strong civic interests outside your career.

Interview Personality: Good-humored and enthusiastic, you are an excellent salesperson. You present an upbeat, athletic, energetic image. Your sense of humor wins fans, but some of you may have to work on developing tact and diplomacy.

CAPRICORN RISING

Lucky Career Tips: Since Libra rules your career sector, you could be especially successful in fields that promote justice and fairness, such as the legal profession, or in a position where you are called upon to mediate or judge. You might also shine in any Venusian profession, such as fashion, the arts, or the promotion, sale, or creation of beautiful things—or work that deals with relationships, such as the single-girls' mentor, Helen Gurley Brown, editor of *Cosmopolitan* magazine. You work especially well in partnership with another. It is doubly important that your working environment be tasteful and harmonious. You have a talent for appealing to popular tastes and lifestyles.

Interview Personality: You come across as a serious, conservative, disciplined worker. But you could also choose the traditional flair of Fred Astaire. Not a frivolous type, you aim to be taken seriously, which could be intimidating. You'll easily adapt to present the classiest impression appropriate to your business.

AQUARIUS RISING

Lucky Career Tips: Your ideal job is one where you can wield power and transform other lives in some way, especially if you can enhance individual rights or promote freedom. You may head for a career in research, investigation, or probing psychological depths. In business, you are attracted to powerful positions and can be quite manipulative, focusing all your efforts on reaching the top. You may have extremes of success/failure during the course of your working life, depending on the political and cultural orientation of your time. But you also have a marvelous ability to bounce back from setbacks. You could be happiest working free lance—or alone, rather than in a regimented environment.

Interview Personality: Like daredevil Evil Knievel you're charismatic and individualistic—you know how to get attention, sometimes in a startling way that shakes everyone up. You'll dress to please yourself—never mind the dress codes. Be sure to find a business that appreciates your eccentric side, one with a cause or principles you believe in.

PISCES RISING

Lucky Career Tips: Growth, plus freedom of choice should be your career criteria. You have high goals and the faith to achieve them. You project enthusiasm for any products and ideas you sell, elevating them to the highest level. You also have a great gift for inspiring others. You are determined to be the best you can be, like ice-skater

Rising Signs—A.M. Births

	1 AM	2 AM	3 AM	4 AM	5 AM	6 AM	7 AM	8 AM	9 AM	10 AM	11 AM	12 NOON
Jan 1	Lib	Sc	Sc	Sc	Sag	Sag	Sag	Cap	Cap	Aq	Aq	Pis
Jan 9	Lib	Sc	Sc	Sag	Sag	Sag	Cap	Cap	Aq	Pis	Ar	Tau
Jan 17	Sc	Sc	Sc	Sag	Sag	Cap	Cap	Aq	Aq	Pis	Ar	Tau
Jan 25	Sc	Sc	Sag	Sag	Sag	Cap	Cap	Aq	Pis	Ar	Tau	Tau
Feb 2	Sc	Sc	Sag	Sag	Cap	Cap	Aq	Pis	Pis	Ar	Tau	Gem
Feb 10	Sc	Sag	Sag	Sag	Cap	Cap	Aq	Pis	Ar	Tau	Tau	Gem
Feb 18	Sc	Sag	Sag	Cap	Cap	Aq	Pis	Pis	Ar	Tau	Gem	Gem
Feb 26	Sag	Sag	Sag	Cap	Aq	Aq	Pis	Ar	Tau	Tau	Gem	Gem
Mar 6	Sag	Sag	Cap	Cap	Aq	Pis	Pis	Ar	Tau	Gem	Gem	Cap
Mar 14	Sag	Cap	Cap	Aq	Aq	Pis	Ar	Tau	Tau	Gem	Gem	Can
Mar 22	Sag	Cap	Cap	Aq	Pis	Ar	Ar	Tau	Gem	Gem	Can	Can
Mar 30	Cap	Cap	Aq	Pis	Pis	Ar	Tau	Tau	Gem	Can	Can	Can
Apr 7	Cap	Cap	Aq	Pis	Ar	Ar	Tau	Gem	Gem	Can	Can	Leo
Apr 14	Cap	Aq	Aq	Pis	Ar	Tau	Tau	Gem	Gem	Can	Can	Leo
Apr 22	Cap	Aq	Pis	Ar	Ar	Tau	Gem	Gem	Can	Can	Leo	Leo
Apr 30	Aq	Aq	Pis	Ar	Tau	Tau	Gem	Can	Can	Can	Leo	Leo
May 8	Aq	Pis	Ar	Ar	Tau	Gem	Gem	Can	Can	Leo	Leo	Leo
May 16	Aq	Pis	Ar	Tau	Gem	Gem	Can	Can	Can	Leo	Leo	Vir
May 24	Pis	Ar	Ar	Tau	Gem	Gem	Can	Can	Leo	Leo	Leo	Vir
June 1	Pis	Ar	Tau	Gem	Gem	Can	Can	Can	Leo	Leo	Vir	Vir
June 9	Ar	Ar	Tau	Gem	Gem	Can	Can	Leo	Leo	Leo	Vir	Vir
June 17	Ar	Tau	Gem	Gem	Can	Can	Can	Leo	Leo	Vir	Vir	Vir
June 25	Tau	Tau	Gem	Gem	Can	Can	Leo	Leo	Leo	Vir	Vir	Lib
July 3	Tau	Gem	Gem	Can	Can	Can	Leo	Leo	Vir	Vir	Vir	Lib
July 11	Tau	Gem	Gem	Can	Can	Leo	Leo	Leo	Vir	Vir	Lib	Lib
July 18	Gem	Gem	Can	Can	Can	Leo	Leo	Vir	Vir	Vir	Lib	Lib
July 26	Gem	Gem	Can	Can	Leo	Leo	Vir	Vir	Vir	Lib	Lib	Lib
Aug 3	Gem	Can	Can	Can	Leo	Leo	Vir	Vir	Vir	Lib	Lib	Sc
Aug 11	Gem	Can	Can	Leo	Leo	Leo	Vir	Vir	Vir	Lib	Lib	Sc
Aug 18	Can	Can	Can	Leo	Leo	Vir	Vir	Vir	Lib	Lib	Sc	Sc
Aug 27	Can	Can	Leo	Leo	Leo	Vir	Vir	Lib	Lib	Lib	Sc	Sc
Sept 4	Can	Can	Leo	Leo	Leo	Vir	Vir	Vir	Lib	Lib	Sc	Sc
Sept 12	Can	Leo	Leo	Leo	Vir	Vir	Lib	Lib	Lib	Sc	Sc	Sag
Sept 20	Leo	Leo	Leo	Vir	Vir	Vir	Lib	Lib	Sc	Sc	Sc	Sag
Sept 28	Leo	Leo	Leo	Vir	Vir	Lib	Lib	Lib	Sc	Sc	Sag	Sag
Oct 6	Leo	Leo	Vir	Vir	Vir	Lib	Lib	Sc	Sc	Sc	Sag	Sag
Oct 14	Leo	Vir	Vir	Vir	Lib	Lib	Lib	Sc	Sc	Sag	Sag	Cap
Oct 22	Leo	Vir	Vir	Lib	Lib	Lib	Sc	Sc	Sc	Sag	Sag	Cap
Oct 30	Vir	Vir	Vir	Lib	Lib	Sc	Sc	Sc	Sag	Sag	Cap	Cap
Nov 7	Vir	Vir	Lib	Lib	Lib	Sc	Sc	Sc	Sag	Sag	Cap	Cap
Nov 15	Vir	Vir	Lib	Lib	Sc	Sc	Sc	Sag	Sag	Cap	Cap	Aq
Nov 23	Vir	Lib	Lib	Lib	Sc	Sc	Sag	Sag	Sag	Cap	Cap	Aq
Dec 1	Vir	Lib	Lib	Sc	Sc	Sc	Sag	Sag	Cap	Cap	Aq	Aq
Dec 9	Lib	Lib	Lib	Sc	Sc	Sag	Sag	Sag	Cap	Cap	Aq	Pis
Dec 18	Lib	Lib	Sc	Sc	Sc	Sag	Sag	Cap	Cap	Aq	Aq	Pis
Dec 28	Lib	Lib	Sc	Sc	Sag	Sag	Sag	Cap	Aq	Aq	Pis	Ar

Rising Signs—P.M. Births

	1 PM	2 PM	3 PM	4 PM	5 PM	6 PM	7 PM	8 PM	9 PM	10 PM	11 PM	12 MIDNIGHT
Jan 1	Tau	Gem	Gem	Can	Can	Leo	Leo	Leo	Vir	Vir	Vir	Lib
Jan 9	Tau	Gem	Gem	Can	Can	Leo	Leo	Leo	Vir	Vir	Vir	Lib
Jan 17	Gem	Gem	Can	Can	Can	Leo	Leo	Vir	Vir	Vir	Lib	Lib
Jan 25	Gem	Gem	Can	Can	Leo	Leo	Leo	Vir	Vir	Lib	Lib	Lib
Feb 2	Gem	Can	Can	Can	Leo	Leo	Vir	Vir	Vir	Lib	Lib	Sc
Feb 10	Gem	Can	Can	Leo	Leo	Leo	Vir	Vir	Lib	Lib	Lib	Sc
Feb 18	Can	Can	Can	Leo	Leo	Vir	Vir	Vir	Lib	Lib	Sc	Sc
Feb 26	Can	Can	Leo	Leo	Leo	Vir	Vir	Lib	Lib	Lib	Sc	Sc
Mar 6	Can	Leo	Leo	Leo	Vir	Vir	Vir	Lib	Lib	Sc	Sc	Sc
Mar 14	Can	Leo	Leo	Leo	Vir	Vir	Lib	Lib	Lib	Sc	Sc	Sag
Mar 22	Leo	Leo	Leo	Vir	Vir	Lib	Lib	Lib	Sc	Sc	Sc	Sag
Mar 30	Leo	Leo	Vir	Vir	Vir	Lib	Lib	Sc	Sc	Sc	Sag	Sag
Apr 7	Leo	Leo	Vir	Vir	Can	Lib	Lib	Lib	Sc	Sc	Sag	Sag
Apr 14	Leo	Vir	Vir	Vir	Lib	Lib	Lib	Sc	Sc	Sc	Sag	Cap
Apr 22	Leo	Vir	Vir	Lib	Lib	Lib	Sc	Sc	Sc	Sag	Sag	Cap
Apr 30	Vir	Vir	Vir	Lib	Lib	Sc	Sc	Sc	Sag	Sag	Cap	Cap
May 8	Vir	Vir	Lib	Lib	Lib	Sc	Sc	Sag	Sag	Sag	Cap	Cap
May 16	Vir	Vir	Lib	Lib	Sc	Sc	Sc	Sag	Sag	Cap	Cap	Aq
May 24	Vir	Lib	Lib	Lib	Sc	Sc	Sag	Sag	Sag	Cap	Cap	Aq
June 1	Vir	Lib	Lib	Sc	Sc	Sc	Sag	Sag	Cap	Cap	Aq	Aq
June 9	Lib	Lib	Lib	Sc	Sc	Sag	Sag	Sag	Cap	Cap	Aq	Pis
June 17	Lib	Lib	Sc	Sc	Sc	Sag	Sag	Cap	Cap	Aq	Aq	Pis
June 25	Lib	Lib	Sc	Sc	Sc	Sag	Sag	Cap	Cap	Aq	Pis	Ar
July 3	Lib	Sc	Sc	Sc	Sag	Sag	Cap	Cap	Aq	Aq	Pis	Ar
July 11	Lib	Sc	Sc	Sag	Sag	Sag	Cap	Cap	Aq	Pis	Ar	Tau
July 18	Sc	Sc	Sc	Sag	Sag	Cap	Cap	Aq	Aq	Pis	Ar	Tau
July 26	Sc	Sc	Sag	Sag	Sag	Cap	Cap	Aq	Pis	Ar	Tau	Tau
Aug 3	Sc	Sc	Sag	Sag	Cap	Cap	Aq	Aq	Pis	Ar	Tau	Gem
Aug 11	Sc	Sag	Sag	Sag	Cap	Cap	Aq	Pis	Ar	Tau	Tau	Gem
Aug 18	Sc	Sag	Sag	Cap	Cap	Aq	Pis	Pis	Ar	Tau	Gem	Gem
Aug 27	Sag	Sag	Sag	Cap	Cap	Aq	Pis	Ar	Tau	Tau	Gem	Gem
Sept 4	Sag	Sag	Cap	Cap	Aq	Pis	Pis	Ar	Tau	Gem	Gem	Can
Sept 12	Sag	Sag	Cap	Aq	Aq	Pis	Ar	Tau	Tau	Gem	Gem	Can
Sept 20	Sag	Cap	Cap	Aq	Pis	Pis	Ar	Tau	Gem	Gem	Can	Can
Sept 28	Cap	Cap	Aq	Aq	Pis	Ar	Tau	Tau	Gem	Gem	Can	Can
Oct 6	Cap	Cap	Aq	Pis	Ar	Ar	Tau	Gem	Gem	Can	Can	Leo
Oct 14	Cap	Aq	Aq	Pis	Ar	Tau	Tau	Gem	Gem	Can	Can	Leo
Oct 22	Cap	Aq	Pis	Ar	Ar	Tau	Gem	Gem	Can	Can	Leo	Leo
Oct 30	Aq	Aq	Pis	Ar	Tau	Tau	Gem	Can	Can	Can	Leo	Leo
Nov 7	Aq	Aq	Pis	Ar	Tau	Tau	Gem	Can	Can	Can	Leo	Leo
Nov 15	Aq	Pis	Ar	Tau	Gem	Gem	Can	Can	Can	Leo	Leo	Vir
Nov 23	Pis	Ar	Ar	Tau	Gem	Gem	Can	Can	Leo	Leo	Leo	Vir
Dec 1	Pis	Ar	Tau	Gem	Gem	Can	Can	Can	Leo	Leo	Vir	Vir
Dec 9	Ar	Tau	Tau	Gem	Gem	Can	Can	Leo	Leo	Leo	Vir	Vir
Dec 18	Ar	Tau	Gem	Gem	Can	Can	Can	Leo	Leo	Vir	Vir	Vir
Dec 28	Tau	Tau	Gem	Gem	Can	Can	Leo	Leo	Vir	Vir	Vir	Lib

Dorothy Hamill or baseball's Pete Rose, and you'll get the higher education necessary to do so. You tend to attract notice, have a strong theatrical quality—you may be attracted to politics, religion, education, or drama. You're always aiming for something higher, need a career that provides plenty of room to advance—and you tend to move ahead in bursts rather than a slow, steady climb.

Interview Personality: You'll express the most artistic, theatrical, and imaginative side of your sun sign. Like Phil Donohue, you'll come across as empathetic, a good listener who is able to cuc in to where others are coming from—a valuable interview asset. You may be quite dramatic in the way you present yourself, as a "character" like baseball's Yogi Berra or author Norman Mailer.

11

The Stars of Gemini

Have you ever noticed how often celebrities fit the archetype of their sun sign? Could Madonna be anything but a dazzling Leo golden girl? How about Diana Ross as the prototype of a dynamic Aries woman. You can easily find the Taurus musical talent and strong focus in Barbra Streisand, the Cancer sensitivity in Tom Cruise and Geraldo Rivera, the Aquarian charisma in the "mustache trio" of Burt Reynolds, Tom Selleck, and Clark Gable.

You can also compare other planets with the celebrity members of your sign using the "Look Up Your Planets" chapter. It's fun to find out how much you have in common—as well as the significant differences. You may be able to see how other planetary placements have colored their personalities and public image. It's an interesting way to sharpen your skills in astrology and apply what you have learned so far.

The following list contains the stars' birthdays and years wherever possible. Take the birthday of someone who fascinates you and do your own astrological study! Look up Venus and Mars to learn about their tastes and romantic preferences, Pluto and the outer planets for their audience appeal, Jupiter for their luck, and Saturn their trials. (If you're curious about celebrities of other sun signs, you'll find many celebrity birthdays listed in the annual edition of the *World Almanac*, which is available in the reference section of your local library or bookstore.)

Michael Sarrazin (May 22, 1940)
Joan Collins (May 23, 1933)
Marvelous Marvin Hagler (May 23, 1952)
Rosemary Clooney (May 23, 1928)

Priscilla Presley (May 24, 1945)
Patti LaBelle (May 24, 1947)
Ian MacKellen (May 25, 1939)
Connie Sellacca (May 25, 1955)
Miles Davis (May 25, 1926)
John Wayne (May 26, 1907)
James Arness (May 26, 1923)
Stevie Nicks (May 26, 1948)
Peggy Lee (May 26, 1920)
Philip Michael Thomas (May 26, 1949)
Allen Carr (May 27, 1941)
Vincent Price (May 27, 1911)
Ramsey Lewis (May 27, 1935)
Lou Gossett, Jr. (May 27, 1935)
Ian Fleming—creator of "James Bond" (May 28, 1908)
Gladys Knight (May 28, 1944)
Bob Hope (May 29, 1903)
Latoya Jackson (May 29, 1956)
Meredith MacRae (May 30, 1944)
Winona Judd (May 30, 1964)
Tom Berenger (May 31, 1950)
Don Ameche (May 31, 1908)
Brooke Shields (May 31, 1965)
Marilyn Monroe (June 1, 1926)
Gustav Mahler (June 1, 1860)
Brigham Young (June 1, 1801)
Lisa Hartman (June 1, 1956)
Ron Wood (June 1, 1947)
Cleavon Little (June 1, 1939)
Sally Kellerman (June 2, 1938)
Hedda Hopper (June 2, 1890)
Tony Curtis (June 3, 1925)
Colleen Dewhurst (June 3, 1928)
Bruce Dern (June 4, 1936)
Dennis Weaver (June 4, 1924)
Bill Moyers (June 5, 1934)
Rosalind Russell (June 5, 1912)
Bjorn Borg (June 6, 1956)
Tom Jones (June 7, 1940)
Gauguin (June 7, 1848)
Prince (June 7, 1958)
Joan Rivers (June 8, 1933)

Jackie Mason (June 9, 1931)
Michael J. Fox (June 9, 1961
Cole Porter (June 9, 1893)
Judy Garland (June 10, 1922)
Gene Wilder (June 11, 1935)
Jacques Cousteau (June 11, 1910)
Ally Sheedy (June 12, 1962)
Vic Damone (June 12, 1928)
George Bush (June 12, 1924)
Basil Rathbone (June 13, 1892)
Donald Trump (June 14, 1946)
Boy George (June 14, 1961)
Mario Cuomo (June 15, 1932)
Jim Belushi (June 15, 1954)
Barry Manilow (June 17, 1942)
Isabella Rossellini (June 18, 1952)
Paul McCartney (June 18, 1942)
Kathleen Turner (June 19, 1954)
Mariette Hartley (June 19, 1940)
Cyndi Lauper (June 20, 1953)
Errol Flynn (June 20, 1909)
Danny Aiello (June 20, 1933)
Lionel Richie (June 20, 1950)
Jane Russell (June 21, 1921)

12

Gemini Self-Discovery

The Gemini Man

Gemini is a restless spirit, with a mind always seeking out new interests. Because you tap into the eternal undercurrents of life, you treat life as a game, sensing that the here and now is not all there is. And your intelligent mind is always looking for new moves—new ways to play it.

Since predictable routines can be depressing to a natural free-lancer, you may be far more comfortable in business and social life than in an intense one-to-one relationship. You tend to walk away from difficult situations involving emotions, especially romantic ones. One reason that depth of feeling may be difficult for you to understand is because you are primarily mental rather than emotional. You'd rather turn to whatever or whoever is new and different than work through long-standing or deep-rooted problems. As President George Bush said: "I'm not an emotional kind of guy." Some Geminis avoid emotional responsibilities by refusing to grow up—they become the Peter Pans of the zodiac—and losing their grip on reality if they have to deal with serious matters or crises. The rock singers Boy George and Prince embody this type of Gemini.

Gemini can communicate with any other type without intruding, always keeping the proper distance with a touch of wit. You need to socialize, because even though you love to read, you learn from direct experience. You usually slip away from anyone who would tie you down. The key to keeping you around is to make you feel you'll be missing out on an exciting experience otherwise—and Gemini can't bear to miss out!

The Gemini Husband

The Gemini man is not averse to beauty, but he's really looking for his twin soul, a partner who will be a mental companion as well as a lover. Stability, security, or physical amenities are not as high priority as with other signs; however, his bright mind can devise ways to earn a steady and sometimes spectacular income. Many of this sign often juggle two jobs—or careers—simultaneously. He is best suited to a free-thinking woman who can adapt to changes and not object too strenuously to his being constantly on the move. She should also enjoy contact with many different people and be willing to live with many projects in various stages of completion. The Gemini man keeps a youthful, fun-loving view throughout his life, and is one of the most amusing, interesting companions. He may not give a woman emotional reassurance as often as she would like, but she will never be bored.

The Gemini Woman

The Gemini woman has a mind of her own and many different facets to her personality. She's not likely to fulfill any roles in the traditional way. Even the Geminis with a conservative, maternal facade (such as Barbara Bush) are up-to-date and with-it—and probably know a little bit about almost everything. If you don't have a college education, you've probably done an excellent job of educating yourself. Your mind races so fast that you often know the answers before the question is asked!

You have the advantage of being a quick study, a fast learner who can match wits and "spin on a dime," like Gemini Joan Rivers—or Joan Collins. You rarely get too attached to anything or anyone, and you can adapt to a new situation quickly.

Face it, you'd be miserable in a life of routine. Often you'll do two things at once—hold down two jobs, combine a job with a personal interest, talk on two telephones, have two love affairs simultaneously. But you prefer to keep your distance from people or situations—it's more fun to keep your options open, isn't it? After all, something or someone more exciting might appear.

Can we talk? At some point, you've got to figure out where you're going, get some "grounding." Otherwise you could become like those lost Gemini girls, looking somewhere "Over the Rainbow," as Judy Garland and Marilyn Monroe—both Geminis—did. It is important for you to reconcile the twins within—that is, your feminine emotions with your detached "masculine" intelligence. When you're using your excellent mind in the right way, you can find the combination of stimulation and security that is your real "pot of gold."

The Gemini Wife

The Gemini woman usually prefers to keep working after marriage, so she can delegate the more mundane chores to someone else. And an interesting job gives her the change of scene and social contact she needs to keep from getting bored. Geminis often marry more than once: it's not easy to find a man who can match your wit and intelligence, give you the space you need, yet provide solid support. Gemini is rarely the sentimental type wife—you like a full social life, with some games, frivolity, and style. You love to flirt and need a mate who won't get too jealous. But if there is room in your marriage for personal freedom, Gemini provides a life of sparkle and changes that is ever fresh.

13

The Gemini Family

The Gemini Parent

You Geminis take a great interest in your child's different stages, as the young personality unfolds. You may find the early babyhood years most difficult, when the child is dependent and needs steady routine care. After the child learns to communicate, you'll take on the role of teacher, introducing the child to the world of ideas and mental pursuits, helping with homework and making difficult subjects easier to understand. One of your greatest assets as a parent is your own insatiable curiosity about the world, which you can communicate to the child. Gemini children are introduced early to the world of ideas and books. You are also an excellent coach, teaching your child social abilities and the art of handling others at an early age. As your child matures, your youthful ever-fresh outlook makes you a wonderful friend and companion through the years.

The Gemini Stepparent

Your sense of humor will often come to the rescue in the initial stages of starting up a new family. But you're also a communicator who can quickly get shy youngsters to open up and difficult personalities to communicate. Gemini's talk-power and natural sociability makes family gatherings seem more like parties, where everyone has fun together. Since you have many outside activities and interests, the children will be able to have as much time as they need alone—you're not the type to smother. Soon your new family will find that you are a fun-loving addition to their lives, a wise adviser, and an excellent noncompetitive companion.

The Gemini Grandparent

You're the grandparent who is the life of the party, up on all the latest family gossip as well as what's happening with the rest of the world. Visits with you are full of laughter and good stories! You'll take special interest in your grandchildren's education (like Barbara Bush, you may have a large extended family that reaches out to the children of your community) and support them in whatever career path they choose. You'll give your own children plenty of space to rear the grandchildren as they please—never interfering with Mother's rules or taking over the grandchildren's upbringing. "Never complain" was the motto of the Duchess of Windsor and could be yours, too—you accentuate the positive and keep a cheerful attitude (after all, Norman Vincent Peale, the author of *The Power of Positive Thinking* was a Gemini!)—an upbeat grandparent who still finds life an interesting adventure!

14

Your Gemini Healthwatch

Geminis are natural jugglers, but if you take on too many activities, you could be thrown off balance when problems crop up in several areas at once. Gemini's nerves are your vulnerable point, especially when you try to do everything and put your emotional ties on hold. Sometimes it takes a real crisis for you to deal with irritating family and partnership demands.

The trick for Gemini is to build a solid support system. Get someone to handle the organizational detail work, follow-through tasks and chores, so that you can do the mental work that truly interests you, have fun with your loved ones, and take time out to explore those areas that fascinate you. Read a good book or do a crossword puzzle.

A Gemini who's tied down is a Gemini under stress. Although you can't always sidestep situations where you are closed in and forced to stay put, you can spice up your life with networking and power lunches and a variety of social contacts. Get a good multiline telephone system or a computer with modem to communicate with the outside world. If your work is solitary, get involved in group activities or special-interest clubs after-hours.

Gemini's weak spots are the lungs, hands, and nervous system. Pay special attention to the air quality where you work. Try to avoid smoking and air-polluted environments. An air ionizer in your home or office can make a big difference. It's also a good idea to avoid windowless rooms.

Massage is a wonderful stress reliever for Gemini. Either giving or receiving it is a form of communication as well as relaxation. Investigate the different kinds of massage—reflexology, polarity, shiatsu, Swedish —and give yourself a special treat.

Relaxing activities should appeal to you mentally and have a social aspect. Avoid anything too routine or repetitious. Racquet sports use Gemini's well-coordinated arms and hands. Yoga would be excellent to calm your nerves, focus your concentration, and increase your breathing capacity. You may also like to play team sports—softball, baseball, lacrosse—which make good use of your great hand-eye coordination. Jogging or rhythmic aerobics will strengthen your lungs.

Hobbies can be Gemini health savers. You could combine two of them, such as hiking and nature photography, travel and writing. Take a weekend seminar in your favorite hobby at a resort. When not moving about, you can relax and mind-travel in a book. Most Geminis are omnivorous readers: pack the latest best-seller when you go on a business trip to take your mind off work. New Age relaxation techniques such as mind control and visualization could also help you maintain a disciplined, focused, positive attitude.

Healthy Gemini Vacations

Gemini getaways should have mental interest, a variety of activities, and social life. Steer clear of desert islands, unless you are studying or writing about them. You'd prefer lots of good conversation in a Welsh pub, the sparkling social life of Newport, Rhode Island, golfing in Maine, a tennis resort in South Carolina, or exploring the antiquities of Egypt.

15

Gemini Astro-Outlook for 1992

Protect yourself from possible robbery or other monetary security pressures during the opening week of January. Forge full steam ahead in partnerships up until January 8, and then build up your economic and social security during the rest of the month. Your long-range and long-distance interests are more protected and travel ventures get increasing support during February. Between February 18 and the middle of March is an excellent time to mix business with pleasure away from home base.

There can be some conflicts about savings, investments, and tax shelters this year. Be open to new ideas from unexpected sources. Uranus favors changes and new approaches, whereas Neptune is more bullish, tricky, but also magical. Your love life is illuminated for you on and about April 17.

Social expansion potential is good during April and May, with door-opening opportunities in your hands during May. You can find a new direction in health and work matters on and about May 16.

Push your personality assets during late May when Venus and Mercury join the sun in your sign, but pull back from any possible confrontations with partners around the middle of June, when the moon is eclipsed in Sagittarius. Wealth production and earning power can waver somewhat as June comes to a close and the sun is totally eclipsed in your second house.

Take advantage of good opportunities in studies, hobbies, and the learning processes during July and leave long-range, long-distance, and travel decisions until mid-August. Saturn remains a damper on travel now and then as it moves through your ninth house, but August and September are ideal periods for finding your way around obstacles, with your love department spotlighted in late September. Your energy and clout are phenomenal during the August–September interval, and it is during this period that you can control, direct, claim, initiate, and originate successfully.

After October 11, count on much good luck in your love life, because Jupiter has just assumed control of your fifth house of romance. You can achieve your heart's desire, so to speak, during the remaining months of 1992. Obstacles in travel are far fewer after October 16, when Saturn resumes direct movement in Aquarius.

Extract power from the past during the first half of November, and push all wealth production matters hard. Marriage and partnerships also count heavily as November wanes.

Play December by ear, keeping a low profile and hugging the walls, so to speak, around the ninth, when the moon is totally eclipsed in Gemini. Be sure you are not being misquoted or misinterpreted and avoid energy-drainers and gossips. The holidays are more expensive than you anticipated, and some of the old traditions may have to be dropped this year.

16

Eighteen Months of Day-by-Day Predictions:

JULY 1991

Monday, July 1 (Moon in Aquarius to Pisces 12:51 p.m.)   Check details in connection with an upcoming holiday. You'll be involved in a celebration but there could be a dispute about where and when. Relatives might be saying, "It's possible we might not even participate!" Stress balance, deliberation, good-will. Taurus and Scorpio figure prominently.

Tuesday, July 2 (Moon in Pisces)   Your career gets a boost, prestige swings upwards. You'll get written verification about your career, business, or promotion. Accept an invitation to a special social affair. Today's scenario highlights change, travel, variety, and unique ways of communicating. Virgo and another Gemini play significant roles. The lucky number is 5.

Wednesday, July 3 (Moon in Pisces to Aries 10:34 p.m.)   A guest in your home talks about promotion, production, your involvement in a unique program. But someone may be envious of your talent. Be diplomatic and watch out for the green-eyed monster. Check the invitation list for a celebration tomorrow.

Thursday, July 4 (Moon in Aries)   Your psychic impressions are on target. A secret is revealed. You'll learn plenty during today's holiday festivities. What had been a mystery will be clarified. A clandestine arrangement involves Pisces and another Gemini. An introduction to someone of the opposite sex could be the start of something big.

159

Friday, July 5 (Moon in Aries) The emphasis falls on power, authority, responsibility, an intensified love relationship. Today's lunar position accents fulfillment; you can win friends and influence people, if you use your powers of persuasion. You're lucky in matters of speculation now, especially if you stick with number 8. A Capricorn can be helpful, now.

Saturday, July 6 (Moon in Aries to Taurus 4:52 a.m.) Lucky lottery numbers: 1, 10, 9, 27, 36, 45. At the races: number 2 post position in fourth race; exacta: 4 and 6. Hot numbers combination: 2 and 4, 4 and 6, 3 and 5. You'll complete a long-standing project, assignment. Attention also centers around popularity, creativity, a love relationship. Pay attention to an Aries.

Sunday, July 7 (Moon in Taurus) Be independent; you can to make use of information previously withheld. A Taurus helps make the proper contact. You could be involved with a jury or court. Light is shed on a situation which had been obscured. A young Leo wants to be on your side!

Monday, July 8 (Moon in Taurus to Gemini 7:42 a.m.) Follow your intuition. Attention centers around a teaching program, special organization, or a lecture that inspires. Communicate with someone temporarily confined to home or hospital. You could also be invited to participate in special behind-the-scenes tour. Your lucky number is 2.

Tuesday, July 9 (Moon in Gemini) What begins as a minor effort will gather momentum today. The moon in your sign reflects popularity, initiative, personality, sensuality. You'll be at the right place at the crucial moment. You'll also be part of a dramatic announcement. As social activities accelerate, you'll be more aware of your wardrobe, general appearance, or body image.

Wednesday, July 10 (Moon in Gemini to Cancer 8:03 a.m.) You can set your own pace today. It will be necessary to revise, review, or tear down and rebuild on a more suitable structure. Some people will be overbearing and might attempt to intimidate. Your position is strong, you need not fear retaliation.

Thursday, July 11 (Moon in Cancer)   The new moon position highlights money, payments, collections, income potential. An exchange of ideas with Sagittarius proves beneficial and could involve a member of opposite sex. Flirtation lends spice, and a clash of concepts inspires progress. One thing is certain—the status quo will no longer suffice.

Friday, July 12 (Moon in Cancer to Leo 7:35 a.m.) Post position special: number 2 P.P. in fourth race; pick six: 6, 2, 3, 2, 4, 8. You'll be rid of a burden which belonged to another in the first place. You strike a chord of universal appeal. Someone with a love problem will consult you. Invitation to travel is sincere and will involve an Aries or Libra.

Saturday, July 13 (Moon in Leo)   Define terms to avoid sensationalism. The key is to perfect techniques, to investigate a reunion with a Pisces or Virgo relative. The action could involve trips, visits, a clash of ideas. A project started approximately three weeks ago can now be revived. Try number 7 today.

Sunday, July 14 (Moon in Leo to Virgo 8:12 a.m.) The lunar position highlights showmanship, children, affairs of the heart. The emphasis falls on intensity, dedication, responsibility, the challenge of a deadline. In matters of law, justice is on your side. An older person, possibly a father figure, serves as a reliable advisor. Cancer and Capricorn figure prominently. Your best bet is number 8.

Monday, July 15 (Moon in Virgo)   Winning colors: various shades of red. Attention centers around an older woman, possibly an aunt or mother. Property appraisal figures in today's scenario. The emphasis is on safety, security, removal of hazards associated with your automobile. An aggressive person—possibly an Aries—might appear frightening but actually is on your side.

Tuesday, July 16 (Moon in Virgo to Libra 11:34 a.m.) You'll be getting more information about safety, security, your building code. Take the initiative in making inquiries. Play up your talent and creativity. The direct approach brings the desired results. You'll be invited to attend a unique festival by a Leo.

Wednesday, July 17 (Moon in Libra) The aspects favor sensuality, emotional reactions, and psychic impressions. You may reunite with an estranged relative at a family dinner tonight. A Cancer talks about money, how to earn more of it. You'll be complimented on ability to analyze character by an Aquarian.

Thursday, July 18 (Moon in Libra to Scorpio 6:41 p.m.) You'll be in the mood to celebrate. Show how creative you can be. Accept an invitation to an unusual social affair. Focus on design or a relationship with a young person. You'll have luck in speculation, especially by sticking with number 3.

Friday, July 19 (Moon in Scorpio) Nothing happens halfway today—it is all out or forget it. The emphasis falls on personnel, employment, pets, and people who rely upon your judgment. You are capable now of bringing order out of chaos. The puzzle pieces fall into place. You'll be able to read a pattern. Taurus and Scorpio figure prominently. Play number 4 to win.

Saturday, July 20 (Moon in Scorpio) Post position special: number 3 P.P. in second race; exacta: 1 and 3; Pick six: 1, 3, 4, 7, 3, 1. Be ready for change, travel discovery, a revelation about someone of the opposite sex. Discretion is necessary when handling an intimate situation. Scorpio could be jealous.

Sunday, July 21 (Moon in Scorpio to Sagittarius 5:17 a.m.) A family gathering restores harmony. Focus on a domestic adjustment, gifts, music, or a visit to the park or zoo. A young person would rather be with you than anyone else in the world! An oblique approach is better this time than direct confrontation. This message will become crystal clear. Libra plays an important role.

Monday, July 22 (Moon in Sagittarius)   The emphasis falls on whether or not to cooperate with someone who was guilty of deception. Wait and see. Time is on your side. Don't be cajoled into making a snap decision. Focus on intrigue, mystery, glamour, or marriage. You'll discover the answers by looking beyond the immediate. A Pisces figures prominently.

Tuesday, July 23 (Moon in Sagittarius to Capricorn 5:56 p.m.)   You'll have important dealings with older people today, especially men in authority. You'll account for past efforts and could have legal matters pending. Make certain that documents are in order. You might have to meet a deadline. The current cycle highlights public relations, reputation, necessity for putting forth your case in a forceful way.

Wednesday, July 24 (Moon in Capricorn)   You're finished with a burden that sapped you emotionally and financially, the other party will now begin to make payments. Dig deep, and study cryptic messages. Clues are available; you'll detect them. Aries and Libra can be helpful. Your lucky number is 9.

Thursday, July 25 (Moon in Capricorn)   You'll make a fresh start, you'll also get to heart of romantic matters. Your psychic impressions are on target. You'll attract the opposite sex, some of whom will be dedicated and sincere. Today's scenario features showmanship, variety, entertainment, and sex appeal. Leo is involved. Your lucky number is 1.

Friday, July 26 (Moon in Capricorn to Aquarius 6:49 a.m.)   Steer clear of a family dispute. The full moon position coincides with interest in the occult, mantic arts, and sciences. A heavy drinker could make promises which lack foundation. Stick to creative projects today. There's a strong love connection tonight! Cancer, Capricorn, and Aquarius are important now.

Saturday, July 27, (Moon in Aquarius) Lucky lottery numbers: 2, 11, 27, 3, 30, 6. A good lunar aspect coincides with dissemination of information, education, and possible participation in a publishing program. You'll be concerned with the learning progress, with philosophy and theology. Resolutions about diet and nutrition will surface again.

Sunday, July 28 (Moon in Aquarius to Pisces 6:35 p.m.) Deal with abstract matters while remaining practical, today. Some will feel there is conflict, but you'll understand that complexities actually lend spice and ultimately provide inspiration. Answers are not simple but they are available.

Monday, July 29 (Moon in Pisces) Attention centers around achievement, prestige, promotion. Written material gives you a subtle edge on the competition. You come out ahead if you present an original format or concept. A clash of ideas with an attractive person actually brings you closer. Know it, respond accordingly.

Tuesday, July 30 (Moon in Pisces) Post position special: number 2 P.P. in fourth race; exacta: 3 and 6. Hot numbers combinations: 3 and 2, 2 and 6, 4 and 1. Be independent, daring, pioneering! A major domestic adjustment takes place that contains subtle overtones. There are no outright arguments, but there is concern about an arrangement, design, or budget.

Wednesday, July 31 (Moon in Pisces to Aries 4:21 a.m.) A higher-up makes sincere promises, but could have the order canceled. Keep your options open; be more self-reliant. Be open-minded without being gullible. Look behind the scenes—someone is actually attempting to manipulate events. Refuse to be a puppet on a string. Your winning number is 7.

AUGUST 1991

Thursday, August 1 (Moon in Aries)　Suddenly it seems that all of your desires, past and present, are on the front burner. The cycle is high in connection with romance, speculation, and fulfillment. Today's aspects favor messages, writing, reading, a short trip that could involve a relative. Virgo, Sagittarius, and another Gemini are part of the action. Lucky number is 5.

Friday, August 2 (Moon in Aries to Taurus 11:32 a.m.)　Elements of timing, and luck continue to ride with you. Attention also centers around family relationships, a domestic adjustment, the realization that the financial picture is brighter than you thought. The moon continues to occupy a section of chart related to friends, hopes, wishes, romance. A Taurus has plenty to say.

Saturday, August 3 (Moon in Taurus)　Lucky lottery numbers: 2, 11, 20, 13, 22, 6. A secret is exposed, revealing that what you feared is only a paper tiger. The opposition melts. Terms will be defined; you'll have access to information previously withheld. Get in touch with someone confined to home or hospital. A Pisces or Virgo figures prominently.

Sunday, August 4 (Moon in Taurus to Gemini 3:55 p.m.)　You'll be saying, "At last I'm getting results!" Focus on secrets, institutions, hospitals, and special interest groups. Today's scenario features a deadline or insurance policies. Pay attention to tax and license requirements. You'll be dealing with older people, especially men and the sign of Cancer.

Monday, August 5, (Moon in Gemini)　The moon in your sign highlights your personality, showmanship, ability to put ideas across in a meaningful way. It's a dramatic day when you'll meet someone who stimulates your creative forces. A new love is not only on the horizon, but could be right next to you. Dining in an out-of-the-way place comes as a surprise, spontaneous decision.

Tuesday, August 6 (Moon in Gemini to Cancer 5:47 p.m.) Stress independence, creativity, initiative. A contact made yesterday bears fruit. Your sense of direction is restored. A special note: Avoid heavy lifting. You'll get to the heart of matters. Today's scenario features discretion, hidden meanings, subtle clues. Leo and Aquarius figure prominently. The lucky number is 1.

Wednesday, August 7 (Moon in Cancer) A woman, very likely born under Cancer, will play an important role in helping achieve your goal. Focus on income, personal possessions, and special investment. The scenario highlights security, property, or a family relationship. An Aquarian who had been out of sight makes a sudden and flashy return. Keep your sense of perspective. The lucky number is 2.

Thursday, August 8 (Moon in Cancer to Leo 6:10 p.m.) Post position special: number 5 P.P. in seventh race; exacta: 1 and 3; daily double: 1 and 4. Forces tend to be scattered, pulling you in numerous directions. Your sense of humor becomes a valuable ally. Special note: Remember your resolutions about diet and nutrition. Sagittarius and another Gemini play paramount roles.

Friday, August 9 (Moon in Leo) You're on more solid ground despite detours, delays, postponements. Today's scenario highlights trips, visits, and relatives who want the best for you but really are financially embarrassed. Check references; be positive about rights and permissions. Locate documents, including your birth certificate.

Saturday, August 10 (Moon in Leo to Virgo 6:35 p.m.) The new moon position emphasizes short trips, visits, and a dialogue with a Leo whose ideas can be considered grandiose. Focus also on children, variety, showmanship, speculation, sex appeal. You'll emerge from an emotional cocoon in a rush. You'll be saying, "Here I am and all of us can smile!"

Sunday, August 11 (Moon in Virgo)   Attention centers around family, home, and security, today. You'll be conscious of values and prices. An older person is on your side, will be there during any crisis period. A family discussion relates to moving, residence, domesticity, the possibility of a major purchase. Libra plays a role.

Monday, August 12 (Moon in Virgo to Libra 8:52 p.m.)   Yesterday's events continue to be of concern. You'll be involved with real estate or organization matters. It's a good time to throw out excess material and streamline your operations. Separating fact from wishful thinking when a Pisces reveals a secret desire. For actual answers, you must look behind the scenes. The lucky number is 7.

Tuesday, August 13 (Moon in Libra)   Be discriminating. Choose quality over quantity. A lively Virgo says, "I can help you make the right choice!" Another Gemini is also in the picture, possibly declaring, "Concentrate on durability!" In the long run, you'll have to rely upon your own judgment. You'll have luck with number 8.

Wednesday, August 14 (Moon in Libra)   Your efforts will be received with favor, especially by those at a distance. This means today could feature travel, communication, and ability to overcome language barriers. Focus on romance, search, discovery, excitement, sensuality. You'll have luck in matters of speculation, especially with this triple play: 3, 6, 9.

Thursday, August 15 (Moon in Libra to Scorpio 2:34 a.m.)   The key is to concentrate, to finish one task at a time. Stick to your own style. Today's aspects bring you charisma, originality, and favorable publicity. Someone of the opposite sex is genuinely interested in your welfare. Something that had been hidden will be uncovered. This revelation will prove beneficial. An Aries is involved.

Friday, August 16 (Moon in Scorpio)   Follow through on a hunch. You'll locate the right people, you'll be at a special place at a designated time. Plainly, today's scenario indicates you'll be where the action is. Attention centers around employment, pets, dependents, general health. A relative says one thing but apparently is forgetful and does something entirely different. The lucky number is 2.

Saturday, August 17 (Moon in Scorpio to Sagittarius 12:11 p.m.)   Post position special: number 5 P.P. in seventh race; alternate selection: number 2 P.P. in third race. Hot numbers combinations: 3 and 6, 1 and 4, 2 and 5. Stress versatility, humor, and your ability to overcome shyness about your body image. Your attractiveness is apparent, but remarks by a sharp-tongued person are aimed at deflating your confidence. Watch a Sagittarian.

Sunday, August 18 (Moon in Sagittarius)   You'll learn where you stand with someone connected with law, real estate, communication. Today's spotlight falls on partnership, publicity, special appearances, and marriage. You are on solid ground but you must pay close attention to the small print. There is a possibility of a hidden clause. Scorpio plays a top role.

Monday, August 19 (Moon in Sagittarius)   The lunar position highlights rights and permissions, added recognition, and your ability to state your case in a convincing way. The emphasis falls on communication, relatives, and a dialogue with one about to embark upon a short trip. Someone of the opposite sex is drawn to you, wants more than mere flirtation. Your lucky number is 5.

Tuesday, August 20 (Moon in Sagittarius to Capricorn 12:35 a.m.)   You might be saying, "I can hardly believe it but it does seem that everything is coming up roses!" The emphasis falls on emotional ties, commitments, and a legal sanction to your relationship. Your domestic situation changes, you'll be happier despite added responsibility and expense. Today's scenario features art, music, gifts, luxury items, romance.

Wednesday, August 21 (Moon in Capricorn)   You'll blend the practical with the imaginative. Focus on balance, security, serenity, an end to woe connected with someone who makes both threats and promises. You'll be asked to handle finances connected with one close to you, possibly your partner or mate. Taurus and Scorpio play dominant roles.

Thursday, August 22 (Moon in Capricorn to Aquarius 1:27 p.m.)   This can be your power-play day! Credit that had been withheld will be freely acknowledged. A love relationship intensifies. A business or career coup is featured. You'll have more responsibility and a greater chance for promotion or financial reward. Someone who has authority will say, "You are the right person!" The lucky number is 8.

Friday, August 23 (Moon in Aquarius)   Idealism rules. Altruism plays a major role. Focus on philosophy, theology, and spiritual values. You'll have the feeling of being transformed. An overseas journey or venture could be part of today's excitement. You'll locate what had been missing—you'll also thank a relative who helped you approximately nine months ago.

Saturday, August 24 (Moon in Aquarius)   Post position special: number 7 P.P. in third race. Hot numbers combinations: 1 and 4, 2 and 6, 5 and 5. You're due to make fresh start, to get to heart of romantic matters. Be original and daring! Enthusiasm will replace indifference. Leo and Aquarius take notice.

Sunday, August 25 (Moon in Aquarius to Pisces 12:52 a.m.)   Today's full moon accents journeys, higher education, spiritual values, attraction to someone who encourages your emotional growth. You'll have a chance to fulfill your potential The scenario also highlights character analysis, family relationships, joint efforts, intuitive reaction to one who wants something for nothing. The lucky number is 2.

Monday, August 26 (Moon in Pisces)   Diversify, contact someone in authority. The moon at the top of your chart coincides with promotion, direction, career, production. You'll be trusted with a product which requires careful handling. Keep your options open; realize those in charge have qualms about your purpose or motive. Play it safe with number 3.

Tuesday, August 27 (Moon in Pisces to Aries 10:01 a.m.)   A Pisces wants proof and references. Ride with the tide. Restrictions will be removed. Be willing to tear down in order to rebuild on a solid base. A Pisces boss seeks reassurance, but wants your vote of confidence. Say it with a smile. "You are my friend as well as boss!"

Wednesday, August 28 (Moon in Aries)   Lucky lottery numbers: 9, 1, 10, 28, 41, 5. Today brings change, travel, variety! You can sell your ideas. A relationship that promised passion could turn out to be strictly cerebral. The scenario also highlights trips, visits, and dialogue with a relative who had been missing. Another Gemini and Virgo play roles.

Thursday, August 29 (Moon in Aries to Taurus 5 p.m.)   Those who doubted you will now be saying, "Your performance was outstanding!" You'll successfully use publicity, powers of persuasion. You could have a career or business promotion. Take a creative approach with speculation and romance. Taurus, Libra, and Scorpio figure prominently. Count on number 6.

Friday, August 30 (Moon in Taurus)   It won't be easy for others to fool you, but you could fall victim to self-deception. Be realistic, especially in assessing property value. Define terms; consult the experts. Your automobile might need a tune-up. The plumbing in your apartment or home demands attention. Virgo is helpful, now.

Saturday, August 31 (Moon in Taurus to Gemini 10:03 p.m.)   Accept a challenge involving a deadline. Check references, be aware of dates of policies. An older person could be overlooking details. A love relationship commands attention, is not entirely smooth. You'll learn plenty about security, finance, long-range prospects. A close associate reveals separation from parents.

SEPTEMBER 1991

Sunday, September 1 (Moon in Gemini)   Keep your equilibrium; agree to a reasonable request by a family member. You'll be presented with a gift, actually something that had been borrowed and repaired. You might be saying to yourself, "I never expected to see this again!" Taurus, Libra, and Scorpio figure prominently. Stick with number 6.

Monday, September 2 (Moon in Gemini)   The moon in your sign, plus other factors, reveals a degree of introspection. You'll say, "I don't care what it takes, I want to improve!" You'll be your own most severe critic. During the cycle high a crisis passes, and you emerge whole and victorious. You'll have access to private notes, to confidential information from a Pisces.

Tuesday, September 3 (Moon in Gemini to Cancer 1:20 a.m.)   The emphasis falls on power, authority, production, and an intensified love relationship. You'll feel more assured and secure. There will be reason to celebrate. Your popularity zooms upward; you'll add to your wardrobe; you'll also resolve to pay more attention to your diet, nutrition. Cancer and Capricorn play outstanding roles.

Wednesday, September 4 (Moon in Cancer)   A flatterer really wants something for nothing. Protect your assets, demand more than mere whispered promises. Focus on money, payments, collections; you can transform a hobby into a moneymaking enterprise. Look beyond the immediate. Actions now could have far-reaching consequences. Aries plays a role.

Thursday, September 5 (Moon in Cancer to Leo 3:13 a.m.)   Stress independence, style, creativity, and a willingness to fight for your rights. Get to the heart of

171

matters. Take the initiative. Be direct. Your money house is activated. By adopting new procedures, you almost assure profit. Love plays a key role. Leo and Aquarius are supportive. Your lucky number is 1.

Friday, September 6 (Moon in Leo) Trust your intuition; a family member who seeks advice is sincere but confused. Be patient; play the waiting game. Within eleven days, missing items will be located or returned. You'll reunite with someone who cares very much but has been waiting for you to make the initial gesture. An Aquarian will figure prominently.

Saturday, September 7 (Moon in Leo to Virgo 4:35 a.m.) Diversify, use showmanship, respond to one who says, "As far as I'm concerned, you've got everything!" Emerge from your emotional cocoon. Accent self-expression, accept a challenge, and realize you deserve to be the center of attention. The spotlight falls on social activity, entertainment, wardrobe, sensitivity about your body image.

Sunday, September 8 (Moon in Virgo) The new moon position highlights property, family relationships, completion of a mission. Check details; bring your source material up to date. An older person, possibly a parent or employer, shares experience in connection with basic values, property, security. A special note: Check automobile tires and brakes!

Monday, September 9 (Moon in Virgo to Libra 6:52 a.m.) Today's aspects favor communication, flirtation, your ability to express yourself in a unique, dynamic way. An attractive person is intrigued but not free to act. You'll set information previously withheld. Family, possibly brothers or sisters, will be involved. Virgo and another Gemini figure prominently.

Tuesday, September 10 (Moon in Libra) Post position special: number 2 P.P. in fourth race; exacta: 3 and 2; pick six: 3, 6, 4, 2, 5, 3. Focus on speculation, elements of timing and luck. Major changes occur at home,

172

where a serious discussion involves budget or income potential. Taurus, Libra, and Scorpio play major roles. Be diplomatic.

Wednesday, September 11 *(Moon in Libra to Scorpio 11:43 a.m.)*   Lucky lottery numbers: 16, 49, 5, 13, 22, 14. Define terms; realize others are not capable of fooling you—but you could fall victim to wishful thinking and self-deception. Demand proof, guarantees, a definition of terms. Romance may be on shaky ground but if it survives, it will last. Virgo has much to say.

Thursday, September 12 *(Moon in Scorpio)*   What happened yesterday is not over. Today's spotlight falls on employment, pets, dependents, and a health report. Your relationship will survive, you'll be whispering sighs of relief. You get the proverbial second chance. Someone close to you may be embarking on short trip. Cancer and Capricorn are in today's picture.

Friday, September 13 *(Moon in Scorpio to Sagittarius 8:15 p.m.)*   Be willing to revise, review, actually dismantle in order to rebuild on a more secure base. Special note: Be willing to let go of a situation that has drained you emotionally and financially. Open lines of communication; there will be opportunity for travel, romance, creativity, even more happiness. The lucky number is 9.

Saturday, September 14 *(Moon in Sagittarius)*   Hot combinations: 1 and 1, 7 and 3, 5 and 5. You're due to make a fresh start in a new direction. A love relationship needs more time. What happened during the past weeks appeared tragic but now you can actually laugh and say, "I'm glad it happened the way it did!" Express yourself; emphasize freedom of thought and action.

Sunday, September 15 *(Moon in Sagittarius)*   A family gathering centers attention on emotional ties, legal obligations, marriage. Circumstances take control of current situation. Give up some authority if the reins will be handed back to you at appropriate time. Protect your image; read the fine print in any legal agreement. Cancer and Aquarius are in the picture.

Monday, September 16 (Moon in Sagittarius to Capricorn 8:04 a.m.)   Focus on idealism, philosophy, theology, higher education. A clash of ideas proves stimulating. A Sagittarian declares, "I don't always agree with you, but you're the most provocative, dynamic person I know!" The emphasis also falls on communication, humor, and sensitivity about your wardrobe, weight, and body image. You could receive a very important proposal. Count on number 3.

Tuesday, September 17 (Moon in Capricorn)   Be practical today. Check past performances. Be aware of records and accounting procedures. Your partner or mate could be inadvertently wasting funds. State your case with authority but also with consideration for feelings. Taurus, Capricorn, and Scorpio figure prominently. You'll locate an article that had been lost, missing, or stolen.

Wednesday, September 18 (Moon in Capricorn to Aquarius 8:58 p.m.)   Post position special: number 3 P.P. in second race; winning colors: navy blue, black. Be ready for change, travel, variety. A written message contains valuable clues or hints. Someone of the opposite sex could be involved. Virgo, Sagittarius, and another Gemini have much to say. Wait five days before you take action!

Thursday, September 19 (Moon in Aquarius)   Dig deep for information. Fascination with the occult will surface. A family member will agree to do it your way! The spotlight is on diplomacy, a domestic adjustment, or ways to increase your income. A romantic blind date could finally become a meaningful relationship. Your lucky number is 6.

Friday, September 20 (Moon in Aquarius)   Define terms, perceive potential, and follow through on first impressions. You will have the urge to travel, communicate, publish, and advertise. You'll meet a spiritual person who, nevertheless, is physically attracted. Ride with one tide; bask in an aura of affection. Pisces plays an outstanding role.

Saturday, September 21 (Moon in Aquarius to Pisces 8:21 a.m.) The answer to your question: Yes, you'll meet a deadline. Check insurance policies and various other financial obligations. A love relationship intensifies, but responsibilities also increase. A long-distance call relates to travel and dissemination of pertinent information. Cancer and Capricorn are in touch now. Lucky number is 8.

Sunday, September 22 (Moon in Pisces) Long-range prospects come into sharp, clear focus. It's a very unusual day that combines fun and games with serious work. Your aspirations are fulfilled; an older person is convinced you can handle the job! You may be asked to travel, to solve a dilemma. All signals are go. Libra plays a dominant role.

Monday, September 23 (Moon in Pisces to Aries 4:56 p.m.) The full moon highlights intuition, romance, emotional responses. A task or assignment is completed; views are vindicated. You'll have special success in dealing with an organization largely composed of women. Be independent, creative, and pioneering. Leo and Aquarius are on your side. The lucky number is 1.

Tuesday, September 24 (Moon in Aries) You'll receive a special reward for service, performance, and ability to perceive events before they occur. Cancer and Aquarius, one possibly related to you, help clear the path, provide inspiration, and might even obtain funding. Your cycle is high and circumstances can take a sudden turn in your favor. Focus on wishes, aspirations, and powers of persuasion.

Wednesday, September 25, (Moon in Aries to Taurus 11:00 p.m.) As your popularity increases, you'll be involved in a charitable, community or political project. You may also be planning a vacation and adding to your wardrobe. A friend may wish he or she had followed your lead! You'll get a good return on your investment. Another Gemini is involved. Your lucky number is 3.

Thursday, September 26 (Moon in Taurus) An Aries helps transform obstacles into stepping-stones. You're going places despite the objections of one who feels important but lacks talent. Take the initiative; show the courage of your conviction. You'll be tested, ask questions. Be sure references are available. Taurus and Scorpio figure prominently.

Friday, September 27 (Moon in Taurus) Questions previously placed on the back burner will now be answered. You'll be invited on a special tour. A hospital visit may be necessary in connection with a relative. Today's scenario features greater freedom of thought and action. Special note: That person you are interested in may want more than mere flirtation.

Saturday, September 28 (Moon in Taurus to Gemini 3:26 a.m.) You lost something of value—it was not stolen. A family member, as it might turn out, merely borrowed. Don't cast the first stone! The spotlight falls on secrets, confinement, mystery, intrigue, the necessity for discretion. Someone of the opposite sex wants attention and attempts to get it by giving you a gift. Be gracious and diplomatic, but refuse to be rushed.

Sunday, September 29 (Moon in Gemini) The moon in your sign, plus the numerical cycle, emphasizes intrigue, mystery, possibly a cult following. This means people with special tastes will appreciate your capabilities and contributions. Some will say, "You are unique, intelligent, attractive!" Pisces, Virgo, and another Gemini play paramount roles. Your lucky number is 7.

Monday, September 30 (Moon in Gemini to Cancer 6:59 a.m.) You'll be making up for lost time. Almost

176

without warning, events transpire in your favor. You could be saying, "This has to be my lucky day!" The spotlight falls on intensity, responsibility, a strong love relationship. The scenario also features production, initiative, and sex appeal. Cancer and Capricorn figure prominently.

OCTOBER 1991

Tuesday, October 1 (Moon in Cancer) Hold off on financial arrangements; an element of deception could exist. The more you delay, the more you play the waiting game, the better for you. A social engagement tonight could lead to a significant relationship. Today's cycle highlights security, personal possessions, and ability to comprehend basic values. A Pisces is involved. Your lucky number is 7.

Wednesday, October 2 (Moon in Cancer to Leo 9:49 a.m.) The accent continues on emergency funds, investments, family disclosures regarding sales and purchases. You'll learn more about various commitments, deadlines, insurance policies. An older person, possibly a parent, will be in your corner. Capricorn and Cancer figure prominently. Play number 8 to win.

Thursday, October 3 (Moon in Leo) Post position special: number 8 P.P. in ninth race; alternate selection: number 3 P.P. in third race; exacta: 1 and 7; daily double; 1 and 3, 6 and 4, 5 and 3. You're due to complete a major project. Your efforts will spread far and wide. You could be active in importing and exporting. An Aries can be helpful today.

Friday, October 4 (Moon in Leo to Virgo 12:45 p.m.) You'll be concerned with the weight or appearance of a product. Recent inquiries bring desired responses. Your ideas are seriously considered. You'll be questioned about tonnage, showmanship, display, production, and distribution. Your creative juices are stimulated. A new love could be on horizon. Yes, celebrate tonight!

Saturday, October 5 (Moon in Virgo)   You'll be invited to join forces with one who understands business and is capable of helping you earn money. Emotions blend with practicality. You'll be concerned with your family, home, property, marital status. A Cancer native says, "You are not really aware of your own potential!" Leo has good ideas.

Sunday, October 6 (Moon in Virgo to Libra 4:01 p.m.)   Be independent, today and don't be afraid to break with family tradition. A fresh opportunity exists to correct past errors. Light is shed on areas previously obscured. A young Aquarius is enthusiastic about your appearance and prospects.

Monday, October 7 (Moon in Libra)   The new moon highlights change, travel, variety, and romance. Nothing happens halfway—for you it will be hot or cold, not lukewarm. Be creative with your appearance by trying a different wardrobe. Project your charisma, personality, sex appeal. Aquarius and Leo take notice.

Tuesday, October 8 (Moon in Libra to Scorpio 9 p.m.) You have been relying on someone who usually is filled with energy and optimism. However, you may now be dealing with a burn-out situation. This means you will have to rely on yourself more heavily. That third person is going to make a change, could leave you high and dry. Virgo is involved. Stick with number 5.

Wednesday, October 9 (Moon in Scorpio)   In dealing in commodities, you could have financial success with silver. You'll have inside information. The emphasis falls on family, security, and domestic adjustment. What you have been seeking is practically handed to you on the proverbial platter. You could be reunited with an old flame. Play number 6 to win.

Thursday, October 10 (Moon in Scorpio)   A secret meeting figures prominently. Legal terms could be open for discussion and possible renegotiation. Don't equate delay with defeat. You are going to have a second chance, terms will be defined and improved. The spotlight falls on employment, basic issues, work methods, and people who rely upon your judgment.

Friday, October 11 (Moon in Scorpio to Sagittarius 4:58 a.m.)   Practical issues surge to the forefront. What had been regarded as nebulous will now be solid. A conservative course brings the desired results. You'll win a legal decision. A relationship heats up. Focus on care of pets; do the job at hand. There could be a significant agreement involving an older Capricorn.

Saturday, October 12 (Moon in Sagittarius)   Finish what you start; realize that a recent rift was more serious than you believed. Protect your interests. Reach beyond previous limitations. An obligation that was serious in the first place can no longer be regarded as your own. Your marital status is in spotlight. Aries and Libra are in the picture.

Sunday, October 13 (Moon in Sagittarius to Capricorn 4:11 p.m.)   It will be necessary to revamp procedures. It's time to stick to your own ideas, style. A love relationship will be on a more stable base. The emphasis is on public relations, your image and reputation. You'll learn more about legal rights and permissions. You'll be offered a new deal by a Leo. Your lucky number is 1.

Monday, October 14 (Moon in Capricorn)   Interest is fanned about hidden affairs, secrets, arcane literature, the mantic arts. You'll be physically attracted to someone who could belong to another. Exercise restraint but don't completely hide your feelings. Cancer and Capricorn figure prominently.

Tuesday, October 15 (Moon in Capricorn)   You'll be dealing with successful people today. Focus on responsibility, a deadline, legal negotiations. Your romantic relationship is strong but could also be stormy. Dig deep for information, especially source material. Forces tend to be scattered. Social activity accelerates. A travel invitation is likely. Play number 3 to win.

Wednesday, October 16 (Moon in Capricorn to Aquarius 5:05 a.m.)   You will be presented with facts, figures, and accounting procedures. The key is to be specific, ask questions, be willing to revise, and seriously consider taking a different direction. A loyal Scorpio wants to help, but could be financially embarrassed. The lucky number is 6.

Thursday, October 17 (Moon in Aquarius)   Post position special: number 3 P.P. in second race. Hot numbers combinations: 1 and 3, 2 and 5, 4 and 3. You've been seeking a change; opportunity is here—a short trip could be start of something big. Focus on written data, especially locating legal papers—including your birth certificate and passport.

Friday, October 18 (Moon in Aquarius to Pisces 4:53 p.m.)   Today's emphasis is on idealism. You have a wonderful chance to show your feelings. Some will say, "You seem ready to give the store away!" It is true—altruism figures prominently. However, keep your guard up, don't give up something of value for a mere whispered promise. Taurus, Libra, and Scorpio play paramount roles.

Saturday, October 19 (Moon in Pisces)   Lucky lottery numbers: 12, 19, 26, 25, 30, 7. Your ambition, career, and participation in a community project take center stage. Your suggestions will be heeded. In your personal life, there could be a minor crisis due to a missed appointment. Focus on time, film, illusion, glamour, and discretion. Pisces will figure prominently.

Sunday, October 20 (Moon in Pisces)   You'll strike a chord of universal appeal. People will be drawn to you; some will consult you about their love problems. What you started approximately nine days ago could now reach fruition. Today features communication, travel, and ability to expand your horizons. An Aries is good company.

Monday, October 21 (Moon in Pisces to Aries 1:33 a.m.) A surprise is due—this relates to the lifting of a burden. You'll be rewarded for past efforts. You'll get credit long deserved. A love relationship is on more solid ground. Reach beyond the immediate. Become more aware of your own potential. A long-distance call from a Libra will verify views. Your best bet is number 9.

Tuesday, October 22 (Moon in Aries) There is a valid reason for optimism on this unusual Tuesday! It might seem almost like Saturday night. You'll make a fresh start; you'll be rid of an obligation which was not yours in the first place. You could have a romantic time with Leo. Play number 1 to win.

Wednesday, October 23 (Moon in Aries to Taurus 6:55 a.m.) The full moon highlights romance, fulfillment, speculation, and ability to win friends and influence people. Your popularity rating moves up; career or business efforts are successful. Make public appearances, and realize others actually will enjoy your progress. Cancer, Capricorn, and Aquarius are on your side.

Thursday, October 24 (Moon in Taurus) Diversify. Stress humor, versatility, intellectual curiosity. A long-distance communication relates to a social affair, possibly a journey. Your cycle moves up following an initial delay. On this day, you'll receive a call or message from one who is temporarily confined to home or hospital. Sagittarius and another Gemini figure in today's plans.

Friday, October 25 (Moon in Taurus to Gemini 10:09 a.m.) Check details; read between the lines. Something important is being kept secret. Within three days, you'll be on top of the situation. Meantime, be discreet and play cards close to your chest. Realize you don't have all information and the story is yet to have an ending. So play the waiting game.

Saturday, October 26 (Moon in Gemini)   Investigate; give full play to your intellectual curiosity. Your cycle is high; circumstances swing in your favor. Your judgment and intuition are likely to be on target. The moon in Gemini accents personality, vivaciousness, elan. Someone of the opposite sex will be inspired by your company!

Sunday, October 27 (Moon in Gemini to Cancer 12:37 p.m.)   Your family will give positive responses to your suggestions and efforts. Home surroundings will be beautified due to gifts. You might be saying, "All this and it is not even my birthday!" Those close to you express gratitude and display affection. Taurus, Libra, and Scorpio figure prominently. Your lucky number is 6.

Monday, October 28 (Moon in Cancer)   The moon emphasizes personal possessions, money, and income. Your mood tends to change as a result of what appears to be a broken promise. This romantic rift can be healed. Define meanings, look behind scenes; remember obligations agreed to less than two months ago. All the puzzle pieces will fit together.

Tuesday, October 29 (Moon in Cancer to Leo 3:21 a.m.)   You're in a fortunate financial and romantic cycle. A relationship which temporarily went off the track is now restored. You'll have more responsibility and a greater chance to hit the financial jackpot. Accept a challenge. The law is on your side. Taurus, Cancer, and Capricorn figure prominently.

Wednesday, October 30 (Moon in Leo)   Emphasize showmanship; be active where design and display are concerned. Focus on entertainment, romance, creativity, and discovery. Long-range prospects will be clarified. A love relationship plays a major role. You'll have luck in matters of speculation, especially with this triple play: 3, 6, 9.

Thursday, October 31 (Moon in Leo to Virgo 6:47 p.m.) People will comment, "You certainly know how to be with youngsters!" Children play important roles, you'll be very much aware of Halloween. Stress creativity, costumes, your ability to provide pleasure. A short trip involves visits, relatives, and retrieving article that had been borrowed and not returned. A Leo figures prominently. The lucky number is 1.

NOVEMBER 1991

Friday, November 1 (Moon in Virgo) You recently asked questions about durability, basic values, and guarantees. Today you'll get the answers; you'll know where you stand, and you'll also understand who is a true friend. A relationship is tested. Older people, possibly parents, give you straight talk about finances.

Saturday, November 2 (Moon in Virgo to Libra 11:13 p.m.) A transaction can be completed to your satisfaction. On a personal level, love plays a major role. A relationship, recently cool, will heat up. A previous obligation is pushed aside, and you need not feel guilty about it. Aries and Libra figure prominently. You can have luck with this triple play: 3, 6, 9.

Sunday, November 3 (Moon in Libra) Light is shed on an area previously prohibited. This involves family relationships, property, money that had been put aside for a proverbial rainy day. Special note: Avoid heavy lifting. A young person discusses romance, a creative project, the immediate future. Leo and Aquarius play significant roles. Your lucky number is 1.

Monday, November 4 (Moon in Libra) Your intuition rings true. Focus on creativity, change, travel, and contact with an admirer of the opposite sex, possibly an Aquarius. You're being pulled in two directions. The key is to test your own capabilities. A reluctant relative is sincere but could be misinformed. A break from tradition is necessary.

Tuesday, November 5 (Moon in Libra to Scorpio 5:09 a.m.)   Post position special: number 5 P.P. in seventh race; exacta: 3 and 3. Hot number combinations: 3 and 5, 4 and 2, 7 and 1. You'll receive a social invitation; you'll also buy some new clothes. Today's emphasis is on style, design, discovery, and emotional reawakening. Gemini and Sagittarius have much to say.

Wednesday, November 6 (Moon in Scorpio)   Lucky lottery numbers: 8, 18, 22, 2, 20, 14. The new moon accents basic issues, practical efforts, pets, cooking, sewing. The employment picture is bright despite a recent misunderstanding. You'll have a chance for a fresh start in a new direction. A young lady becomes your valued ally. Cancer and Capricorn figure prominently.

Thursday, November 7 (Moon in Scorpio to Sagittarius 1:22 p.m.)   You recover what had been lost, missing or stolen. You'll gain through reading, writing. The health report is good, but you must pay more attention to diet, nutrition. A relative, who recently returned from a short journey, will have interesting stories to tell. Virgo, Sagittarius, and another Gemini are good company. Your lucky number is 5.

Friday, November 8 (Moon in Sagittarius)   Attention centers around contracts, special permissions, and publicity. At home, your marital status comes up for review. Be diplomatic without abandoning your principles. Someone wants to wine and dine you, but you are uncertain—there is a gnawing at your conscience. Taurus is involved.

Saturday, November 9 (Moon in Sagittarius)   Lucky lottery numbers: 9, 16, 17, 27, 44, 45. Be open-minded but avoid being gullible. You could be the prime target for someone who seeks something for nothing. Look for loopholes, keep your options open, refuse to make a real estate commitment. Watch Pisces and Virgo. Keep dry!

Sunday, November 10 (Moon in Sagittarius to Capricorn 12:17 a.m.)   Attention centers around legal actions, justice, intentions, and motives. A study of the law would prove tremendous asset. Contact someone whose duty is to represent your interests. Focus also continues on partnership, special appearances, and your marital status. Cancer and Capricorn figure prominently. Play number 8 today.

Monday, November 11 (Moon in Capricorn)   You'll be relieved of an obligation not your own in the first place. Money will change hands. Check percentages and interest rates. You could be asked to be the guardian of special funds, savings, or news about an inheritance. A trust fund could also be in the picture. Interest in unusual subjects, including the occult will be fanned.

Tuesday, November 12 (Moon in Capricorn to Aquarius 1:07 p.m.)   Be independent today. Those who attempt to intimidate you will fail if you take the lead. Focus on style, creativity, and willingness to get to the heart of matters. Someone who recently slipped away will again be heard from, possibly within two months. Leo, Aries, and Aquarius are on hand.

Wednesday, November 13 (Moon in Aquarius)   Lucky lottery numbers: 11, 20, 2, 7, 44, 49. Your ability to interpret trends, motives, and cycles surges to the forefront. Your opinion will be sought regarding character analysis, the actual intentions of one who claims to know a secret. A family dispute will be settled once you show that you actually are neutral.

Thursday, November 14 (Moon in Aquarius)   A good lunar aspect coincides with education, spirituality, romance, and ability to disseminate pertinent information. You'll have more working room, your popularity increases, you'll be invited to attend a prestigious affair. You'll be sensitive about your clothing, appearance, weight, and body image.

Friday, November 15 (Moon in Aquarius to Pisces 1:34 a.m.)   Recent doubts about your abilities and appearance will be dispelled. Someone you admire will return the compliment and might actually state "You look simply marvelous!" You'll be revising, reviewing, possibly rebuilding on more a suitable structure. Taurus, Leo, and Scorpio figure prominently. Your lucky number is 4.

Saturday, November 16 (Moon in Pisces)   The key is to be analytical; take nothing for granted—do some private detective work. Someone may be deliberately playing hide and seek. Three members of the opposite sex are actually interested in your welfare and will protect you from chicanery. Virgo, Sagittarius, and another Gemini figure prominently.

Sunday, November 17 (Moon in Pisces to Aries 11:08 a.m.)   A relative brings good news in connection with your career or business. The pleasure principle is emphasized. Dining out tonight will feature music, goodwill, romance. Your employer or parent provides information that can lead to a promotion, production, or impact where distribution of product is concerned. Libra is in the picture.

Monday, November 18 (Moon in Aries)   What appeared to be a defeat will be transformed into an outstanding performance. The moon position accents romance, style, creativity, and luck in matters of speculation. You are capable now of winning friends and influencing trends. Someone, previously cold, will say, "I really enjoy being with you!" Pisces is involved.

Tuesday, November 19 (Moon in Aries to Taurus 4:49 p.m.)   This can be your power play day! The spotlight falls on money and love, achievement, ability to successfully use charm and salesmanship. An element that had been missing will again be present. Some will say, "You certainly have found yourself!" You'll have luck in matters of speculation, especially by sticking with this triple play: 8, 2,4.

Wednesday, November 20 (Moon in Taurus)   Reach beyond limitation which an envious person attempts to impose. Today's scenario features romance and style. You'll strike a universal chord of appeal. An Aries says, "You can count on me!" You'll get credit for achievement long overdue. Someone in authority will strongly recommend you for assignment or promotion. Your lucky number is 9.

Thursday, November 21 (Moon in Taurus to Gemini 7:23 p.m.)   The full moon position highlights secrets, prophesies, institutions, hospitals, and theatrical performances. You'll make a fresh start. You'll overcome fears, doubts, suspicions. Show your independent pioneering spirit. Be willing to get to the heart of matters. Leo and Aquarius figure prominently. Your best bet is number 1.

Friday, November 22 (Moon in Gemini)   You'll rise above obstacles mainly connected with family and finances. It will turn out that an unusual collection or hobby is worth more than you originally anticipated. The focus is on gardening, coins, and jewelry. Someone of the opposite sex apologizes for a recent outbreak. Stand tall; be willing to forgive without abandoning your principles.

Saturday, November 23 (Moon in Gemini to Cancer 8:26 p.m.)   Lucky lottery numbers: 41, 40, 3, 5, 30, 17. The moon moves into your sign, highlighting attractiveness, personality, bright colors, and a new start in a different direction. Many will be drawn to you; some will indicate, "You are the one person I can trust." Accent humor, perspective, and versatility.

Sunday, November 24 (Moon in Cancer)   You'll finish a project which gives the credit you need to make a career or business advance. The lunar position accents correct judgment. You should also use your intuition. Wear your colors: silver, bright green, yellow. You are going places; a relative will suggest a trip that combines business with pleasure. Your lucky number is 4.

Monday, November 25 (Moon in Cancer to Leo 9:38 p.m.)   The lunar position emphasizes income, special

187

collections, the ability to gain through personal activities. Be ready for change, travel, variety, or contact with someone of the opposite sex who is dynamic, mercurial, and does have your best interests at heart. You'll be active socially; your strength might be depleted; you'll have to recall resolutions about proper rest, diet, and nutrition.

Tuesday, November 26 (Moon in Leo)   Go slow, play the waiting game. What you possess is valuable—your first offer only scratches the surface. Maintain your sense of self-worth. A favor you recently did for a Cancer will be returned—twofold. Be diplomatic and calm in the face of emotional hijinks. Taurus, Libra, and Scorpio figure prominently. Your lucky number is 6.

Wednesday, November 27 (Moon in Leo)   Post position special: number 1 P.P. in sixth race. Hot numbers combinations: 3 and 7, 1 and 4, 2 and 5. You'll have an opportunity to perfect techniques, to get rid of superfluous material. A Pisces will want to do everything he or she can to help you achieve your goal! A short trip will be part of today's scenario and will involve a relative.

Thursday, November 28 (Moon in Leo to Virgo 12:12 a.m.)   Today's emphasis is on showmanship, creativity, or an intensified relationship. What appeared lost will be found alive and kicking. You'll have the proverbial second chance to correct your mistakes, to recover a financial loss. An older person is fascinated and will encourage you to pursue your objective. A Cancer plays an outstanding role.

Friday, November 29 (Moon in Virgo)   You'll learn more about land, real estate, and development of a project. Protect your own interests; be aware of your need for security. Check details; be scrupulous about the fine print. Negotiations that had been continuous for almost two months will now be amicably resolved. A Virgo is in the picture.

Saturday, November 30 (Moon in Virgo to Libra 4:47 a.m.) The lunar position continues to accent conclusions, definitions, and dealings with persons involved with law, land, and real estate. You'll have universal appeal—people will listen to your opinions; many will consult you. The schedule also features romance and a search for a soul mate. Aries is involved. Your lucky number is 9.

DECEMBER 1991

Sunday, December 1 (Moon in Libra) Your feelings dominate logic. Ride with the tide. Focus on family relationships, potential, serious concern about a break from tradition. A long-distance call is necessary if travel plans are to be verified. The spotlight falls on children, adventure, discovery, and sensuality. Aries and Libra figure prominently.

Monday, December 2 (Moon in Libra to Scorpio 11:34 a.m.) A fresh start is indicated. The moon position continues to highlight attractiveness, creativity, sex appeal. A young person wants you to be responsible in a financial transaction. Be interested, sympathetic, encouraging but refuse to cosign. Leo and Aquarius play outstanding roles. Your lucky number is 1.

Tuesday, December 3 (Moon in Scorpio) Basic issues dominate. Focus on home activities such as cooking, repairs, plumbing, sewing. Cancer and Aquarius are genuinely interested in your welfare and will prove it. A relative who is being pulled in two directions seeks your support. Provide encouragement. Number 2 is your best bet.

Wednesday, December 4 (Moon in Scorpio to Sagittarius 8:33 p.m.) Lucky lottery numbers: 28, 8, 22, 14, 15, 1. The key is to diversify and to plan entertainment involving groups concerned with politics, charity, or the community. You'll be looked upon to set an example. Your social life sparkles; you could meet the right person. Sagittarius and another Gemini appreciate your sense of humor.

189

Thursday, December 5 (Moon in Sagittarius) You'll get a good health report. Intricate details unravel in connection with the job at hand. Focus also on skills in the kitchen, mending, repairs aimed at improving your safety. Your material recently submitted will be returned but not rejected. Revisions are required. Scorpio is represented.

Friday, December 6 (Moon in Sagittarius) Post position special: number 3 P.P. in second race; exacta: 3 and 2. The new moon position accents partnership, publicity, legal affairs, marriage. Be ready for diverse explanations from relatives about trips, visits, investigations. The key is to be analytical, to reject accusations without proof. Virgo is involved.

Saturday, December 7 (Moon in Sagittarius to Capricorn 7:41 a.m.) Your attention continues to center around home, domestic issues, budget, and delineation of a message dispatched by a family member who feels offended. Be diplomatic without entering into a silly game of accusations. Reject the temptation to say, "I told you so!" You'll recall this special day, and many will seek your opinions, reactions.

Sunday, December 8 (Moon in Capricorn) Spiritual values surface. Your inner feelings command attention: Focus on mystery, intrigue, the occult. An admirer talks about physical attraction, romance, a possible relationship. But practical matters have yet to be discussed, including payments and debts. Check the deadline on an insurance policy.

Monday, December 9 (Moon in Capricorn to Aquarius 8:27 p.m.) The emphasis falls on responsibility, pressure, a possible controversy with your employer, parent, or older person. Money could be the center of an issue. You'll be asked to meet a challenge and deadline—policies, circumstances, promises are involved. Despite some unpleasantness, there's a chance to make major progress. Number 8 is your best bet.

Tuesday, December 10 (Moon in Aquarius)   A recent mix-up concerning who owns what will be straightened. Money, debts, and payments were involved and concerned one close to you, uncle or aunt, partner or mate. A conclusion is reached regarding holiday activities, visits, a possible journey. A long-distance communication resolves a dilemma. Aries and Libra figure prominently.

Wednesday, December 11 (Moon in Aquarius)   Stress independence, creativity, and a willingness to make a fresh start. The lunar position also accents greater recognition of spiritual values. Get in touch with a relative at a distance. Travel indications are strong, but previous plans simply were not practical. A young person is involved, possibly a Leo. Your lucky number is 1.

Thursday, December 12 (Moon in Aquarius to Pisces 9:20 a.m.)   Your intuition is on target; a family member finally agrees to a plan relating to the upcoming holiday. Tonight features a reunion at a gourmet dinner. You are being pulled in two directions—Cancer and Aquarius relatives figure prominently. Your marital status comes under family scrutiny.

Friday, December 13 (Moon in Pisces)   Diversify; arrange entertainment for your employer or an older relative. Religious observances will be discussed. There is an abundance of talk about the true meaning of a holiday. Focus on diversity, versatility, curiosity, and awareness of your appearance, wardrobe, body image. Luck rides with you if you stick with number 3.

Saturday, December 14 (Moon in Pisces to Aries 8:07 p.m.)   Dig deep for information, realize that someone in authority may decide to test you. Accent the positive, and let others know you are willing to accept more responsibility. You could be seriously considered for promotion. The spotlight falls on leadership, community activity, the ability to arrange a program and to meet a deadline.

Sunday, December 15 (Moon in Aries)   You're due for a pleasant surprise, involving trips, visits, relatives, a prize. You'll gain through reading and writing, formats, submission of suggestions or ideas. When someone of the opposite sex is drawn to you, flirtation, and physical attraction brighten your day. Another Gemini plays a key role. Count on number 5.

Monday, December 16 (Moon in Aries)   Your performance rating will be outstanding. The moon in the eleventh sector of solar horoscope coincides with your ability to win friends and influence people. Your configuration also means advancement in connection with your business, career, and community activity. Your popularity moves up—you could win a contest. Try this triple play: 6, 4, 2.

Tuesday, December 17 (Moon in Aries to Taurus 3:10 a.m.)   Someone wants something for nothing—you might be the target. Know it, be alert, be suspicious of obsequious statements. One who calls you sweetie pie is miles away from being sincere. Look behind the scenes, define meanings, and avoid a get-rich-quick scheme. The lunar position continues to emphasize speculation, popularity, charisma, and physical attraction.

Wednesday, December 18 (Moon in Taurus)   This can be your power play day! Astrological and numerical cycles relate to authority, responsibility, and a chance to hit the financial jackpot. You'll have access to inside information from some one associated with a special interest group, institution, or hospital. Your ideas will be sought in connection with a community or charitable campaign.

Thursday, December 19 (Moon in Taurus to Gemini 6:22 a.m.)   Efforts made yesterday will now bear fruit. Much that occurs continues to be hidden, obscured, behind the scenes. Your influence will be felt where previously doors were closed. Many will hear of you as you strike a chord of universal appeal. Personal horizons will broaden. Aries and Libra are in the picture. Your lucky number is 9.

Friday, December 20 (Moon in Gemini)   Post position special: number 7 P.P. in third race; exacta: 1 and 1; pick six: 2, 4, 7, 1, 3, 1; winning colors: yellow and gold. The moon in your sign highlights initiative, timing, luck, intuition, sex appeal. You'll be at the right place at a crucial moment. Show your independence, style, creativity. Be willing to test your own capabilities.

Saturday, December 21 (Moon in Gemini to Cancer 6:55 a.m.)   The full moon and lunar eclipse in Gemini could indicate this is a night when you fall madly in love. Inhibitions tend to be tossed aside. Emotions dominate logic. Attention centers around a special relationship, marital status, family obligations. An older female, possibly your mother, might ask, "Are you sure?"

Sunday, December 22 (Moon in Cancer)   As a burden is lifted, your financial picture becomes brighter. Attention centers around social activities, communication, a possible purchase which adds to wardrobe. Check legal documents; be positive about deadlines for payments. Another Gemini plays an outstanding role. Your lucky number is 3.

Monday, December 23 (Moon in Cancer to Leo 6:39 a.m.)   You get more about payments, collections, and debts that can be wiped off the books. Some material requires revision but can still be considered a winner. Today's scenario also features mystery, intrigue, a revelation about a trust fund or possible inheritance. A secret investment could come to light.

Tuesday, December 24 (Moon in Leo)   On this Christmas Eve, the moon in Leo accents desires, fulfillment, receipt of large gifts. You'll have more fun with wrappings and ribbons than you might have thought possible. The spotlight also falls on children, variety, communication, and visits. You'll receive a touching tribute from one who recently seemed to go out of your life.

Wednesday, December 25 (Moon in Leo to Virgo 7:24 a.m.)   This Christmas Day will be memorable because harmony is restored on the home front. Music, gifts, and displays of genuine affection mark a family celebration. Taurus, Libra, Scorpio, and Leo will be especially meaningful. A major gift will help beautify surroundings; it will require care, attention, and upkeep.

Thursday, December 26 (Moon in Virgo)   The spotlight falls on home, security, and your sense of discrimination. You'll be grateful for what occurred during the past week, especially on Christmas Day. You are now more analytical about the gifts you gave and received. Don't let the holiday spirit escape. A Pisces who helped you in the past vows to always stand by you!"

Friday, December 27 (Moon in Virgo to Libra 10:38 a.m.)   Post position special: number 6 P.P. fifth race; hot daily doubles: 2 and 4, 6 and 5, 5 and 7, 3 and 3. As a relationship intensifies, you'll know where you stand; love and romance are back on track but not without some bumps. Cancer and Capricorn figure prominently. Funding will be approved.

Saturday, December 28 (Moon in Libra)   Reach beyond your previous limitations today to express your personal style and creativity. The urge to speculate is strong—you'll have luck where before you might have failed. An Aries helps you to use your sales ability, successfully. A Libra admirer also offers support.

Sunday, December 29 (Moon in Libra to Scorpio 5:04 p.m.)   Focus on children, variety, change, travel, and communication. The emphasis continues on emotional responses, speculation, and a willingness to test the waters. You will make a fresh start despite objections by a young relative. A financial obligation is not your own, and you need not be held back by it. Leo and Aquarius play roles. Stick to number 1.

Monday, December 30 (Moon in Scorpio)   As the New Year approaches, you straighten out family relationships; you actually make a resolution which can be maintained. Focus on intellectual curiosity; make inquiries which bring positive responses. Take care of pets, dependents, and polish off basic cooking and sewing chores.

Tuesday, December 31 (Moon in Scorpio)   This can be one of your liveliest New Year's Eve celebrations. Forces are scattered, people say things they might mean at the moment. Be sociable but don't expect others to keep their promises. Accent fun, frolic, moderation. Take special care in traffic; avoid driving with those who have been drinking heavily. A long-distance call brings best wishes from one who left suddenly. Sagittarius and another Gemini figure prominently. Your lucky number is 3.

JANUARY 1992

Wednesday, January 1 (Moon in Scorpio to Sagittarius 2:30 a.m.)   On this first day of 1992, you feel a surge of power, relating to basic issues, employment, communicating with those who share your interests. You'll have a positive inner conviction about your future survival. You'll say, "I made it this far and now I know I can go all the way!" Cancer is involved.

Thursday, January 2 (Moon in Sagittarius)   A long-standing project requires reexamination. Be aware of the state of the art. Toss aside outmoded procedures. Focus on universal appeal, public image, legal affairs, and marital status. Aries and Libra figure prominently. At the track: post-position special—number 8 P.P. in ninth race.

Friday, January 3 (Moon in Sagittarius to Capricorn 2:09 p.m.)   Don't hesitate to start a new project. Be aware, alert, and get to the heart of matters. But avoid heavy lifting. Use brains instead of brawn. If you're seriously considering marriage, take a new and different approach, especially with Leo and Aquarius. Your lucky number is 1.

Saturday, January 4 (Moon in Capricorn)   The new moon, solar eclipse falls in the area of your chart relating to money, which is regulated or processed by a third party or agent. Dig deep for information. Follow a hunch. When two family members vie for your favor, keep your emotional equilibrium. Lucky lottery numbers: 11, 22, 33, 29, 44, 48. An Aquarian plays a role.

Sunday, January 5 (Moon in Capricorn)   Diversify, display humor, and accept a social invitation that might involve a short journey. You could meet a person who eventually will play a significant role in your life. Check insurance payments, and don't neglect bills that are due. Gemini and Sagittarius figure prominently.

Monday, January 6 (Moon in Capricorn to Aquarius 2:59 a.m.)   A grand opportunity exists to rebuild on a solid base. What had been an obstacle might be transformed into a stepping-stone. You'll get a favorable health report. Today's cycle also highlights care of pets, relations with those who rely upon your judgment. Taurus and Scorpio play outstanding roles.

Tuesday, January 7 (Moon in Aquarius)   You'll be telling more than one person, "This is one of the strangest Tuesdays I've ever experienced!" Focus on spirituality, language, and communication. At times you'll feel as if you're floating. You'll be musing, "Even solid objects seem to lack reality!" Gemini, Virgo, and Sagittarius are in the picture.

Wednesday, January 8 (Moon in Aquarius to Pisces 3:52 p.m.)   Attention centers around your home, a family member who seriously contemplates a long journey. Focus continues on spirituality, education, a desire to gain knowledge. The lunar aspect is favorable, and what had been the cause of friction will be removed. Taurus, Libra, and Scorpio figure prominently.

Thursday, January 9 (Moon in Pisces)   The moon enters an area of your chart relating to achievement, prestige, your standing in the community. You'll be presented with what appears to be a legitimate opportunity for financial gain. Caution: Insist on an outline, definition of terms. Pisces and Virgo figure in today's scenario. Your lucky number is 7.

Friday, January 10 (Moon in Pisces)   You'll get results from a direct effort made approximately nine days ago. You've recently met someone who "means business." Ignore rumors, speculations that lack foundation. You're going places—finally. A professional superior will seriously consider promotion.

Saturday, January 11 (Moon in Pisces to Aries 3:22 a.m.)   Lucky lottery numbers: 12, 7, 17, 45, 43, 18. More people are interested in your observations and actions. You now appeal to a wide audience. A love relationship, cool for the past two weeks, will be ignited. Aries and Libra play outstanding roles. A project is completed.

Sunday, January 12 (Moon in Aries)   Today's scenario highlights friends, hopes, wishes, a love relationship. You'll be ruled more by your heart than by logic. Be aware, alert, and protect yourself in emotional clinches. Insist on getting to the core of matters. You'll learn plenty about the aspirations of a loved one. Don't be surprised!

Monday, January 13 (Moon in Aries to Taurus 12:00 noon)   You'll be saying, "This is going to be just the opposite of a blue Monday!" Puzzle pieces fall into place. Your intuition is on target. A reunion with loved one is featured. Elements of timing and surprise work for you. A major wish will be fulfilled. Cancer, Capricorn, and Aquarius are featured.

Tuesday, January 14 (Moon in Taurus)   You'll have more room, and fun will replace gloom. Someone temporarily confined to home or hospital communicates. A serious discussion involves diet and nutrition. Your blood-sugar level requires consideration. Generally, however, you'll have reason to celebrate. What was feared turns out to be the proverbial paper tiger.

Wednesday, January 15 (Moon in Taurus to Gemini 4:55 p.m.)   Lucky lottery numbers: 40, 21, 22, 6, 15, 2. Post-position special: number 4 P.P. in fourth race. Alternate selection: number 7 P.P. in third race. You'll have special luck by sticking with 7 and possibly with this triple play: 3, 7, 1. Taurus, Leo, and Scorpio play significant roles.

Thursday, January 16 (Moon in Gemini)   The moon in your sign, plus other factors, relates to reading and writing, change, travel, sex appeal. You might be declaring, "What a Thursday!" Curiosity is spurred, contacts are made with people who are dynamic, intellectual, and who appreciate your unique talents. Your lucky number is 5.

Friday, January 17 (Moon in Gemini to Cancer 6:26 p.m.)   Although you'll be saying, "Thank God it's Friday," you actually were stimulated this week and are not necessarily happy to see it end. Your judgment and intuition will be accurate. A large home appliance is likely to be obtained. A financial discussion involves a close family member. Your lucky number is 6.

Saturday, January 18 (Moon in Cancer)   Hold off on a money deal. There could be a hidden clause. Keep your own options open. Insist on a clear definition of terms. Tonight could be made for romance. But protect yourself in emotional clinches. Focus on illusion, beauty, the necessity for discretion. A Pisces figures prominently.

Sunday, January 19 (Moon in Cancer to Leo 5:57 p.m.)   Recently a member of the opposite sex complimented you on selection of colors. The full moon occurs in that section of your chart relating to personal possessions, payments, and collections. An article that had been lost, missing, or stolen will be recovered. An older person, possibly a parent, makes peace.

Monday, January 20 (Moon in Leo)   What had been "left hanging" can now be attended to in an efficient way. Today's lunar position emphasizes close relatives, trips, visits, and basic concepts. Perceive potential. Previous limitations will be lifted. The answer to a question concerning a possible journey is affirmative. Aries plays a paramount role.

Tuesday, January 21 (Moon in Leo to Virgo 5:22 p.m.)   Stress initiative, pioneering spirit, the ability to remove yourself from "mob thinking." Some will say you're being selfish, that you are being aloof, that you want only to hear the sound of your own voice. Reject these statements and accusations. Refuse to be held back by mediocrity.

Wednesday, January 22 (Moon in Virgo)   Continue to stress individuality. You'll have luck by sticking with number 2. The moon position highlights completion of a long-standing transaction. The emphasis falls on building material, quality, and durability. An older person says, "You've earned a reward and you will receive it!" Leo is involved.

Thursday, January 23 (Moon in Virgo to Libra 6:43 p.m.)   Diversify, ask questions, reject superficial responses. Property value will be estimated—obtain more than one opinion. You are being considered for what might be a prestigious position. Say, "That's fine, but I can't live on air." That means let others know where you stand. Your lucky number is 3.

Friday, January 24 (Moon in Libra)   It's time to revise, revamp, and remodel. Today's favorable lunar aspect coincides with sex appeal, speculation, the ability to hear the sound of your own voice. This means you develop individual style. A gentle member of the opposite sex wants to provide tender, loving care. Scorpio is represented.

Saturday, January 25 (Moon in Libra to Scorpio 11:32 p.m.)   Correspondence or calls lead to someone who will play an important role in your life. A date or engagement tonight proves exciting and meaningful. A member of the opposite sex makes a declaration of love. Be receptive, but avoid being gullible. Maintain a balance between believing and being foolish.

Sunday, January 26 (Moon in Scorpio)   Spiritual values surface. Attention centers around discovery, children, variety, change of scenery. You'll gain by opening lines of communication. Reading, writing, and the process of learning will be featured. Share knowledge with one who is dynamic, sensitive, and psychic.

Monday, January 27 (Moon in Scorpio)   One who wants something for nothing might feel you are a prime target. Protect your own interests. The spotlight falls on employment, health, pets, and people who rely upon your judgment. Define your terms and work behind the scenes. You'll have access to privileged information. Your lucky number is 7.

Tuesday, January 28 (Moon in Scorpio to Sagittarius 8:20 a.m.)   The spotlight falls on responsibility, deadline, review of an insurance policy. A warranty for an automobile or a large household product could be located. The lunar position continues to accent basic issues, recovery of lost objects, contacting someone who helped with repair work less than two months ago.

Wednesday, January 29 (Moon in Sagittarius)   You'll finish a project; the moon position "guarantees" attention to legal affairs and public relations. Someone from your past makes an appearance, a relationship could be resumed. Attention also centers around partnership, reputation, image, and marriage. Libra will figure prominently.

Thursday, January 30 (Moon in Sagittarius to Capricorn 8:07 p.m.)   The lunar position highlights speculation, a public appearance, added popularity. This cycle reveals you are due to make a fresh start in a new direction. You'll get to the heart of matters. An admirer will say, "It must be your hair or clothes, because you seem like a different person!"

Friday, January 31 (Moon in Capricorn) You'll get a definite answer about a legal problem. Two people are involved; one says let's go, the other insists on a waiting period. Show self-confidence, a sense of your own worth. In matters relating to procedure, choose the unorthodox. Leo and Aquarius figure prominently. Your lucky number is 2.

FEBRUARY 1992

Saturday, February 1 (Moon in Capricorn) Someone who knows plenty about investments, loans, percentages will be part of your Saturday night. What begins as mild assignation could become meaningful. Romance is definitely part of scenario. Lucky Lottery: 9, 19, 10, 27, 28, 44. Aries, Libra will figure prominently.

Sunday, February 2 (Moon in Capricorn to Aquarius 9:09 a.m.) A relative insists, "Let us be together and act as if we are a family!" Focus on unity, spiritual values, gourmet dining tonight. A Cancer wants you to succeed, will lend the benefit of experience. A Capricorn perhaps a bit harsh, says, "Please get going!"

Monday, February 3 (Moon in Aquarius) Experiences 24 hours ago can now be useful. The New Moon accents communication, education, ability to perceive your own potential. A publishing opportunity is imminent. Your intuition rings true. First impressions are on target. Cancer, Capricorn, Aquarius play paramount roles.

Tuesday, February 4 (Moon in Aquarius to Pisces 9:51 p.m.) It comes to you in a flash that you are qualified to take charge of your own destiny! You'll shine at a social affair, people will want to be with you, and the focus will be on versatility, adaptability, and sense of humor. You'll be conscious of your weight and body image. Another Gemini is involved. Your lucky number is 3.

Wednesday, February 5 (Moon in Pisces) The lunar position highlights communication, travel, and romance. You are idealistic, especially this month and this day. Don't permit others to dampen your spirit. Your soul mate is not merely an abstract equation. The concept is more solid, and realistic than might be imagined. Today you'll know it!

Thursday, February 6 (Moon in Pisces) An inquiry made less than one week ago brings a favorable response. This involves a short trip, possibly working with your hands. The emphasis also falls on reading, writing, an exchange of ideas. Someone of the opposite sex is in a mood to flirt. Virgo, Sagittarius, and another Gemini are involved. Plan number 5 to win.

Friday, February 7 (Moon in Pisces to Aries 9:15 a.m.) The spotlight falls on home and a family member who could have made it, or been promoted! Show that you are not envious, express sincere good wishes and congratulations. In your high cycle, you overcome obstacles in a grand manner. Your lucky number is 8.

Saturday, February 8 (Moon in Aries) Define terms, look behind the scenes, be confident in knowing that your fondest hopes and aspirations are due to become realities. This Saturday night features creativity, romance, a definite gain where ambitions are concerned. The financial picture is bright due to career or business advancement.

Sunday, February 9 (Moon in Aries to Taurus 6:36 p.m.) The moon occupies that part of your chart relating to popularity, aspirations, the ability to win friends and influence people. Say your piece and let the chips fall where they may. This can be a powerful day of intensity and dedication, which could give you a chance to hit the financial jackpot. A love relationship grows strong.

Monday, February 10 (Moon in Taurus) Take special care with fire and electricity. Where automobiles are concerned, be wary of "backfire" and spark plugs. A project that had been shunted aside commands attention.

You'll meet an Aries who could become instrumental in transforming wishes into actualities.

Tuesday, February 11 (Moon in Taurus)   Stress independence, and eradicate suspicions based on superstition. Light will be shed on an area previously hidden. You can now get an excellent view of what occurs backstage. You could participate in a television quiz program. Leo and Aquarius figure prominently. Your lucky number is 1.

Wednesday, February 12 (Moon in Aquarius to Gemini 1:08 a.m.)   You are capable of bringing together people with opposing views. The moon moves toward your sign but remains in your "house of seclusion." The emphasis continues on secrets, subconscious thoughts, and dreams that could prove prophetic. You could gain access to information previously censored.

Thursday, February 13 (Moon in Gemini)   The moon in your sign, plus the numerical cycle, reveals a general aura of confusion. On the positive side, this can be transformed into curiosity, humor, versatility, and significant inquiries. You are more conscious now than in previous days of your appearance and wardrobe, of your weight and body image.

Friday, February 14 (Moon in Gemini to Cancer 4:31 a.m.)   Your cycle is high, and you'll receive more tokens of affection on this Valentine's Day than in previous years. A feeling of restriction is temporary. Choose an unorthodox procedure to reach your goals. It's time to remodel, review, and revise. Refuse to be held back by those who lack faith or talent.

Saturday, February 15 (Moon in Cancer)   Be ready for change, travel, variety, and ways of earning more money. An unusual call or message relates to valuables and personal possessions. Focus on reading and writing, adding to your knowledge. You'll be information oriented. Flirtation is also part of today's dynamic scenario. Your lucky number is 5.

Sunday, February 16 (Moon in Cancer to Leo 5:15 a.m.) Stay close to home if possible. Attention centers around beauty, art objects, music, and recognition of spiritual values. Focus on family, domestic issues, and special activities involving those close to you. Strive for harmony and accent diplomacy. Taurus and Libra play key roles.

Monday, February 17 (Moon in Leo) You'll say, "I might have done it yesterday, but I'm certainly going to do it today." Some tasks have been avoided, but you're back in rhythm now, ready to finish what was started one week ago. A short trip involves a Pisces or Virgo relative.

Tuesday, February 18 (Moon in Leo to Virgo 4:47 a.m.) Today's full moon occupies an area of chart associated with romance, speculation, and creativity. Feelings are intense, and nothing happens halfway. Your popularity zooms upward, but be sure to keep your sense of balance and perspective. A long-distance call invites you to an unusual social affair. Your lucky number is 8.

Wednesday, February 19 (Moon in Virgo) Lucky lottery numbers: 5, 16, 24, 35, 18, 44. Attention centers around completion of a long-standing project, negotiation. An older person, possibly a parent, is concerned about the security and durability of a product or property. Aries and Libra figure prominently. Romance is no stranger.

Thursday, February 20 (Moon in Virgo to Libra 5:04 a.m.) Be independent; take a fresh start. You can make progress now if you are discriminating. Choose quality and throw out outmoded methods. You'll attract someone who is revitalized when near you! Leo and Aquarius play dynamic roles. Your lucky number is 1.

Friday, February 21 (Moon in Libra) At the track: post-position special—number 6 P.P. in fifth race. Alternate selection: number 9 P.P. in eighth race. Pick six: 2, 6, 5, 4, 6, 1., A reunion with a relative is indicated.

You'll be dining on food associated with another nation. An Aquarian is good company.

Saturday, February 22 (Moon in Libra to Scorpio 8:11 a.m.) Your intellectual curiosity is aroused by a message or call. Focus on style, creativity, and physical attraction. What appeared out of reach is actually available, very close to home. Lucky lottery numbers: 22, 18, 33, 4, 9, 4. Keep recent diet, exercise, and nutrition resolutions.

Sunday, February 23 (Moon in Scorpio) Stick to rules and regulations. Today's emphasis is on employment, pets, and dependents. Someone who serves you deserves praise. Read between the lines of special source material. You'll be dealing with creative, stubborn people, both giving and taking.

Monday, February 24 (Moon in Scorpio to Sagittarius 3:26 p.m.) Be ready for change, travel, variety, a flirtation that could be transformed into serious relationship. The lunar position highlights a chance encounter with one you previously ignored or took for granted. Virgo, Sagittarius, and another Gemini figure prominently. Your lucky number is 5.

Tuesday, February 25 (Moon in Sagittarius) Domestic adjustment is featured. Attention centers around a partnership, cooperative efforts, and public relations. Get legal papers in order. Check accounts. You'll be concerned with your marital status. Before this evening is over, you'll be involved in a discussion of a singer-entertainer and whether or not that person has real talent.

Wednesday, February 26 (Moon in Sagittarius) The emphasis falls on distance, language, a chance to improve qualifications for a task that could include an overseas journey. Be discriminating, selective, and refuse to be intimidated. Do not equate delay with defeat. Someone who made an initial offer might possibly have lacked authority.

Thursday, February 27 (Moon in Sagittarius to Capricorn 2:33 a.m.) While papers are being shuffled, a long-distance call buoys your spirits. The emphasis falls on universal appeal, completion of a cycle, the testing of a relationship. *Note:* Take care around fire, electricity, and automobiles. Cancer and Capricorn play major roles. You'll have more responsibility along with a chance to hit the financial jackpot.

Friday, February 28 (Moon in Capricorn) The emphasis continues on deadline pressure, a strong love relationship. Tonight you'll say, "I am fully confident that I can fulfill obligations!" The cycle is finished, and you're in a position to review your past and to perceive future potential. Aries is in the picture. Your lucky number is 9.

Saturday, February 29 (Moon in Capricorn to Aquarius 3:34 p.m.) You'll be hearing plenty about "leap year." Take note of your own life and love. A partner or mate is concerned about income, personal possessions, an article that had been lost, missing, or stolen. The answer to this dilemma is to make a fresh start in a different direction.

MARCH 1992

Sunday, March 1 (Moon in Aquarius) Hopes are revitalized—a young person, possibly Leo, seems suddenly to be talking sense instead of nonsense. Attention also centers around style, romance, and creativity. You'll say, "This is a wonderful way to start the month!" But no heavy lifting! Your lucky number is 1.

Monday, March 2 (Moon in Aquarius) Today's agenda features reunions, gourmet dining, relationships that bridge distance and language barriers. The spotlight falls on career, promotion, prestige, and general standing. Someone from another nation talks about food, customs, and employment possibilities. A physical attraction spices up this evening.

Tuesday, March 3 (Moon in Aquarius to Pisces 4:11 a.m.)   A favorable lunar aspect emphasizes education, spiritual values, a possible journey. As your popularity increases, social activities also accelerate. Someone you respect comments on your wardrobe and your weight. Get diet and nutrition advice, if needed. Sagittarius and another Gemini play significant roles.

Wednesday, March 4 (Moon in Pisces)   A decision is reached that favors your career and income. The new moon occupies that area of your chart associated with promotion, direction, authority, and business. Attention centers around references and qualifications. A love affair will be back on track. Your lucky number is 4.

Thursday, March 5 (Moon in Pisces to Aries 3:07 p.m.)   Get promises in writing, and open lines of communication. Someone of the opposite sex makes declarations, tells of intent. You'll be working with your hands. Virgo, Sagittarius, and another Gemini figure prominently. At the track, choose number 3 post position in the second race.

Friday, March 6 (Moon in Aries)   The emphasis falls on domestic adjustment and the ability to make wishes come true. Accent romance, style, creativity, and powers of persuasion. Some will say, "You really seem to know how to win friends and influence people!" Taurus and Libra play outstanding roles. Play number 6 to win.

Saturday, March 7 (Moon in Aries)   Use your ability to read between the lines. Your psychic impressions prove correct. Emphasize glamour, mystery, and intrigue. Be discreet; don't tell all. The lunar position continues to highlight popularity, speculation, and winning ways. Your performance will be rated superb. Your lucky number is 9.

Sunday, March 8 (Moon in Aries to Taurus 12:05 a.m.)   People will talk about getting down to business, but you'll be concerned mainly with spiritual values. Focus on intensity, responsibility, the ability to meet a deadline. A love relationship grows strong. Good news comes via a telephone call or message—it relates to your career or salary.

Monday, March 9 (Moon in Taurus)   A secret meeting could result in a unique tour of a hospital, home, or institution. A long-range project commands attention and could eventually involve a journey. You'll strike a chord of universal appeal. People will be drawn to you, will confide problems and aspirations—an Aries, especially.

Tuesday, March 10 (Moon in Taurus to Gemini 7:03 p.m.)   Show the independence that comes as a result of enlightenment. You'll have more knowledge in connection with "hidden values." You might be receiving or giving a diamond. As your cycle moves up, you'll be at the right place at a crucial moment. Leo plays a paramount role.

Wednesday, March 11 (Moon in Gemini)   Lucky lottery numbers: 30, 5, 33, 35, 45, 1. Relatives who had a disagreement two weeks ago will come together, will agree that feuding accomplishes nothing. Dining out could help break the ice, and provide laughter and relaxation. Cancer, Capricorn, and Aquarius figure prominently.

Thursday, March 12 (Moon in Gemini to Cancer 11:50 a.m.)   You'll be told to dispense with formalities and emphasize friendship and conviviality. The moon in your sign highlights your personality, appearance, and excellent timing. Some will say, "It is a pleasure to be with you!" Show your colors: silver, bright green, yellow. Accept a social invitation. Your lucky number is 3.

Friday, March 13 (Moon in Cancer)   You might be saying, "This has not been unlucky for me!" The lunar position accents income, personal possessions, the ability to locate lost articles. Rules and regulations ultimately favor your cause and aspirations. Check bills, count your change, and be sensitive to your credit rating.

Saturday, March 14 (Moon in Cancer to Leo 2:20 p.m.) This could be a lively Saturday. Today's scenario highlights change, travel, flirtation, a unique communication with a member of the opposite sex. You'll enjoy reading, writing, and satisfying your curiosity. An excellent day for checking with an investment counselor or banker. Another Gemini is involved.

Sunday, March 15 (Moon in Leo) You're likely to be concerned with home appliances, family gatherings, and food. The emphasis falls on security, domestic adjustment, and a surprise visit by a relative. Keep your sense of fitness and humor, and your plans flexible. You'll receive a gift representing a real token of affection. Your lucky number is 6.

Monday, March 16 (Moon in Leo to Virgo 3:13 p.m.) People who make grandiose gestures or promises could be sincere but also misinformed. This applies to relatives or a visitor who seems suddenly to have the solution to all your problems. Rely on your own counsel, meditation, and spiritual values. Define terms and check legal agreements. A Pisces figures prominently.

Tuesday, March 17 (Moon in Virgo) Whether or not you are Irish, you'll be made aware of this "celebration." St. Patrick possibly did rid Ireland of snakes, although history indicates Ireland never had snakes in the first place. Ride with the tide, and enjoy the spirit of today's festivities. Cancer and Capricorn play significant roles. Your lucky number is 8.

Wednesday, March 18 (Moon in Virgo to Libra 3:55 p.m.) The full moon position highlights property, the completion of a transaction aimed at improving your financial security. Stress universal appeal, and refuse to be limited by those who lack foresight. Instead, do all you can to broaden your personal horizons. You'll discover new opportunities in a dramatic way.

Thursday, March 19 (Moon in Libra) This is one of the most exciting, romantic Thursdays you've experienced! There's plenty of activity, change, travel, and variety. Today's scenario features children, speculation, and physical attraction. You'll get to the heart of matters, and you'll also make a fresh start in a different direction.

Friday, March 20 (Moon in Libra to Scorpio 6:20 p.m.) Overcome a tendency to brood. A recent contact with an exciting, dynamic person, possibly a Leo, should be a reason for joy and celebration, not for wondering or brooding. A family member acquiesces to a request relating to property or budget. A Cancer will figure prominently.

Saturday, March 21 (Moon in Scorpio) Focus on people who perform unique services. The key is to be versatile, to look beyond the immediate. As your popularity increases, social activities accelerate. Someone you respect comments on your appearance, wardrobe, or weight. Sagittarius and another Gemini play major roles. Your lucky number is 3.

Sunday, March 22 (Moon in Scorpio to Sagittarius 12:13 a.m.) Be willing to revise, review, and rebuild. Family members talk about a possible inheritance, investments, money that a relative once promised but has not been forthcoming. You'll personally realize that self-reliance is the key to relevant answers. Taurus and Scorpio play outstanding roles.

Monday, March 23 (Moon in Sagittarius) The key is communication, reading and writing, realizing that flirtation might not lead to anything else. Protect yourself in emotional clinches. Two friends, both commanding your respect, express opposite views. Realize that by attempting to please everyone you will please no one. Be yourself!

Tuesday, March 24 (Moon in Sagittarius) Attention centers around your family, home, and marital status. Also commanding attention: your public image, relations with people, legal affairs, and special documents that include birth certificate and passport. The key to accomplishment is diplomacy. By attempting to force issues, you merely succeed in creating animosity.

Wednesday, March 25 (Moon in Sagittarius to Capricorn 10:08 a.m.) In matters of speculation, try this triple play: 3, 7, 1. Your psychic powers become evident. It's best to work alone. Attempting to crowd too many appointments or arrangements would represent an error. Spiritual values surface, and you become more aware of the fact that you must take greater charge of your own destiny.

Thursday, March 26 (Moon in Capricorn) At the track: You'll have special luck by sticking with the number 8 post position. Winning colors: dull purples, gray, green, black. Jockeys born under Pisces are likely to ride in, mounting upset winners. Away from the track, you'll learn of a deadline and chance to hit the financial jackpot.

Friday, March 27 (Moon in Capricorn to Aquarius 10:44 p.m.) In a gambling casino, these six numbers could prove significant, especially while trying your hand at Keno: 80, 72, 9, 5, 8, 44. It's an excellent time for completing a project, for reaching more people, and for checking travel arrangements. You're capable now of overcoming distance and language barriers.

Saturday, March 28 (Moon in Aquarius) Lucky lottery numbers: 19, 1, 27, 35, 34, 15. Stress independence, creativity, and a willingness to get to the heart of matters in connection with style or a member of opposite sex. Do not play second fiddle! You'll learn about a financial arrangement made by a partner or mate.

Sunday, March 29 (Moon in Aquarius) Spiritual values are shared by your family. Attention centers around metaphysical subjects, travel, the ability to communicate abstract concepts. Romance refuses to be a stranger. Strive for universal appeal, and prepare a gourmet dinner for special people, including two members of your family who might be born under Cancer.

Monday, March 30 (Moon in Aquarius to Pisces 11:23 a.m.)   The emphasis falls on communication, publishing, advertising, the ability to promote your product and yourself. There'll be more social activity than usual for Monday. Special: Stick to a resolution concerning diet and nutrition. Your wardrobe will be noticed. Dress to impress.

Tuesday, March 31 (Moon in Pisces)   What you have been waiting for will finally arrive. Filling out forms and red tape were involved, but now you have it and this could add to your financial security. At the track: postposition special—number 4 P.P. in ninth race. Alternate selection: number 7 P.P. in third race.

APRIL 1992

Wednesday, April 1 (Moon in Pisces to Aries 10:04 p.m.)   Usually not many people will fool you, but today family members could help you fall victim to self-deception. Be a sympathetic listener to various woes, but refuse to become inextricably involved. Cooperation is required in connection with your career or business. A money question is resolved.

Thursday, April 2 (Moon in Aries)   Diversify, and show your sense of perspective and humor. Allies are attracted when you laugh at your own foibles. Many express a desire to be with you, to relax, to share your interests. The top person notices that you get more results with smiles. Your lucky number is 3.

Friday, April 3 (Moon in Aries)   The new moon position accents friends, aspirations, and fulfillment of desires. You'll receive a meaningful compliment on your performance. Written material figures prominently. Your popularity zooms upward, and you could win a contest. Use your powers of persuasion. Watch Scorpio.

Saturday, April 4 (Moon in Aries to Taurus 6:18 a.m.)   Projects or contacts begun less than 24 hours ago will bear fruit. Today's emphasis is on variety, communication, speculation, and flirtation. You'll say about this evening: "This is one Saturday night I will remember, and I intend to have a good time!" Response: Right on!

Sunday, April 5 (Moon in Taurus)   A family gathering relates to unique procedures and services. The moon position highlights discretion, secrets, institutions, and visits to those confined to home or hospital. The emphasis also falls on music, art, and reading material. Taurus, Libra, and Scorpio play outstanding roles. Stick with 6.

Monday, April 6 (Moon in Taurus to Gemini 12:33 p.m.)   You'll remember a commitment made yesterday, and you can know it will be fulfilled. The key is to separate facts from illusion. Delay is on your side—play the waiting game. Refuse to be rushed or chided into premature action. Pisces and Virgo figure prominently. Your lucky number is 9.

Tuesday, April 7 (Moon in Gemini)   The moon in your sign highlights your ability to be at the right place at a crucial moment. Focus on power, authority, an intensified love relationship. Make a public appearance, and show your colors: silver, bright green, yellow. Tuesday night you'll say, "I'm glad I did it my way!"

Wednesday, April 8 (Moon in Gemini to Cancer 5:18 p.m.)   You'll finish a key project. A romance flourishes. You'll perceive potential. Your judgment and intuition will be on target. Take the initiative in getting rid of outmoded methods and procedures. Travel plans are currently formulating, if only in your subconscious. Your lucky number is 9.

Thursday, April 9 (Moon in Cancer)   Be ready to revise, review, to imprint your own style. Someone of the opposite sex says, "I can't explain it, but you are more exciting than ever!" It is not necessary to look for reasons. Love dominates; you'll feel fulfilled and capable of getting to the heart of matters. Play number 3 to win.

Friday, April 10 (Moon in Cancer to Leo 8:46 p.m.)
The emphasis falls on family, home, and financial planning. Someone close to you seeks counsel, wants to "form a partnership." There are too many doubts and options. Refuse to make a definite commitment, especially where an investment is concerned. A Cancer plays a role.

Saturday, April 11 (Moon in Leo) Lucky lottery numbers: 2, 20, 31, 4, 17, 19. Rise above petty differences—your intuition is on target and could enable you to pick a profitable number. For you today, your best number could be 3. Diversify, and make an appointment with one knowledgeable about spiritual matters.

Sunday, April 12 (Moon in Leo to Virgo 11:09 p.m.)
Build on a solid base. A relationship that had been sidetracked once again synchronizes with your desires. What starts as a blind date or casual meeting could be transformed into a meaningful relationship. Taurus, Leo, and Scorpio play significant roles. Play number 4 to win.

Monday, April 13 (Moon in Virgo) A trip might be delayed—which could actually be to your advantage. Take special care in traffic, and avoid being with heavy drinkers. Keep company with people capable of staying sober. This message should become increasingly clear. Gemini, Virgo, and Sagittarius are in the picture.

Tuesday, April 14 (Moon in Virgo) Stress creativity, beautify your surroundings, and pay attention to the purchase of theater tickets. A promise made by a relative will be fulfilled—this could include money. Focus on harmony, a special relationship with Taurus, Libra, or Scorpio. Your lucky number is 6.

Wednesday, April 15 (Moon in Virgo to Libra 1:11 a.m.) Be discriminating, select quality, and steer clear of "committees." Be selective, work as an individual, and avoid those persons who want you always to "do it their way." Do it your own way! You'll be concerned with the appearance of home, security, and removal of safety hazards. Bet on number 9.

Thursday, April 16 (Moon in Libra)   Once again you have proof that your own ideas suit you much better than concepts that others would have you follow. Stress authority, power, the ability to work under pressure. Check deadlines for bills, especially those involving your automobile and insurance. Capricorn and Cancer are in the picture.

Friday, April 17 (Moon in Libra to Scorpio 4:10 a.m.)   Today's full moon position highlights emotional responses, physical attraction, the ability to say with conviction, "I do love you!" The scenario also highlights speculation, the excitement of a discovery, and successful dealings with children. Aries and Libra play meaningful roles.

Saturday, April 18 (Moon in Scorpio)   Just three days ago you made a resolution to "do it my way." Now take the initiative, express your ideas, actually "do it your way." The emphasis on basic issues, dependents, and care of pets. Leo and Aquarius figure prominently. Your lucky number is 1.

Sunday, April 19 (Moon in Scorpio to Sagittarius 9:40 a.m.)   You need cooperation if today is to be constructive. Focus on family, safety, and security. The lunar position accents health, work methods, pets, and people who rely upon you. Special: A vision or psychic impression is on target. Cancer and Capricorn play paramount roles. Count on number 2.

Monday, April 20 (Moon in Sagittarius)   Wishes have been coming true in a surprising way. Today you might now realize that you do have plenty for which to be thankful! Legal papers are needed if a partnership is to be formed. Focus also on popularity, social activity, and marital status. A Sagittarian is in the picture.

Tuesday, April 21 (Moon in Sagittarius to Capricorn 6:41 p.m.)   At the track: post-position special—number 4 P.P. in ninth race. Alternate selection: number 6 P.P. in second race. Pick six: 4, 6, 2, 1, 3, 5. Be ready to revise, review, and renovate. A question concerns love, validity, and durability. Almost any delay will work in your favor. Scorpio plays a role.

Wednesday, April 22 (Moon in Capricorn) Lucky lottery numbers: 8, 18, 32, 22, 5, 10. You'll profit through communication, a short trip, the written word. You'll be involved with a dynamic, restless, creative person. You'll be working with your hands, and you'll learn more about machinery and typewriters. Virgo plays a role.

Thursday, April 23 (Moon in Capricorn) Domestic issues dominate. Money relating to your partner or mate also figures prominently. You'll learn more about hidden assets, a possibile inheritance. Today's scenario features secrets, a physical attraction, or liaison with someone who might not be free to express true feelings. Your lucky number is 6.

Friday, April 24 (Moon in Capricorn to Aquarius 6:38 a.m.) Avoid self-deception. See places and people as they actually exist. Interest in the occult is stimulated. A series of coincidences convinces you that there is someone up there. Define terms, look beyond the immediate, and check references. An insurance agent should be questioned for proof.

Saturday, April 25 (Moon in Aquarius) Get started on architectural plans and contacts necessary for a journey. The key is to show initiative, originality, a pioneering spirit. Love figures prominently—get directly to the point with Leo and Aquarius. The lunar aspect coincides with philosophy, education, and communication.

Sunday, April 26 (Moon in Aquarius to Pisces 7:20 p.m.) Look for potential. Almost everything points to sensitivity, idealism, and closeness to a soul mate. Yes, you are romantic, and you also know what is best for you despite possible derision from those who are "little people." Stress confidence, and welcome contact with Aries and Libra. Your lucky number is 9.

216

Monday, April 27 (Moon in Pisces)   Make a fresh start, stress independence, and stick to your own style. Someone attempts to inveigle you into joining a committee. Declare with conviction, "Thanks but no thanks!" This will be a most interesting Monday because events transpire that permit you to express views to the right people at a propitious moment.

Tuesday, April 28 (Moon in Pisces)   Suddenly cooperation comes from many quarters. People previously lukewarm now heat up, seek your company and opinions. A relative says, "I've changed my mind, let's do it your way!" Special: Protect your left eye from possible injury. Cancer and Capricorn figure in a fascinating scenario.

Wednesday, April 29 (Moon in Pisces to Aries 6:13 a.m.)   You're on brink of a major discovery. Give full play to curiosity and investigative talents. If you are a good reporter, you'll discover a clue that puts you over the top. You'll shine at a social affair, people will insist you are lucky and might ask you for winning numbers. A Sagittarian is in the picture.

Thursday, April 30 (Moon in Aries)   The moon moves to an area of your chart representing fulfillment, luck, money, and romance. This is not your imagination; you are on solid ground and this means you get anything you want via powers of persuasion. Don't let this day slip by without accomplishment. Try this triple play for luck—4, 2, 1.

MAY 1992

Friday, May 1 (Moon in Aries to Taurus 2:09 p.m.) This could be one of your most exciting Friday nights! Focus on popularity, speculation, and winning social ways. A wish is fulfilled in a way that combines drama and humor. A long-distance call elevates your spirits as your views are vindicated. Sagittarius and another Gemini figure prominently. Your lucky number is 3.

Saturday, May 2 (Moon in Taurus)   Lucky lottery numbers: 20, 6, 15, 2, 38, 5. The new moon emphasizes glamour, secrets, the ability to perceive what is happening backstage. Focus on details, mechanical objects, and dealings with those in authority. Taurus, Scorpio, and Aquarius figure prominently.

Sunday, May 3 (Moon in Taurus to Gemini 7:28 p.m.   You'll be working with your hands and sharing ideas with relatives. Routine changes, short trips, and visits are featured. Get your ideas on paper. You'll enjoy Sunday in the park. What you feared turns out to be a "paper tiger." That means you actually have nothing to fear. Your lucky number is 5.

Monday, May 4 (Moon in Gemini)   If you misplaced an article of clothing Sunday, it will be located this afternoon. You'll discover that many are drawn to you, want to confide, desire to become allies. Consciously or not, you have struck a chord of universal appeal. The financial picture is brighter than originally anticipated.

Tuesday, May 5 (Moon in Gemini to Cancer 11:09 p.m.)   Define your terms, and perfect techniques. The moon in Gemini emphasizes independence, originality, the ability to turn circumstances to your advantage. Display your colors: silver, bright green, yellow. A situation arises that requires the utmost discretion. Pisces figures prominently.

Wednesday, May 6 (Moon in Cancer)   Circumstances continue to turn in your favor. Stress confidence and timing. First impressions prove correct. A relationship grows strong but requires attention and added responsibility. You'll be sensitive to weather conditions. Cancer and Capricorn play major roles. Count on number 8.

Thursday, May 7 (Moon in Cancer)   Events come full circle. Recent experiences seem to repeat themselves. Obviously, you might be asking, "Is this déjà vu?" Today's scenario features completion of a project, romance. The moon in Cancer highlights protecting valuables. You'll find ways of increasing your income and adding to special collections.

Friday, May 8 (Moon in Cancer to Leo 2:07 a.m.) A new approach results in financial gain. You'll also locate an article that had been lost, missing, or stolen. Emphasize independence. Pay attention to your right eye if it was recently injured or under strain. Leo and Aquarius provide encouragement and stimulation. Your lucky number is 1.

Saturday, May 9 (Moon in Leo) An older woman insists she is under duress. This possibly is a relative recently returned from a short trip. Show interest and sympathy, but don't get involved. A Saturday night celebration could offer gourmet dining with Cancer, Capricorn or Aquarius.

Sunday, May 10 (Moon in Leo to Virgo 4:56 a.m.) There is plenty of pretense this month—today you expand your horizons, gain a legitimate glimpse of your own potential. The emphasis falls on entertainment, visits, and recognition of spiritual values. A social gathering lifts your spirits as you are complimented on your versatility, ideas, and sense of humor.

Monday, May 11 (Moon in Virgo) Only yesterday you pierced a curtain of pretense, possible deception. Now you face issues squarely, which could involve the price of a property. Be ready to dismantle for ultimate purpose of rebuilding on a more solid base. Taurus, Aquarius, and Scorpio play outstanding roles.

Tuesday, May 12 (Moon in Virgo to Libra 8:05 a.m.) These are exciting times, and you might be declaring, "By using my own judgment I seem to have made some very important discoveries—I'll continue to do so!" Today's scenario features flirtation, an invitation to examine photographs or artwork. Virgo, Sagittarius play key roles.

Wednesday, May 13 (Moon in Libra) A domestic adjustment is featured—you'll be concerned with a possible partnership, your public image, or your marital status. Strive for balance, and give logic equal time with emotional responses. Work that had been put aside now requires almost immediate attention. A Libra figures prominently.

Thursday, May 14 (Moon in Libra to Scorpio 12:15 p.m.) Some will accuse you of "keeping secrets." Sticks and stones can break your bones but a verbal assault will soon evaporate into nothing. Continue to be discreet. A good lunar aspect coincides with speculation, excitement, and physical attraction. Pisces and Virgo play important roles. Your lucky number is 7.

Friday, May 15 (Moon in Scorpio) The lunar position highlights work, health, and care of pets. You'll be concerned with power, authority, and an intensified relationship. There is a chance for a promotion, a raise, or a new job. You could actually be deluged with offers. Cancer and Capricorn are very much in the picture.

Saturday, May 16 (Moon in Scorpio to Sagittarius 6:22 p.m.) Lucky lottery numbers: 8, 17, 18, 22, 33, 45. Today's full moon highlights publicity, legal documents, and marriage. Someone whose views are opposite your own will, nevertheless, offer to cooperate. Scorpio, Aries, and Libra are part of the exciting events. Avoid handling knives.

Sunday, May 17 (Moon in Sagittarius) Stress independence. Realize that legal rights and ramifications require your attention. Recently you omitted an item on a purchase list. Make up for it now, express yourself, tell your side of story. The moon in Sagittarius relates to spiritual values, justice, travel, language, and distance. Your lucky number is 1.

Monday, May 18 (Moon in Sagittarius) Focus on food, diet, digestion, and the ability to locate an article that had been missing. Someone says, "Why not really settle down—now!" The answer is that you do not need outside interference. Spotlight on character analysis, intuition, the ability to select winning numbers.

Tuesday, May 19 (Moon in Sagittarius to Capricorn 3:13 a.m.)   Your horizons expand, you have a feeling that you'll soon be on the move. That certainly could be correct, especially from an intellectual standpoint. Your curiosity will be satisfied by someone from a foreign land. Focus on permits, special license, and legal document. Your lucky number is 4.

Wednesday, May 20 (Moon in Capricorn)   At the track: post-position special—number 4 P.P. in sixth race. Alternate selection: number 3 P.P. in second race. Pick six: 1, 3, 2, 5, 5, 4. The moon in Capricorn highlights dealings with agents and financial aspects relating to your partner or mate. An inheritance is considered.

Thursday, May 21 (Moon in Capricorn to Aquarius 2:43 p.m.)   The key is to make inquiries, check your calendar, be aware of appointments and dates. A surprise invitation could find you dining out tonight. Be prepared for change, variety, the possibility of short trip. A close relative, possibly your brother or sister, relates a message and expects much gratitude in return.

Friday, May 22 (Moon in Aquarius)   Someone close to you, possibly a relative, reminds you of a meeting that occurred less than 24 hours ago. The lunar position accents spiritual values, distance, and in-laws. A young person might respect your opinions despite what anyone else might claim!

Saturday, May 23 (Moon in Aquarius)   The lunar position highlights travel and distribution of pertinent information. Romance on a "high level" is also featured. Serious discussions could revolve around the subject of your soul mate. Define terms, and separate fact from illusion. There could be a secret skeleton in the closet.

Sunday, May 24 (Moon in Aquarius to Pisces 3:25 a.m.)   Someone persists in placing obstacles in your

221

path. Speak out—refuse second-hand goods. An older relative wants everything to fall into place. Be as cooperative as possible without abandoning promises, and principles. You'll be asked to meet a deadline. A relationship intensifies.

Monday, May 25 (Moon in Pisces)   Finish what you start, and realize that you are on the brink of an exciting adventure. Today's cycle highlights fulfillment of wishes, the ability to win friends and influence people. You'll have luck in matters of speculation, especially by sticking with number 9. Aries plays a major role.

Tuesday, May 26 (Moon in Pisces to Aries 2:53 p.m.)   You're ready for a fresh start. You'll get to the heart of matters. Romance could smolder, finally catch fire. The moon is in that lucky part of your chart, which coincides with popularity and gain as result of business or career activities. Someone you meet could eventually play an important part in your romantic life.

Wednesday, May 27 (Moon in Aries)   Lucky lottery numbers: 9, 19, 1, 10, 44, 46. The moon in Aries emphasizes initiative, originality, and sex appeal. Your eleventh sector is activated. Translated, this means you can get almost anything desired. Just ask! A relative who made a promise supporting your efforts may now find it inconvenient.

Thursday, May 28 (Moon in Aries to Taurus 11:16 p.m.)   The realization strikes home that you can indeed call your own shots. You could win a contest; some insist you could go into politics. Focus on humor, gifts, and visits. Pay special attention to diet and nutrition. Sagittarius and another Gemini will figure prominently. Your lucky number is 3.

Friday, May 29 (Moon in Taurus)   You might be saying, "This appears to be too good to last, but it is lasting and I'm going to enjoy it!" Money comes from sources interested in your career and business. The social whirl also continues—some will comment on your charm and aplomb. Taurus and Scorpio are in the picture.

Saturday, May 30 (Moon in Taurus)   Stretch your hands, check your nails, and be aware that many people will be looking at your fingers, wrists, and arms. Be prepared to enjoy yourself; refuse to feel guilty because a relative is temporarily incapacitated. A unique message concerns a possible journey. Virgo is represented.

Sunday, May 31 (Moon in Taurus to Gemini 4:19 a.m.)   This is an excellent time for being with family, attending religious services, and gaining understanding of spiritual values. You'll enjoy a wonderful feeling of peace. The lunar position represents a favorable cycle, means that lost articles will be recovered. Taurus figures prominently.

JUNE 1992

Monday, June 1 (Moon in Gemini)   The new moon in your sign coincides with excitement, timing, a fresh procedure. You'll agree that this is a most unusual Monday. Your vigor returns, and you actually exude personal magnetism. The lunar position accents independence, individuality, and physical attraction. Taurus and Scorpio figure prominently.

Tuesday, June 2 (Moon in Gemini to Cancer 6:58 a.m.)   You met someone Monday and you'll hear from that person by tonight. Focus on home, domesticity, music, harmony, the receipt of a token of affection. Your judgment and timing will be accurate. People will comment favorably on your apparel and appearance. Virgo plays a major role. Your lucky number is 5.

Wednesday, June 3 (Moon in Cancer)   Almost as if by magic, a wish comes true in connection with money. The emphasis falls on large household items, automobiles, luxury items. Someone close to you will notice how romantic you are these days! Accept this as a compliment. Taurus and Scorpio figure prominently.

Thursday, June 4 (Moon in Cancer to Leo 8:35 a.m.) A money "proposition" requires further study. Terms must be clarified. Separate fact from illusion. Today's lunar position highlights payments, collections, the ability to locate an article that had been lost, missing, or stolen. Pisces and Virgo play outstanding roles. Your best bet is number 7.

Friday, June 5 (Moon in Leo) At the track: postposition special—number 9 P.P. in eighth race. Alternate selection: number 3 P.P. in second race. Pick six: 1, 3, 4, 2, 5, 8. You'll have luck by staying close to an older person, possibly a parent or employer. Cancer and Capricorn figure prominently.

Saturday, June 6 (Moon in Leo to Virgo 10:28 a.m.) The moon position highlights ideas, concepts, welcoming a relative recently returned from a short trip. You go full circle. The search for your soul mate could result in a reunion with an old flame. This will be a Saturday night to remember! Aries and Libra play paramount roles.

Sunday, June 7 (Moon in Virgo) A fresh start is favorable—be direct and get to the heart of matters. Focus on security, property, a long-standing negotiation. You'll be with someone who makes you feel comfortable. A young person seeks your counsel. Combine spiritual advice with romance.

Monday, June 8 (Moon in Virgo to Libra 1:33 a.m.) The emphasis is on discrimination, intuition, the ability to settle a family dispute. The focus continues on romance, the unorthodox, an element of surprise. A long-distance call relates to possible vacation travel. Cancer, Capricorn, and Aquarius figure prominently. Your lucky number is 2.

Tuesday, June 9 (Moon in Libra) Diversify, accept a social invitation—it's possible that your eyes will meet those of a special person across the room. Indeed, this could be a unique day and evening—creative juices will flow. Your popularity increases, and your sense of humor will be noted. A Sagittarian is involved.

Wednesday, June 10 (Moon in Libra to Scorpio 6:27 p.m.) Patience pays dividends. A relationship that floundered will be back on track. You'll be dealing with a dynamic, creative, and unorthodox person. You'll be saying, "At last I'm out of the rut!" Lucky lottery numbers: 10, 7, 16, 6, 25, 24. Taurus and Scorpio play significant roles.

Thursday, June 11 (Moon in Scorpio) Someone you helped in the past, possibly a relative, is ready to repay a debt. Today's cycle highlights dependents, pets, work methods, the ability to locate proper personnel. A member of the opposite sex who stands by your side will prove loyal. Virgo, Sagittarius, and another Gemini play key roles.

Friday, June 12 (Moon in Scorpio) Stay close to home if possible. Today's scenario highlights domesticity, employment, a gift from neighbor reflecting "high esteem." Stress harmony, music, and art, Don't hide your talents. A late supper has all earmarks of sophistication, glamour. Taurus, Libra, and Scorpio are in the picture.

Saturday, June 13 (Moon in Scorpio to Sagittarius 1:29 a.m.) Look beyond the immediate for long-range potential. A vacation or holiday plan apparently lacks substance. Today's scenario features illusion, romance, necessity for discretion. Someone who enjoys gossip could make you their prime target. Pisces plays a role. Your lucky number is 7.

Sunday, June 14 (Moon in Sagittarius) Today's scenario features power, authority, and legal decisions. The emphasis falls on partnership and marriage. You might be seriously discussing the possibility that there will be an addition to your family. A financial contact made eight days ago could now bear fruit. Cancer and Capricorn play roles.

Monday, June 15 (Moon in Sagittarius to Capricorn 10:50 a.m.)   A relationship is tested. This current cycle indicates a beginning or an end. No longer is there middle ground. A decision is reached about rights and permissions. You'll win over the opposition, and former adversaries will want to become allies. Keep the door ajar and play number 9 to win.

Tuesday, June 16 (Moon in Capricorn)   At the track: winning colors: purple, gray, green, black. Post-position special: number 1 P.P. in sixth race. Alternate selection: number 7 P.P. in third race. Pick six: 4, 2, 7, 1, 3, 1. Today's lunar position highlights money belonging to another, transfer of valuables, and dealings with an insurance agent.

Wednesday, June 17 (Moon in Capricorn to Aquarius 10:19 p.m.)   Two days ago the full moon and lunar eclipse related to contracts, legal negotiations, and your public image. Much was negative, but now you make what many consider a "remarkable comeback." Your intuition is on target; your ability to analyze character is spotlighted. An Aquarian is in the picture.

Thursday, June 18 (Moon in Aquarius)   Fluorescent lighting requires review, could be harmful if not used intelligently. Diversify, display humor, and be willing to laugh at your own foibles. Attention centers around your wardrobe, general appearance, and body image. Vacation activity accelerates. Your lucky number is 3.

Friday, June 19 (Moon in Aquarius)   Today's lunar aspect emphasizes travel, philosophy, and education. On a personal level, you could fall madly in love. There is mental attraction first, followed by physical. You could actually locate the person of your dreams or soul mate. Scorpio is represented. Your lucky number is 4.

Saturday, June 20 (Moon in Aquarius to Pisces 11:00 a.m.) Lucky lottery numbers: 2, 11, 8, 33, 31, 45. A breakthrough shows you where you stand. Your confidence builds and you'll play second fiddle to no one! Be ready for change, travel, variety, an unusual adventure initiated by the written word. Virgo plays a role.

Sunday, June 21 (Moon in Pisces) You get a proverbial second chance to fulfill your potential. Business combines with pleasure. The emphasis is on entertainment and spiritual values, a gift that helps beautify your home. The money picture brightens almost in a flash. Taurus, Libra, and Scorpio figure prominently. Your lucky number is 6.

Monday, June 22 (Moon in Pisces to Aries 11:03 a.m.) Someone who claims you have a temper might plead, "Please don't blow a fuse!" The rug could be pulled out from under you when a promise made in all sincerity might be withdrawn. Focus on money, solidity, illusion, and backstage maneuvers. Pisces figures prominently. Your lucky number is 7.

Tuesday, June 23 (Moon in Aries) Racetrack special: winning colors—sea green, mauve. Post-position special: number 3 P.P. in second race. Alternate selection: number 9 P.P. in eighth race. Pick six: 1, 3, 4, 8, 5, 8. Focus on intensity, power, authority, and the ability to deal with the rules and regulations.

Wednesday, June 24 (Moon in Aries) An attorney might be selling you a bill of goods. You now are in a position to take greater charge of your own destiny. Many will correctly proclaim, "You are a winner!" The moon position highlights your powers of persuasion, friends, romance, and emotional fulfillment. Aries is represented.

Thursday, June 25 (Moon in Aries to Taurus 8:28 a.m.) A fresh start in a new direction proves just what the "doctor ordered." Love is on the horizon, friendship could be transformed into a serious relationship. Take the initiative, be direct, stress independence of thought and action. A special note: Avoid heavy lifting. Leo is represented.

Friday, June 26 (Moon in Taurus) Secrets surface. Skeletons rattle in the closet. As your cycle moves up, your timing and judgment will improve. A Taurus will not necessarily agree with you but would not desert you! Your intuition is on target. A former teacher returns, is ready to assist. Play number 2 today.

Saturday, June 27 (Moon in Taurus to Gemini 2:14 p.m.) You'll be pulled away from accounting procedures, details, and contracts. Many will say, "Come with us—this is holiday time and all of us are going to celebrate!" Be flexible, and keep your options open. As your popularity increases, you could win contest. Your lucky number is 5.

Sunday, June 28 (Moon in Gemini) The Moon in your sign helps you organize, and enables you to really understand a relationship. People comment on your personality, humor, and versatility. Special: You'll be sensitive about your wardrobe, weight, and body image. A long-distance call verifies your travel plans.

Monday, June 29 (Moon in Gemini to Cancer 4:42 p.m.) Be ready for excitement, flirtation, the ability to analyze character, especially via graphology. Examine checks and accounting figures. Remember the dictum, "Figures don't lie, but liars figure!" Protect yourself in close quarters. Virgo, Sagittarius, and another Gemini are on hand.

Tuesday, June 30 (Moon in Cancer) The new moon and solar eclipse is in that part of your horoscope representing money, valuables, and personal possessions. You could be wheeling and dealing. Some will proclaim you an excellent "horse trader"! Focus on decorating, remodeling, and improving your domestic situation. Your lucky number is 6.

JULY 1992

Wednesday, July 1 (Moon in Cancer to Leo 5:15 p.m.)   Holiday preparations begin—make lists, check expenses, and decide how you're going to celebrate. Open lines of communication. A member of the opposite sex wants to put you in the holiday spirit. Lucky lottery numbers: 7, 17, 20, 30, 5, 10. Virgo and Sagittarius are in the picture.

Thursday, July 2 (Moon in Leo)   At the track: post-position special—number 2 P.P. in fourth race. Alternate selection: number 5 P.P. in seventh race. Pick six: 1, 2, 3, 2, 6, 2. You will have special luck, at the track and otherwise, by sticking with number 9. Also, try this triple play: 3, 6, 9.

Friday, July 3 (Moon in Leo to Virgo 5:37 p.m.) Define terms, be sure you have been "in touch" with those who are to help you celebrate tomorrow's holiday. Attention centers around trips, visits, relatives, and ideas that can be transformed into viable concepts. A dream-like romance could come down to earth.

Saturday, July 4 (Moon in Virgo)   You could have a Fourth of July to remember! Observe safety rules and regulations. The lunar position highlights home, security, a possible danger of conflagration. Enjoy fireworks without starting a blaze. Cancer and Capricorn play major roles. Your lucky number is 8.

Sunday, July 5 (Moon in Virgo to Libra 7:27 p.m.) You'll be thankful for this Sunday. A family gathering proves beneficial. Focus on universal appeal, romance, love, giving and receiving. Some will say, "You are a truly amazing person!" A mission will be accomplished. A long-distance call will verify future vacation or holiday plans.

Monday July 6 (Moon in Libra)   A fresh start is indicated. A love relationship gets off the ground. You feel more secure and confident about the future. A special note: Avoid heavy lifting. Some will complain about the weather, but you'll be saying, "This suits me just fine!" Leo and Aquarius play outstanding roles.

Tuesday, July 7 (Moon in Libra to Scorpio 11:53 p.m.) Emotions tend to push logic aside. Today's scenario highlights reunions and protestations of love. You'll have special luck in dealings with women. By making a public appearance, you'll win allies and possibly gain financial support. A Cancer plays an important role.

Wednesday, July 8 (Moon in Scorpio) Diversify, look beyond the immediate to long-range potential. You'll note that your popularity has moved up despite some disagreements with friends or relatives. A clash of ideas provided stimulation, but did not create adversaries. Another Gemini plays a role. Your lucky number is 3.

Thursday, July 9 (Moon in Scorpio) A low-key approach brings the desired results. The emphasis falls on diet, nutrition, and locating key personnel. You'll be working with your hands; featured will be repairs, mending, and food preparation. Be aware of the fine print and where to find source material. Taurus and Scorpio are in the picture.

Friday, July 10 (Moon in Scorpio to Sagittarius 7:17 a.m.) Check signatures. Protect your assets. Locate credit cards and other documents. Today's scenario features the written word, credit rating, a flirtation that could become serious. Virgo, Sagittarius, and another Gemini figure prominently. At the track, stick with number 5 post position.

Saturday, July 11 (Moon in Sagittarius) The emphasis falls on marital status, general appearance, and contractual obligations. Be aware of your rights and permissions. An important domestic adjustment takes place tonight. Be diplomatic, especially when discussing finances. Taurus, Libra, and Scorpio play significant roles.

Sunday, July 12 (Moon in Sagittarius to Capricorn 5:19 p.m.)   Spiritual values surge to the forefront. Terms will be defined, and you'll learn to separate fact from illusion. A spiritual counselor could help resolve a dilemma. You'll have the opportunity to look behind the scenes. The view might be disturbing but also informative.

Monday, July 13 (Moon in Capricorn)   Today's emphasis is on power, authority, the ability to meet a deadline. Money related to your partner or mate commands attention. You'll learn more about a possible inheritance. You'll also become knowledgeable about investments and secret hiding places. Capricorn plays a role. Play number 8 today.

Tuesday, July 14 (Moon in Capricorn)   The full moon position promotes interest in the occult. Focus on glamour, intrigue, a physical attraction. Many preconceived notions will be tossed aside. You'll be able to revise, review, and rebuild on a more suitable base. Aries and Libra are in picture. Number 2 is lucky for you.

Wednesday, July 15 (Moon in Capricorn to Aquarius 5:03 a.m.)   Lucky lottery numbers: 6, 39, 8, 10, 14, 5. Do plenty of investigating to satisfy your curiosity, and refuse to be cajoled by superficial explanations. Don't rest merely at knowing something happened—find out why. Dig deep for information, organize your notes, and highlight research.

Thursday, July 16 (Moon in Aquarius)   Define terms and streamline techniques. You're due for a second chance—think about new outlets for your talents. Today's scenario features distance, language, the possibility of a journey. A romantic mood tonight relates to your search for a soul mate. A Cancer is involved. Your lucky number is 1.

Friday, July 17 (Moon in Aquarius to Pisces 5:44 p.m.)   Some will concede that you are altruistic! Keep your perspective and sense of humor. Focus on your intellectual curiosity, your ability to see various points of view. Important contacts can be made at a social gathering. Another Gemini could help show you the way.

Saturday, July 18 (Moon in Pisces)   Lucky lottery numbers: 1, 8, 18, 12, 7, 36. The key is to be specific, to check details, to be alert for hidden clauses. The lunar position highlights promotion, production, responsibility, and contacts with very important persons. A unique person finds you charming!

Sunday, July 19 (Moon in Pisces)   You'll receive written notification that a request will be fulfilled. Focus on harmony and communication with one who has been out of town. It's a good day for trips, visits, a possible reunion with a close relative. Reading material, started for pleasure, could provide a solution to a dilemma.

Monday, July 20 (Moon in Pisces to Aries 6:07 a.m.)   Go slow, and be diplomatic. This applies especially to family relationships. An agreement will be reached about a significant domestic adjustment. The spotlight falls on money, security, the sale or purchase of an art object or luxury item. A musical performance or entertainment could highlight this evening.

Tuesday, July 21 (Moon in Aries)   Many wishes come true as if in a sudden rush. The lunar position occupies an area of your chart related to friends, desires, aspirations, and luck in matters of speculation. Romance will cease to be a stranger. You'll say, "I'm getting what I asked for and I hope I can make the most of it!"

Wednesday, July 22 (Moon in Aries to Taurus 4:36 p.m.)   You'll have plenty of pressure and responsibility, but the pay is mighty fine! Translated, this means despite hardships and some obstacles, rewards will be ample. Focus also on a deadline, an intensified relationship, a decision affecting your security. Capricorn is represented.

232

Thursday, July 23 (Moon in Taurus)   The cycle is completed—you learn where you stand and what to do about it. You could be part of a hospital tour; you'll relate to home, institutions, and museums. Idealism mingles with practicality. The spotlight falls on love, romance, the search for your soul mate. Aries plays a paramount role.

Friday, July 24 (Moon in Taurus)   Stress independence, confidence, a willingness to get to the heart of matters. You'll have new insight on a problem. Someone close to you could be released from confinement. A special note: Avoid heavy lifting. Leo and Aquarius figure prominently. Your lucky number is 1.

Saturday, July 25 (Moon in Taurus to Gemini 11:44 a.m.)   The moon moves to your sign, which represents your high cycle. You'll bring together relatives who had been involved in a financial dispute. Focus on mediation and property appraisal. By tonight, you'll realize that romance is present and will not be a stranger. It's possible you could be dining near a lake or ocean. Count on number 4.

Sunday, July 26 (Moon in Gemini)   Diversify, accept a social invitation. Amid gaiety you'll also recognize spiritual values. The emphasis falls on trips, visits, and long-distance communication. You'll be fascinated by education and philosophical concepts. Your judgment, timing, and intuition all are on target. Play number 3 to win.

Monday, July 27 (Moon in Gemini to Cancer 3:08 a.m.)   Be willing to tear down for the ultimate purpose of rebuilding on a more suitable structure. Today's lunar position accents money, personal possessions, and valuables. Check accounting procedures, set familiar with license or tax requirements. An unusual relationship stimulates your creativity.

Tuesday, July 28 (Moon in Cancer)   Today's scenario features discovery, adventure, change, travel, a variety of experiences. Although you might be spending more than usual, you'll also be sure to get your money's worth. Someone of the opposite sex wants more than a one-night stand! Virgo and another Gemini play roles.

Wednesday, July 29 (Moon in Cancer to Leo 3:39 a.m.) The new moon is in the area of your chart relating to brothers, sisters, trips, and contacts with lively people, most of whom have something to sell. Have fun, engage in flirtation, but protect yourself at close quarters. Taurus, Libra, and Scorpio figure prominently. Your lucky number is 6.

Thursday, July 30 (Moon in Leo) At the track—you might have luck with number 7. Post-position special: number 1 P.P. in sixth race. Pick six: 6, 1, 2, 4, 4, 1. Don't neglect this triple play: 3, 7, 1. Away from the track devise a method for economizing and get rid of superfluous material.

Friday, July 31 (Moon in Leo to Virgo 3:01 a.m.) An older relative, possibly your brother or sister, talks about money and love. Be a good listener but refuse to become deeply involved. Today could also bring deadlines, more responsibilities, and a chance to make a successful investment. A Cancer plays a significant role. Your lucky number is 8.

AUGUST 1992

Saturday, August 1 (Moon in Virgo) You'll receive plenty of clues, signals that you are loved. Today's emphasis is on security, a domestic adjustment, property appraisal. You could receive a gift, perhaps a diamond. This will not be an ordinary Saturday night! Taurus, Libra, and Scorpio play outstanding roles. Your lucky number is 6.

Sunday, August 2 (Moon in Virgo to Libra 3:17 a.m.) It's a good time for meditation and recognition of a higher power. You'll be on solid ground in much of what you do, including a dialogue with a relative. See others as they are, not merely as you wish they might be. Don't fall victim to self-deception.

Monday, August 3 (Moon in Libra)   Be open-minded without being gullible. The lunar position accents speculation, creativity, and physical attraction. A young person asks questions, expecting you to provide the answers. Keep a tight rein on discipline without arbitrarily expressing opinions. Leave enough room for freedom but not license.

Tuesday, August 4 (Moon in Libra to Scorpio 6:16 a.m.)   You'll finish a project that had been hanging on for almost three months. Know when to leave it alone. A relationship has sparked, but the fire has yet to be ignited. Don't push, crowd, cajole, chide, or threaten. This message will become crystal clear. Your lucky number is 9.

Wednesday, August 5 (Moon in Scorpio)   Lucky lottery numbers: 10, 8, 17, 26, 44, 5. You're due to make a fresh start, to take greater charge of your own destiny. A special note: Protect your right eye from possible injury. An older man, possibly your father or employer, has much to say about where you should be and what you should do.

Thursday, August 6 (Moon in Scorpio to Sagittarius 12:57 p.m.)   Focus on employment, key personnel, a health report. A relative, recently returned from a trip, complains of difficulty in breathing. Make suggestions but also realize you can't force anyone to take proper precautions. Cancer and Aquarius are in the picture.

Friday, August 7 (Moon in Sagittarius)   You'll be getting more clues to what you are all about! Focus on entertainment and social activity. Be willing to test your creative skills. Look at the big picture and leave details for another time. You'll be conscious of your wardrobe, weight, and body image. Another Gemini plays a major role.

Saturday, August 8 (Moon in Sagittarius to Capricorn 11:00 p.m.)   Lucky lottery numbers: 17, 8, 9, 30, 5, 49. You'll be asked to re-create a recent happening. Focus on testing and questioning. Pressure is exerted by one concerned with clues, visions, and impressions. Read between the lines, and have the necessary material at hand. Taurus and Scorpio figure prominently.

Sunday, August 9 (Moon in Capricorn)   Reach beyond previous expectations. A relationship undergoes a serious test. Attention centers around legal documents and decisions involving travel and marriage. Keep your faith; refuse to be discouraged by someone who obviously is resentful or envious. Aries and Libra play outstanding roles.

Monday, August 10 (Moon in Capricorn)   You might be asking yourself whether to spend money on fixing things up. The answer is affirmative. Be diplomatic in connection with the budget and financial prospects. However, don't be weak. The message will become crystal clear. Your lucky number is 6.

Tuesday, August 11 (Moon in Capricorn to Aquarius 11:07 a.m.)   An unusual method brings the desired results. Look at the financial prospects of one close to you, either a partner or mate. There will be interest in hidden affairs, the occult, a possible inheritance. Pisces and Virgo figure prominently.

Wednesday, August 12 (Moon in Aquarius)   You'll be dealing with older persons, especially older men. Today's lunar position highlights philosophy, religion, communication, and travel. Some will say, "You certainly are being studious these days!" Accept this as compliment. Significant domestic changes occur, which could involve a change in living arrangements.

Thursday, August 13 (Moon in Aquarius to Pisces 11:51 p.m.)   Today's full moon highlights discovery, speculation, a physical attraction. You'll learn that although perfection is evasive, there is opportunity for an

236

expression of love. The scenario features illusion, glamour, the need for discretion. Someone wants to tell tales out of school.

Friday, August 14 (Moon in Pisces)   The emphasis is on independence, a fresh start. Be willing to test your capabilities. You'll learn the truth about a new acquaintance. Romance, style and creativity are in the air. The lunar position continues to accent communication, speculation, a strong love relationship. Your lucky number is 1.

Saturday, August 15 (Moon in Pisces)   This is one Saturday you won't soon forget! Focus on celebration, entertainment, and contact with someone who can boost your career. You'll successfully mix business with pleasure. The moon position emphasizes ambition and the ability to overcome obstacles.

Sunday, August 16 (Moon in Pisces to Aries 12:11 p.m.)   Tensions are relieved, and relaxation should be the order of the day. There is plenty of movement, however, because of relatives, calls, messages, and invitations. Your intellectual curiosity will be stimulated. You'll also gain an overview of where you are going and why. Your lucky number is 3.

Monday, August 17 (Moon in Aries)   Be willing to tear down to rebuild on a more suitable structure. The lunar position accents friends, hopes, wishes, and emotional fulfillment. Use your charm and powers of persuasion. Scorpio and Aquarius contact you with almost duplicate propositions.

Tuesday, August 18 (Moon in Aries to Taurus 11:10 p.m.)   A well-intentioned friend could be misinformed. Be aware and alert, especially in traffic. Focus on romance and the stimulation of your creative juices. You could be invited to dine or dance by one who previously seemed indifferent. Stick with number 6.

Wednesday, August 19 (Moon in Taurus)   Lucky lottery numbers: 33, 36, 10, 9, 1, 45. Dress up your product. Make contacts involving distribution or display. On a personal level, a date that starts out in an ordinary way could wind up as an exciting experience, featuring wining and dining. Libra figures prominently.

Thursday, August 20 (Moon in Taurus) Today's scenario features behind-the-scenes activity, institutions, schools, a possible tour of a hospital or nursing home. Get in touch with one temporarily confined. The accent is on glamour, mystery, and intrigue. But play cards close to your chest. Yes, someone is attempting to peek. Your lucky number is 7.

Friday, August 21 (Moon in Taurus to Gemini 7:36 a.m.) What at first appeared irrelevant could actually mean plenty, and might even have much to do with your future, especially where finances are concerned. The emphasis is on responsibility and a strong love relationship. You're going places, but not in the direction you originally planned.

Saturday, August 22 (Moon in Gemini) Finish what you start, and realize that you are actually in control of your own fate. The moon in your sign highlights initiative, originality, and pioneering spirit. Long-range prospects come into sharp, clear focus. The answer to a question: Yes, you could actually be madly in love.

Sunday, August 23 (Moon in Gemini to Cancer 12:36 p.m.) Stress independence, creativity, and style. Go forward despite minor objections, suspicions, and doubts. There no longer is any benefit in hanging onto the past. Someone you trusted broke faith and does not deserve a second, third, or fourth chance. Leo and Aquarius figure prominently. Your lucky number is 1.

Monday, August 24 (Moon in Cancer) Trust your intuition. Use your unique talent as a character analyst. Someone who fascinates you is tricky, restless, and quixotic. In actuality, you see much of yourself in that person. Smile for a while, but protect yourself in clinches.

Someone could be planning an illegal punch. Play it safe with number 4.

Tuesday, August 25 (Moon in Cancer to Leo 2:15 p.m.) At the track: post-position special—number 5 P.P. in seventh race. Alternate selection: number 8 P.P. in ninth race. Pick six: 3, 6, 7, 4, 2, 1. Winning colors: emerald green, white. Diversify, and pay more attention to your appearance, wardrobe, diet, and nutrition.

Wednesday, August 26 (Moon in Leo) You could feel like this is going to be your lucky day! It could be, especially if you filter out rumors, tales, and stories. Get the facts, and realize a relative does mean well but does not have the necessary information. Taurus and Scorpio figure prominently. Your lucky number is 4.

Thursday, August 27 (Moon in Leo to Virgo 1:46 p.m.) The emphasis falls on showmanship, sex appeal, a willingness to make public appearances. Open lines of communication, read and write, articulate opinions. An attractive person is interested but possibly wants no more than a mere summer flirtation. Leo and Virgo play roles.

Friday, August 28 (Moon in Virgo) Today's new moon accents security, family, property, the conclusion of negotiations. Some might be saying, "It seems as if you are starting all over!" In truth, however, you are merely taking a new tack, finishing with a flourish. A relative is serious and is sincere about making amends for a recent error.

Saturday, August 29 (Moon in Virgo to Libra 1:11 p.m.) Define terms, and be discriminating. The key is to select quality rather than quantity. What appears to be lost is only temporary. You finish strong, well ahead of the competition. You'll be dealing with a mysterious person who claims to be psychic.

Sunday, August 30 (Moon in Libra) On this last Sunday of the month, you recognize spiritual values. A favorable lunar aspect brings the focus on children, change, variety, freedom of thought and action. Someone of the opposite sex expresses feelings, is somewhat shy, possibly embarrassed. Wisdom and understanding are required.

Monday, August 31 (Moon in Libra to Scorpio 2:38 p.m.) You'll finish an important assignment. A love relationship could be back on track. The moon in Libra stimulates physical attraction, style, the ability to hear the sound of your own voice. You could meet a Libra who makes you ponder your own true feelings. Your lucky number is 9.

SEPTEMBER 1992

Tuesday, September 1 (Moon in Scorpio) Consideration of new employment should be taken seriously. Avoid acting in haste. Someone who makes promises could be more interested in romance than a job assignment. Be independent but avoid arrogance. Pisces and Virgo figure prominently. Count on number 7.

Wednesday, September 2 (Moon in Scorpio to Sagittarius 7:50 p.m.) Lucky lottery numbers: 22, 33, 18, 8, 44, 45. The emphasis falls on responsibility, pressure, a strong love relationship. You might be saying, "I'm going to give my best; it could be my lucky Wednesday night!" Cancer and Capricorn play meaningful roles. Check expiration dates for credit cards.

Thursday, September 3 (Moon in Sagittarius) Round out an effort associated with distance, language, or travel. It's important to keep resolutions concerning diet and nutrition. A recent addition to your wardrobe revealed a minor weight problem. The lunar position continues to highlight pets, dependents, a job application. Aries plays a major role.

Friday, September 4 (Moon in Sagittarius) Attention revolves around independence, a fresh start, serious consideration of your partnership or marital status. Make a public appearance and let others know your true feelings. A youthful listener could become your strongest supporter. Special note: Avoid heavy lifting.

Saturday, September 5 (Moon in Sagittarius to Capricorn 5:06 a.m.)   Your intuition rings true. A coalition can be created despite a clash of ideas. Two members of your family seem intent on arguing about property or finances. Rise above it. You'll be offered an unusual assignment that could eventually bring huge profits. Cancer and Aquarius play roles.

Sunday, September 6 (Moon in Capricorn)   The spotlight is on spiritual values, philosophical concepts, and expression of abstract formulas. What was hidden will be revealed. Someone close to you confides a problem relating to money and love. A legal document will be located—you'll celebrate by participating in an entertainment program.

Monday, September 7 (Moon in Capricorn to Aquarius 5:08 p.m.)   This need not be the proverbial blue Monday if you realize that rules and restrictions could ultimately work in your favor. A delay should not be equated with defeat. Money is available, but credit ratings should be verified. Taurus and Scorpio play significant roles. Your lucky number is 4.

Tuesday, September 8 (Moon in Aquarius)   The emphasis falls on communication, movement, and travel. Some promises apparently are being made to be broken. Be aware, alert, and ready to express your desires in writing. You'll meet a left-handed person who stimulates your creative process. Virgo, Sagittarius, and another Gemini figure in today's scenario.

Wednesday, September 9 (Moon in Aquarius)   A favorable lunar aspect coincides with education, publishing, the ability to spread the word. But you'll also be concerned with changes at home. Your security could be

241

threatened by someone who seems intent on a spending spree. Taurus and Libra figure prominently.

Thursday, September 10 (Moon in Aquarius to Pisces 5:56 a.m.)   Someone who repeats a ribald rhyme wants to attract your attention. Refuse to be shocked—instead say, "How lovely and foolish!" You'll be attracted to another person who is playing hard to get. Pisces and Virgo are part of the day's excitement.

Friday, September 11 (Moon in Pisces)   This can be your power-play day! A contact made 11 days ago will bear fruit. The emphasis falls on business, career, and activities connected with the community and government. A Friday night date could represent the start of "something big." Cancer and Capricorn play important roles. Your lucky number is 8.

Saturday, September 12 (Moon in Pisces to Aries 6:02 p.m.)   The full moon falls in an area of your chart associated with achievement, responsibility, and daring. You'll be taking a chance on romance. You won't be limited by a commitment that should not have been agreed upon in the first place. You'll be rescued from a trap involving finances or broken promises.

Sunday, September 13 (Moon in Aries)   Leave the door ajar. This means don't burn bridges. The lunar position highlights fulfillment, speculation, the ability to win friends and influence people. This will be one Sunday during which you'll give thanks in an enthusiastic manner. You are on solid ground in connection with emotional responses and fiscal responsibility.

Monday, September 14 (Moon in Aries)   Be ready to revise written material, such as an information kit, or policy. An admirer confides, "I'm serious, I want more than a one-night stand!" A wish will be fulfilled based on your popularity, intuition, and sense of adventure. Your lucky number is 2.

Tuesday, September 15 (Moon in Aries to Taurus 4:47 a.m.) Be flexible today; accept a social invitation, say yes to a challenge. The action could include dancing, investment tips, a long-distance call relating to a possible journey. You'll be more conscious of your wardrobe and the necessity for legal clearances. Sagittarius and another Gemini figure prominently.

Wednesday, September 16 (Moon in Taurus) The moon moves into an area of your chart relating to dreams, visions, institutions, and unique tours. You could be involved with the film or television media. Some will comment on your charm and fresh approach. Lucky lottery numbers: 22, 4, 16, 31, 45, 6. Taurus plays an outstanding role.

Thursday, September 17 (Moon in Taurus to Gemini 1:40 p.m.) What appeared to be a missed opportunity turned out to be a minor error. This will be corrected, the cycle moves up, and you'll be at the right place at the appropriate time. Today's lunar position accents secret information. You'll have access to a document that tells the "true age." Play number 5 to win.

Friday, September 18 (Moon in Gemini) Today's cycle is high enough for a major domestic change or adjustment. A family member talks about funding and hiding places. It is important to be diplomatic, to make concessions without abandoning your principles. The moon in your sign emphasizes personality and sex appeal. Someone says, "I'm not fooling, I want you to myself!"

Saturday, September 19 (Moon in Gemini to Cancer 7:09 p.m.) The lunar cycle continues high—this evening could feature glamour, intrigue, and clandestine arrangements. Focus on secrecy, illusion, film, and the need for discretion. You'll meet someone who could prove instrumental in promoting your business or career. Pisces plays a paramount role.

Sunday, September 20 (Moon in Cancer) You'll say, "I really do have something to celebrate!" Good news is received about the location of a lost article. Focus also on payments, collections, the opportunity to increase your income. On this Sunday, you'll learn more about timing, deadlines, and insurance policies relating to theft.

Monday, September 21 (Moon in Cancer to Leo 11:19 p.m.) The emphasis falls on long-range projects. You can now extend your influence beyond previous limitations. Idealism mingles with practicality—money and love are spotlighted. Your search for a "soul mate" will not be fruitless. Aries and Libra will figure prominently. Your lucky number is 9.

Tuesday, September 22 (Moon in Leo) Today's scenario highlights trips and visits. Keep your plans flexible. A close relative, possibly a brother or sister, needs a favor, and will soon ask for it. Stress independence; be willing to make a fresh start in a new direction. Leo and Aquarius are important to you today. Your lucky number is 1.

Wednesday, September 23 (Moon in Leo) Lucky lottery numbers: 23, 5, 1, 10, 36, 37. Get to the heart of matters, be direct, and take the initiative. You'll learn more about property, professional appraisals, and removal of safety hazards. A needed repair could involve plumbing. Aquarius and Cancer play meaningful roles.

Thursday, September 24 (Moon in Leo to Virgo 12:08 a.m.) Diversify, and insist on additional space. Be in touch with one confined to home or hospital. You'll be complimented on your sense of humor, your general appearance. Open lines of communication. Required legal documents could include a passport. Another Gemini adores being with you!

Friday, September 25 (Moon in Virgo to Libra 11:55 p.m.) Be discriminating, and choose quality. Today's scenario features personnel, tests, lists, and mechanical devices. Focus also on home repairs, the necessity for remodeling and revising. Give some serious thought to your lifestyle. A temporary delay need not be regarded as a defeat. Your lucky number is 4.

Saturday, September 26 (Moon in Libra)   Today's new moon position highlights sensuality, personality, the ability to imprint your special style. Focus also on children, variety, and the adventure of discovery. Your creative juices will be stirred—and this time you'll follow through! A Sagittarian plays a top role.

Sunday, September 27 (Moon in Libra)   Focus on a reunion, spiritual values, restoring domestic harmony. A family member wants to talk about relocating. Be receptive and diplomatic. A money question concerns automobile insurance, a possible sale or purchase. Taurus is involved. Play number 6 to win.

Monday, September 28 (Moon in Libra to Scorpio 12:44 a.m.)   Define terms, refuse to be chided into making a snap decision. Someone who makes an initial promise could be sincere but also misinformed. Focus on sex appeal, and the ability to deal successfully with restless individuals who seek vocational guidance. A love relationship heats up.

Tuesday, September 29 (Moon in Scorpio)   This is your power-play day. Accept the responsibility of a challenge or deadline. A relationship grows strong—a commitment is made and, if you are playing games, this could be a serious blunder. This message will become crystal clear. Cancer and Capricorn figure prominently. Your lucky number is 8.

Wednesday, September 30 (Moon in Scorpio to Sagittarius 4:33 a.m.)   Finish the task at hand. A relationship recently survived the critical stage. On this day, reach an understanding about commitment or future prospects. Some experiences seem to repeat themselves. This could cause you to ask, "Is this déjà vu?" Aries and Libra play a significant role. Your lucky number is 9.

Thursday, October 1 (Moon in Sagittarius) Perhaps you thought you might get away with being only half-committed. Now, however, you learn the game is serious, the water is hot, there is insistence on commitment—emotional and legal. This can be your power-play day—you can emerge with victory and reward. Capricorn is involved.

Friday, October 2 (Moon in Sagittarius to Capricorn 12:29 p.m.) Stress universal appeal, reach more people, and be sensitive to public relations. Check contractual obligations. More people are drawn to you, many confide problems, others want you to be their guest. Be gracious, but refuse to allow your energy to be sapped. Aries figures prominently.

Saturday, October 3 (Moon in Capricorn) Lucky lottery numbers: 3, 10, 8, 26, 44, 45. Post-position special: number 8 P.P. in first race. Alternate selection: number 1 P.P. in sixth race. You'll have special luck by sticking with number 1. Stress independence, creativity, and style. Leo is represented.

Sunday, October 4 (Moon in Capricorn to Aquarius 11:53 p.m.) Consider the feelings of an older person without becoming inextricably involved with a financial problem. The emphasis falls on women, a reunion with a loved one. Gourmet dining is featured during the late afternoon. By going to a public place, you restore confidence in those who thought you were "confined."

Monday, October 5 (Moon in Aquarius) Confusion exists about payments, debts, signatures, and credit rating. Money belonging to another somehow gets in your hands, and this should not be permitted to become a lingering problem. The financial status of a partner or mate commands attention. Play number 3 to win.

Tuesday, October 6 (Moon in Aquarius) If you're puzzled by a legal tangle or red tape, ask questions. The lunar aspect is favorable and coincides with communication, travel, and education. You'll meet Scorpio and Aquarius persons who seem to "vibrate" with your physical prowess. Your own creative juices will be stimulated. Your lucky number is 6.

Wednesday, October 7 (Moon in Aquarius to Pisces 12:38 p.m.)   What begins as friendship or blind date could be transformed into a meaningful relationship. Idealism blends with the consideration of your material needs. The key is to be generous while protecting yourself in emotional clinches. This message will become startlingly clear. Virgo figures prominently.

Thursday, October 8 (Moon in Pisces)   Focus on home and family relationships. Your standing in the community is highlighted—an authority figure declares, "We really would appreciate your cooperation and participation." You'll receive a gift, possibly candy or flowers. Someone is very much enamored of you. Taurus is involved.

Friday, October 9 (Moon in Pisces)   Define terms, and separate fact from illusion. Someone who makes promises is sincere but could be misinformed—or financially embarrassed. For answers, look behind the scenes, make inquiries, and arrange for a tour. Pisces and Virgo play major roles. For luck, stick with number 7.

Saturday, October 10 (Moon in Pisces to Aries 12:36 a.m.)   Discussions can revolve around unusual pets, including turtles and rabbits. You'll be aware of longevity, time, the general health of older relatives. Financial questions remain, but answers can be obtained and you are aware of this. You no longer will be kept in the dark.

Sunday, October 11 (Moon in Aries)   The full moon position highlights satisfaction, fulfillment, the ability to restore a friendship that had gone off-track. The emphasis falls on romance, creativity, deep emotional involvement. In various activities, your performance rating will

247

be "outstanding." You could win a contest. Number 9 will be lucky today.

Monday, October 12 (Moon in Aries to Taurus 10:48 a.m.) The emphasis falls on powers of persuasion, the ability to win friends and influence people. Your perception is accurate. A romance could flourish if you take the direct approach. A special note: Avoid heavy lifting. A young person could become a big fan. Business and career activities pay dividends now.

Tuesday, October 13 (Moon in Taurus) An intuitive flash enables you to discriminate between rumor and fact. There had been reports that disparaged a family member. Almost as if hit by a lightning bolt, your sense of perception is heightened. You'll feel so much better that you could make this Tuesday night a time for celebration!

Wednesday, October 14 (Moon in Taurus to Gemini 7:08 p.m.) Lucky lottery numbers: 32, 2, 12, 14, 30, 7. Attention revolves around social activities, a special invitation, a long-distance call possibly related to holiday travel. A special note: Keep resolutions about diet and nutrition. You'll be more aware of your wardrobe and body image.

Thursday, October 15 (Moon in Gemini) Check details, and be aware of source material. Attention continues to revolve around secret meetings, clandestine arrangements. Accept an invitation to tour an institution, hospital, gallery, or museum. Taurus and Scorpio figure prominently. Your lucky number is 4.

Friday, October 16 (Moon in Gemini) You'll feel released from bondage. There is greater freedom of thought and action. The moon in your sign, plus the numerical cycle, emphasizes your personality and sex appeal. You'll read and write, you'll also put your ideas across in an entertaining, dramatic way.

Saturday, October 17 (Moon in Gemini to Cancer 1:36 a.m.) You become more aware of style and fashion, perhaps the sound of your own voice. Show your colors: silver, bright green, yellow. Your intuition and judgment will hit the mark. Be confident and willing to make a fresh start. A major domestic change is now possible and advantageous.

Sunday, October 18 (Moon in Cancer)   Good news is received about the location of an object that had been lost, missing, or stolen. One close to you says, "Let's get out today—we are getting cabin fever!" Spiritual values command attention. Terms will be defined, putting an end to brooding. A Pisces is involved.

Monday, October 19 (Moon in Cancer to Leo 6:01 a.m.)   The work week gets off to a "passive" start. Responsibilities, hanging over from three months ago, surface. There are deadlines, policies to be paid, a relationship is strong but possibly stormy. You'll be dealing with older persons in positions of authority.

Tuesday, October 20 (Moon in Leo)   Finish what you start, and realize that plans for visits or trips could be subject to change. Refuse to accept negative suggestions about your limitations. You're going places; today you'll know it, and you need not fall victim to assertions by a gloomy Gus. Your lucky number is 9.

Wednesday, October 21 (Moon in Leo to Virgo 8:27 a.m.)   Stress independence, showmanship, and romantic flair. Someone you want to impress does you a favor, actually wants you to succeed in courtship. Confidence is restored as a result. Focus on style, creativity, and originality. You need no longer play second fiddle.

Thursday, October 22 (Moon in Virgo)   Attention revolves around property, basic values, the needs of an older family member. Focus on a secure, long-standing relationship. You're being pulled in two directions, but you can find a highly original solution. Relatives will see it your way. Count on number 2.

Friday, October 23 (Moon in Virgo to Libra 9:39 a.m.) You win friends and allies by being flexible, willing to laugh at your own foibles. Keep an open mind without being gullible. You'll shine at any informal social affair. Expand your horizons. Look beyond the immediate, and close gaps represented by language or distance.

Saturday, October 24 (Moon in Libra) Lucky lottery numbers: 6, 7, 24, 5, 15, 33. The lunar position highlights romance, style, and sensuality. Attention also revolves around children, variety, and experimentation. You'll get your money's worth in connection with property or a special service. Taurus and Scorpio figure prominently.

Sunday, October 25 (Moon in Libra to Scorpio 11:04 a.m.) The new moon could symbolize the beginning of a unique relationship. You'll gain via the written word. Suddenly you perceive spiritual values previously obscured. An attractive admirer pays a meaningful compliment. Your morale soars upward as a result. Your lucky number is 5.

Monday, October 26 (Moon in Scorpio) A happy reunion celebrates the return of a Prodigal Son. Domestic tranquility can be restored. Be diplomatic without abandoning your principles. The lunar position accents basic issues, repairs, mending, the study of recipes. Taurus, Libra, and Scorpio figure prominently.

Tuesday, October 27 (Moon in Scorpio to Sagittarius 2:29 p.m.) A recent contact with a Scorpio looms larger than you originally anticipated. You're provided with a method of computing, more efficient techniques. The money question relating to a distant relative will be answered. Define terms, and pay close attention to your psychic impressions.

Wednesday, October 28 (Moon in Sagittarius) The emphasis falls on marital status, partnership, and legal affairs. Your position is strong despite threats and objections. The location of a document will prove valuable.

An older person, although harsh at times, does have your best interests at heart. Cancer and Capricorn play significant roles.

Thursday, October 29 (Moon in Sagittarius to Capricorn 9:18 p.m.) Long-range prospects are highlighted. Focus on communication, publishing, a continuing search for your soul mate. Give full play to your intellectual curiosity. A long-distance call, possibly from overseas, provides highlight. Be aware of basic values. Aries and Libra are part of today's scenario.

Friday, October 30 (Moon in Capricorn) An answer received some months ago can now be put to work. Take an independent course, reject those who insist on forming committees. Stand tall, you have plenty of support from loved ones. A fresh approach brings the desired results. Your credit rating requires personal attention.

Saturday, October 31 (Moon in Capricorn) Trust your intuition. Rise above petty differences sparked by a family feud over money. Share knowledge, and learn by teaching. Maintain idealism while keeping both feet on the ground. Someone who helped you about 11 months ago returns to the scene and can again become a valuable ally.

NOVEMBER 1992

Sunday, November 1 (Moon in Capricorn to Aquarius 7:43 a.m.) You'll feel as if this Sunday was made especially for you. Focus on romance and love. Express yourself. Your influence extends beyond previous limitations. A project that had been dormant will once again be alive and kicking. Aries and Libra play outstanding roles.

Monday, November 2 (Moon in Aquarius) Be direct, and make inquiries about a long-range project. You may be idealizing one who is only physically attractive.

You'll gain much from the written word, especially poetry. Someone who had been absent could make a dramatic "comeback." Leo figures prominently.

Tuesday, November 3 (Moon in Aquarius to Pisces 8:13 p.m.)   You'll learn more about your health, especially a recent digestive problem. Focus on diet and nutrition. The emphasis also falls on social activity, experimentation, and intellectual curiosity. You'll be more conscious about your wardrobe, general appearance, weight, and body image. Your lucky number is 2.

Wednesday, November 4 (Moon in Pisces)   Diversify, and look beyond the immediate. Both the lunar and numerical cycles highlight movement, communication, the ability to communicate important information. You'll receive a gift or prize—possibly to augment your wardrobe. A long-distance call helps you solve a holiday travel dilemma.

Thursday, November 5 (Moon in Pisces)   The moon position highlights career, business, prestige, the ability to deal with higher-ups. You'll be on more solid ground, but there are still some restrictions. Rules and regulations should be followed because eventually they prove beneficial. Check source material. Your lucky number is 4.

Friday, November 6 (Moon in Pisces to Aries 8:19 a.m.)   At the track: post-position special—number 3 P.P. in second race. Alternate selection: number 6 P.P. in fifth race. Pick six: 5, 3, 2, 8, 6, 2. What begins as a tour or excursion could lead to a fascinating experience. Virgo, Sagittarius, and another Gemini figure prominently.

Saturday, November 7 (Moon in Aries)   Lucky lottery numbers: 17, 10, 1, 9, 45, 6. A significant domestic adjustment takes place—be diplomatic. A gift would smooth the way to peace and harmony. A wish will be fulfilled in a manner that pleases and excites. Focus on a friendship that could be transformed into love. Taurus is involved.

Sunday, November 8 (Moon in Aries to Taurus 6:19 p.m.) Define terms, and agree to a secret meeting. The lunar position indicates events turn dramatically in your favor. You'll earn plaudits and money as result of career or business activities. Some very important people might declare, "You are a superb salesperson!"

Monday, November 9 (Moon in Taurus) The emphasis falls on power, authority, the ability to find out what's happening behind the scenes. Focus on hospitals, institutions, museums, and unique tours. As your romantic inclinations intensify, you'll have to declare your intentions. Cancer and Capricorn are featured.

Tuesday, November 10 (Moon in Taurus) Funds that were being withheld will be released. Today's full moon position highlights secrets, backstage maneuvers. Someone attempts to manipulate, to divert money that belongs to you. Guard your possessions, and let others know you are not without allies. Aries and Taurus play major roles.

Wednesday, November 11 (Moon in Taurus to Gemini 1:49 a.m.) Some will express amazement at your ability to read character. Spotlight your interest in the occult arts and sciences, including astrology, numerology, and graphology. A teacher will ask, "Can this be taught?" Be direct, take the initiative, and reject false modesty. Your lucky number is 1.

Thursday, November 12 (Moon in Gemini) It might be fun to learn chess or bridge today. The moon in your sign highlights originality, personality, and sex appeal. You'll contact fascinating people who want to learn, to experiment, to broaden horizons. Circumstances take a sudden turn in your favor.

Friday, November 13 (Moon in Gemini to Cancer 7:19 a.m.) This could actually be your lucky day. Toss off fears, suspicions, and superstitions. This will be a lively Friday night; you'll shine at social affair. Someone you admire observes that you really do seem to have it all together! Sagittarius and another Gemini figure prominently.

Saturday, November 14 (Moon in Cancer)   Reject someone who advocates what amounts to playing Russian roulette. This means be practical, realize that you are on the right track and need not be concerned with one who attempts to undermine your efforts. The financial picture grows bright—you'll know it by tonight.

Sunday, November 15 (Moon in Cancer to Leo 11:23 a.m.)   Your cycle continues high, especially where personal possessions are concerned. A review of figures reveals that your stock or valuables could bring more money than originally anticipated. Young persons figure in today's scenario—you'll be questioned, tested, and you will not be found wanting.

Monday, November 16 (Moon in Leo)   A short journey could figure in today's scenario, which involves a close neighbor or relative. What had been missing will be recovered. A stockbroker, banker, or accountant desires discussion. Be amiable, but refuse to be intimidated. This meaning will become crystal clear. Libra plays a role. Your lucky number is 6.

Tuesday, November 17 (Moon in Leo to Virgo 2:28 p.m.)   The emphasis falls on versatility, humor, the ability to locate someone who had been in hiding. Examine your own motives. Ask yourself, "Is it money or love?" A mystery will be solved and your sense of direction will be restored as a result. Pisces and Virgo play prominent roles.

Wednesday, November 18 (Moon in Virgo)   This can be a powerful day for dealing with property values. You're presented with facts and figures concerning insurance or deadlines. A love relationship heats up. You'll be confronted by someone associated with authority, or law. You'll have success in dealing with men. Capricorn is in the picture.

Thursday, November 19 (Moon in Virgo to Libra 5:03 p.m.) You'll take greater charge of your own destiny. Someone who truly has your best interests at heart will declare, "Go ahead, you do know what you're doing!" Refuse to be held back by an obligation that was not your own in the first place. Enlarge your horizons. Aries plays a role. Your lucky number is 9.

Friday, November 20 (Moon in Libra) A fresh start is required if your potential is to be fulfilled. A favorable lunar aspect coincides with added knowledge and greater awareness of your spiritual values. Focus also on travel, publishing, and a "hot romance." Leo and Aquarius figure prominently. Bet on number 1.

Saturday, November 21 (Moon in Libra to Scorpio 7:52 p.m.) Diversify, show your feelings in a humorous manner. A long-distance call relates to a unique social affair. You'll be more sensitive about clothing, general appearance, weight, and body image, keep resolutions associated with diet and nutrition. Cancer and Aquarius are in the picture.

Sunday, November 22 (Moon in Scorpio) You might be asking questions about an upcoming holiday—Thanksgiving. Make plans, and extend invitations. Keep an open mind and be flexible. You might be invited to partake of a dinner that does not exactly coincide with traditional holiday cuisine. Someone who is a "hard worker" asks to be of service.

Monday, November 23 (Moon in Scorpio) Stick to "hard news." Leave fluff, rumors, and speculation for another time. A frank discussion helps clear the air. Passions tend to rule logic. Be brief and concise. Let others know you do mean business. Once this is done, you'll be happier and efforts will be rewarded. Your lucky number is 4.

Tuesday, November 24 (Moon in Scorpio to Sagittarius 12:01 a.m.) The new moon occupies an area of your chart relating to cooperative efforts, partnership, publicity, legal affairs, and marriage. Take a fresh point of view in all of these areas. Be ready for a variety of experiences, the adventure of discovery, a flirtation that could be transformed into a serious relationship.

Wednesday, November 25 (Moon in Sagittarius) Attention revolves around your home, marital status, and family relationships. You'll beautify surroundings, with help from one who previously opposed you. A clash of ideas now proves stimulating. Today's activities also feature flowers, music, and gifts representing tokens of affection. Libra plays a role.

Thursday, November 26 (Moon in Sagittarius to Capricorn 6:38 a.m.) Somehow today blends mystery and intrigue with spiritual values. Tradition combines with "something different." Reflection on this Thanksgiving Day will show you are not alone, that indeed there is plenty for which to give thanks. Pisces plays an outstanding role. Your lucky number is 7.

Friday, November 27 (Moon in Capricorn) The emphasis is on promotion, production, and an intensified relationship. An investment proves beneficial and profitable. Focus also on organization, order, patterns, a relationship with one in authority. A directive is issued, and you are singled out for a unique honor. A Cancer is involved.

Saturday, November 28 (Moon in Capricorn to Aquarius 4:19 p.m.) Lucky lottery numbers: 10, 28, 32, 17, 22, 18. A long-range project can be completed. Today's scenario features speculation, universal appeal, a strong love relationship. You'll be rid of a burden, which was a losing proposition. A special note: Be extremely cautious around fire and electricity.

Sunday, November 29 (Moon in Aquarius) Spiritual values surface. The emphasis is on a search for your soul mate. Stress independence, style, and creativity. Physical attraction is part of the excitement—you'll say, "It's good to feel this way once again!" Take the lead, and realize you no longer are going to play second fiddle.

Monday, November 30 (Moon in Aquarius) Focus on idealism, generosity, favors that are repaid. Your intuition rings true; you'll be at right place. An Aquarian will declare, "You know plenty about various subjects without actually having formal knowledge!" Take this as a sincere compliment. A Cancer wants to dine with you—and the sooner the better!

DECEMBER 1992

Tuesday, December 1 (Moon in Aquarius to Pisces 4:23 a.m.) You might feel that you have found someone with whom you blend mentally and physically! Focus on style, creativity, a chance to make up for lost time. Today brings communication, travel, a strong love relationship. Leo and Aquarius figure prominently. Your lucky number is 1.

Wednesday, December 2 (Moon in Pisces) The spotlight falls on security, family relationships, a reunion. Pay attention to property values, durable goods, your marital status. You'll learn a valuable lesson about "when to let go." Cancer and Capricorn play outstanding roles. Check accounting procedures.

Thursday, December 3 (Moon in Pisces to Aries 4:49 p.m.) Diversify and coordinate efforts. The lunar position helps you communicate with those in high positions. You meet important people if you circulate socially. You'll be asked to give special consideration to your favorite charity. Sagittarius and another Gemini play roles. Play number 3 to win.

Friday, December 4 (Moon in Aries) Almost without effort you locate the "right keys." What had been evasive is available. Focus on references, details, and basic issues. A wish will be fulfilled in an unpredictable way. A Scorpio helps you locate a missing mechanical part. Aquarian also plays a significant role.

Saturday, December 5 (Moon in Aries) Someone of the opposite sex pays a meaningful compliment. This is one Saturday night you'll celebrate in a traditional way. The aspects favor communication, style, flirtation, and the ability to profit from the written word. Virgo and another Gemini figure prominently. Your lucky number is 7.

Sunday, December 6 (Moon in Aries to Taurus 3:16 a.m.) Someone who left the door open proffers a combination of promise and apology. The spotlight falls on family, spiritual values, and shared experiences. A surprise dinner invitation could be featured. Enjoy yourself while remembering recent resolutions about nutrition and diet. Libra figures prominently.

Monday, December 7 (Moon in Taurus) A strange experience exists—you feel as if you did this two days ago. The emphasis falls on secrets, glamour, mystery, déjà vu. The need for discretion will become obvious. Lines of communication open in connection with one confined to home or hospital. A secret meeting plays an important role.

Tuesday, December 8 (Moon in Taurus to Gemini 10:37) What had been nebulous becomes solid. Today's agenda revolves around trips, tours, museums, and hospitals. A relationship intensifies—you might be asking if this could be the real thing? Keep your guard up, refuse to give up something of value for a mere whispered promise. Cancer is involved.

Wednesday, December 9 (Moon in Gemini) The full moon and lunar eclipse occur in your sign. Your world might appear to be as if on a wild merry-go-round. Reach for the brass ring. What had been holding you back is gone. You'll be free to show emotions, products. Aries and Libra figure prominently. Your lucky number is 9.

Thursday, December 10 (Moon in Gemini to Cancer 3:05 p.m.) Someone you respect correctly advises you to get started in a new direction! Play up your personality and sex appeal. Wear your own colors—silver, bright green, yellow. You'll be working with your hands, and puzzle pieces will fall into place. A recent favor will be returned.

Friday, December 11 (Moon in Cancer) Your intuition is on target—you learn "where the money is." An object that had been lost, missing, or stolen will be located. Relatives tend to pull you in different directions. It's best to heed your own counsel. Cancer and Aquarius play significant roles. Your lucky number is 2.

Saturday, December 12 (Moon in Cancer to Leo 5:47 p.m.) Lucky lottery numbers: 14, 12, 4, 20, 2, 22. By diversifying, you move around obstacles rather than smashing into them. Meanings will become crystal clear. You'll learn that people do care, that you no longer stand alone. Sagittarius and another Gemini play major roles.

Sunday, December 13 (Moon in Leo) It's time to revise, review, to tear down and rebuild on more solid ground. The emphasis revolves around relatives and visits. You'll make do with the material at hand. Recent actions concerning an investment will pay dividends. A family member repays a debt.

Monday, December 14 (Moon in Leo to Virgo 7:56 p.m.) Be ready for change, travel, variety, the necessity for displaying showmanship. It's a good day for communication, writing, a unique relationship with someone special. A former teacher returns, and is once again ready to become your vigorous ally. Virgo, Sagittarius, and another Gemini play roles.

Tuesday, December 15 (Moon in Virgo) The spotlight falls on desire, sensuality, and the settlement of dispute with a close relative, possibly your brother or sister. Attention revolves around home, security, the value of a gift. Advice comes from all corners—some of it is actually practical. Go slow, and highlight diplomacy. Your lucky number is 6.

Wednesday, December 16 (Moon in Virgo to Libra 10:33 p.m.)   Someone could be attempting a classical "cover up." The key is to be discriminating. Select quality over quantity. Focus also on security, the ability to conclude a long-standing transaction. Relatives have different opinions regarding appraisal, the sale or purchase of property. Your lucky number is 7.

Thursday, December 17 (Moon in Libra)   The emphasis is on power, authority, a strong love relationship. An older person, possibly a parent or employer, is willing to talk about money and how you can obtain more of it. With regard to a relationship—it is serious. If playing games, you are merely fooling yourself. Your lucky number is 8.

Friday, December 18 (Moon in Libra)   No matter what your chronological age, you will be in the mood for romance! This applies especially if you were born during the early morning hours. No matter what your exact time of birth, you apply lessons learned from a recent experience. Focus on creativity, style, and variety.

Saturday, December 19 (Moon in Libra to Scorpio 2:20 a.m.)   Yesterday you broke free from restrictions —an emotional rut. Today you show greater freedom of thought and action. The spotlight is on romance, style, and the ability to let others know exactly how you feel. A young person might take a page from your book!

Sunday, December 20 (Moon in Scorpio)   Strive to bring your family together. The key is cooperation—give special consideration to one who might be temporarily restricted or confined. The lunar position accents care of pets, dependents, your general health. What had been hidden will be revealed—to your advantage. Your lucky number is 2.

Monday, December 21 (Moon in Scorpio to Sagittarius 7:44 a.m.) You won't need a "wake up call." Your biological clock will do the work—you'll know where to go, what to do, and you'll be at the right place at a crucial moment. The emphasis is on diversity, versatility, the ability to work with your hands. Someone who was previously indifferent could confess "true feelings."

Tuesday, December 22 (Moon in Sagittarius) The focus is on your marital status, the ability to present a case before the court of public opinion. Be sure legal papers are in order. Two friends who previously seemed to be harmonious will now reveal conflicts. Be interested and sympathetic without becoming inextricably involved.

Wednesday, December 23 (Moon in Sagittarius to Capricorn 3:04 p.m.) Give full play to your intellectual curiosity. You'll recover a lost article. It's possible you could hit the financial jackpot with these lucky lottery numbers: 3, 9, 18, 6, 34, 45. At the track: post-position special—number 3 P.P. in second race. Alternate selection: number 6 P.P. in fifth race.

Thursday, December 24 (Moon in Capricorn) The new moon and solar eclipse falls in the area of your chart relating to mystery, intrigue, and the financial status of one close to you. It's Christmas Eve—a debt could be wiped out, focus on deep feelings, giving and receiving, a realization that love is present. You could also receive news about a debt, credit, or possible inheritance.

Friday, December 25 (Moon in Capricorn) The spirit of today's holiday looms large—you'll have a different outlook, faith will be restored, and you'll be reunited with a loved one. The emphasis is also on legal ties, commitments, and the ability to relate to one who previously appeared cold. Spiritual values also dominate this fascinating day.

Saturday, December 26 (Moon in Capricorn to Aquarius 12:43 a.m.) Less than 24 hours ago many aspirations appeared to lack a practical base. By late afternoon, however, you realize you are on the right track. Focus on reality, timing, the ability to deal successfully with older people, including men in authority. Capricorn is represented.

Sunday, December 27 (Moon in Aquarius) Spiritual counsel helps you decide regarding motive, direction, and purpose. You'll reach beyond your previous limitations. Focus on distance, language, and travel. A special note: Be cautious around fire and sharp objects. Automobile transmission and electrical outlets require attention. Aries plays a role.

Monday, December 28 (Moon in Aquarius to Pisces 12:28 p.m.) Emphasize independence, your pioneering spirit. A favorable lunar aspect coincides with communication, travel, and an ability to reach a larger segment of the public. Once again spiritual values surface. You learn the meaning of "psychic income." Leo and Aquarius figure prominently. Your lucky number is 1.

Tuesday, December 29 (Moon in Pisces) You recently lent a helping hand to one close to you, possibly a relative. The favor will be returned—a family member might not be satisfied, but in truth you are fortunate. Refuse to enter a dispute over finances or interest rates. An Aquarian is in the picture.

Wednesday, December 30 (Moon in Pisces) Focus on your career, business, prestige, a possible promotion. Lucky lottery numbers: 30, 17, 12, 25, 33, 10. Accept an invitation for New Year's Eve, but keep your options open. The spotlight is on entertainment, the ability to get your "second wind." Another Gemini lifts your spirits.

Thursday, December 31 (Moon in Pisces to Aries 1:07 a.m.) Avoid conflicting dates or appointments. A party celebration could present a dilemma where you are wanted in two places at once. Only through diplomacy can you avoid a jealousy dispute. The original celebration could be out of the question due to a change of itinerary. Taurus and Scorpio figure prominently. Your lucky number is 4.

ABOUT THIS SERIES

This is one of a series of
twelve Day-by-Day Astrological Guides
for the signs in 1992
by Sydney Omarr

ABOUT THE AUTHOR

Born on August 5, 1926, in Philadelphia, Omarr was the only person ever given full-time duty in the U.S. Army as an astrologer. He also is regarded as the most erudite astrologer of our time and the best known, through his syndicated column (300 newspapers) and his radio and television programs (he is Merv Griffin's "resident astrologer"). Omarr has been called the most "knowledgeable astrologer since Evangeline Adams." His forecasts of Nixon's downfall, the end of World War II in mid-August of 1945, the assassination of John F. Kennedy, Roosevelt's election to a fourth term and his death in office . . . these and many others are on record and quoted enough to be considered "legendary."

"...I do not walk alone!"

ALAN CARTER

A woman, writing to Alan Carter recently, said: *"My first Unitology Forecast began in 1982 — and the renewals have continued to see me through the seven years since. As I sit here thumbing through the many pages, I realize how much strength I have drawn from knowing I do not walk alone! These forecasts have aided me in focusing on the reality about me, as well as the reservoir of strength within."*

Many people simply can't believe their eyes when they read their Unitology Forecast for the first time. Even those who have followed its guidance for years are repeatedly astonished at the uncanny insight into the most personal areas of their life.

Following are typical excerpts from letters to Mr. Carter: *"I received a forecast last year from you and could not believe what you'd 'seen' for me...it was so accurate it was amazing! My new love, whom you indicated would come into my life, is one of the people I am requesting this year's forecast for."* L.C., CA *"The Unitology Forecast was by far the best description of my character, desires, aspirations, outlook and beliefs ever received throughout a long lifetime."* A.M., FL *"I feel I owe you a letter of profound thanks: you have probably saved my life these past couple of years. I have had other readings and have paid handsome sums too, but no one has given me a better one than you, and for a small price."* C.B., NJ *"My recent Unitology Forecast is the best I have ever read. You have a beautiful personal touch that the computer horoscopes done now cannot come close to in comparison."* D.D., VA

For over fifty years, the Unitology Forecast has been the guiding light and helping hand for people from all walks of life, thousands of whom have remained faithful clients for decades, and for good reason — **THEY GET THE HELP THEY NEED!**

The rare qualities of sincerity, warmth and understanding are evident on every page of Alan Carter's **UNITOLOGY FORECAST** with **SPECIAL NOTATIONS**. This is a **FULL YEAR'S** forecast, regardless of when you order. Over **13,000 words** of sincere guidance (which many clients feel they cannot do without), by a caring astrologer-counselor, **not** an impersonal computer.

You'll be amazed at Mr. Carter's ability to accurately describe YOUR year ahead! **TEST HIM NOW!** Send for your **UNITOLOGY FORECAST** with **SPECIAL NOTATIONS** individually prepared for your birthdate. **PRINT:** month, day, year, place, and hour of birth (if known), and include **$19.95** plus **$3.50** toward postage and handling Outside U.S. make checks payable in U.S. funds only. Allow 3 to 4 weeks for careful completion and delivery. 100% satisfaction guaranteed or full refund. **MAIL TO: ALAN CARTER, BOX 807, DEPT. 02 INDIANAPOLIS, IN 46206-0807.**

LET THE INCREDIBLE "SIXTH
BRING YOU WEALTH AND LOVE

To Joyce Jillson —
Best Wishes from the White House
G. Bush

JOYCE JILLSON MAKES NEWS!

Perhaps you've seen Joyce with Merv Griffin, Mike Douglas and John Davidson. You may have caught her on the *CBS Evening News* with Dan Rather, with Ted Koppel on *Nightline* or on *Entertainment Tonight*. You may be one of the millions who read her perceptive column every day in over 100 newspapers across North America. And books by Joyce Jillson have made the New York Times best-seller list.

In the past 20 years, the world of astrology has undergone great changes. Since all the math necessary to interpret the charts is done by her computer, **Joyce's psychic knowledge and advice is now available to you!**

Now thanks to Joyce Jillson, you will receive your personal **Lucky Numbers**, **Lucky Days** and **Lucky Signs**!

"Put my name in lights. I went on a trip to Las Vegas. I taped my Lucky Number to the flap of my purse. I won $1,111.00!" —J.C., Black Creek, Wisconsin.

What will tomorrow bring?

Wouldn't it be useful to know when important events in your life are going to happen? How would you respond? What will you experience emotionally, intellectually and psychologically? And how will these experiences affect your life.

Your transits can provide valuable clues to various trends or stages of personal growth. This is especially true for the slower moving outer planets—Jupiter through Pluto. The transits for these planets are long lasting and profound in their psychological consequences. Many occur only once in a lifetime. The Astral Forecast is all about the outer planets.

This horoscope provides a reliable tool for astrological forecasting. The Astral Forecast will show you how the outer transits affect your sense of timing, that is, the times that are appropriate for you to take certain kinds of actions and inappropriate for others. This horoscope includes every significant transit to your outer planets that occurs in a twelve-month period. You can use your Astral Forecast to better understand how the outer planets affect such important life issues as career, child rearing, love, marriage and more.

For example, when Jupiter is in the first house, this transit represents a major growth cycle in your life. This is the best time for you to explore who you really are as an individual. Under this transit, you will feel more secure about yourself and the impression you make on others. Therefore, understanding yourself and your influ-

ence on others can make this transit an especially powerful and important time in your life. This is also a time for learning and gaining new experience. All this is part of your present need for personal growth, which affects not only yourself, but also the way you deal with the world as a whole. This is one time when persons and resources are likely to be drawn to you, and you should take constructive advantage of them.

A unique document You can find out in advance what your transits are going to be. But if you do it on your own, you will have to consult several astronomical tables to find the positions of each of the transiting planets every day and then compare them mathematically to the positions of the planets at the time of your birth.

There's an easier way to learn of your transits. Our IBM computer will handle all the calculations and provide you with information on all your outer transits based on your exact time and place of birth. With the Astral Forecast you not only receive the

most accurate calculation of your personal transits for the next twelve months, you will also receive an extensive printout interpreting the character and significance of your individual transits.

Your Astral Forecast is the most accurate and authoritative guide to the outer transits that you can receive. It is based on the work of Robert Hand, one of America's most famous astrologers, and the author of several astrology books.

Low Price Like all Astral Research horoscopes, the Astral Forecast is inexpensive. For just $25.50 you can have the same kind of advice that would otherwise cost you hundreds of dollars. This low price is possible because the astrological data is stored in our computer, and can be easily formatted and printed. Also, the mathematical calculations can be done in a matter of minutes. Your only cost is the cost of putting your personal information into the computer, producing one copy and then mailing it.

Money-Back Guarantee When you order your Astral Forecast, you receive an unconditional money-back guarantee. This means you can return your Astral Forecast within 30 days and get a full refund of the purchase price. We take all the risk.

Order your Astral Forecast today. Discover how the transits can bring energy to each part of your personality, fulfill your potential and help you gain more control over your own life.

© 1991 Astral Research, Inc.